NEW RALPH

Managing From
The Heart

Managing From The Heart

Unfolding Spirit in People and Organizations

Arun Wakhlu

Foreword by Dr M.B. Athreya

Response Books
A division of Sage Publications
New Delhi/Thousand Oaks/London

First published in 1999 by

Response Books
A division of Sage Publications India Pvt Ltd
32 M–Block Market, Greater Kailash–I
New Delhi 110 048

Sage Publications Inc	**Sage Publications Ltd**
2455 Teller Road	6 Bonhill Street
Thousand Oaks, California 91320	London EC2A 4PU

Published by Tejeshwar Singh for Response Books, lasertypeset by Innovative Processors, New Delhi, and printed at Chaman Enterprises, Delhi.

Library of Congress Cataloging-in-Publication Data

Wakhlu, Arun., 1955–
   Managing from the heart: unfolding spirit in people and organizations/Arun Wakhlu.
     p. cm.
   Includes bibliographical references and index.
   1. Organizational behaviour. 2. Psychology, Industrial.
   3. Work—Psychological aspects. 4. Quality of work life. I. Title.
   HD58.7.W253   1999   158.7—dc21 98–33288

ISBN: 0–7619–9303–7 (US–HB) 81–7036–767–0 (India–HB)
       0–7619–9304–5 (US–PB) 81–7036–768–9 (India–PB)

Production Team: R.A.M. Brown and Santosh Rawat

This book is lovingly dedicated to you, dear Heart!

≈ *Contents* ≈

• Verbal and Non-verbal Communication • Modes of
Communication • Listening and Total Receptivity
• Blocks to Listening • Benefits of Listening • Action Ideas
for Improving Your Listening • Expressing Oneself
and Assertiveness • Steps in Assertive Communication
• Interpersonal Communication • Solving Problems and
Resolving Conflicts • Ideas for Playful Action

≈ *Foreword* ≈

*I*t is a special task of joy to write a foreword to a book that can bring effectiveness and happiness to many managers, and the many more they lead and impact. The initial thrust of management theory was to train people to manage from the 'head'. The stress was on techniques for task analysis and decisions; structure for command; and systems for scheduling and control. Later, the awareness came that management and working processes have also to be from the 'heart', in addition to the head. Much of the 'heart-related' writing was from the Western paradigms of behavioural science. Many readers of this book may be aware of 'models' based on these paradigms, such as the hierarchy of needs of Abraham Maslow; Theories X and Y of Douglas McGregor; hygiene factors and motivations of Herzberg; needs for achievement, affiliation and power of David Mclelland, and so on. To these were added the Japanese concepts and practices of Zen, quality circles, Kaizen, etc.

More recently, there has been a realization in India that in addition to adapting useful foreign management ideas, we should also rediscover, research and evolve Indian concepts, idioms and methods. These may be of value to both Indian and international managers. Arun Wakhlu's book belongs to this stream of writing blending many value-oriented ideas and thoughts from different cultures. As the title indicates, he is exploring ways to manage from the 'heart'. One distinctive feature of Indian heritage is the belief that human affairs, including management, should go even beyond the mind and the intellect, and involve the soul. The book's sub-title hints at this, by recognizing the need to unfold the 'spirit' in people and in the organizations where they work.

In such a book, the writer and the reader have an opportunity to straddle psychology and philosophy; work and life; self and the world. For example, while reading Wakhlu's stress on 'insight' in the first chapter, students of Sri Aurobindo will recognize his emphasis on intuition. Similarly, 'inspired action' brings to mind the *Gita*. Two Indian gifts greatly welcomed in the developed world have been *yoga* and meditation. With economies growing and the problems of managing organizations and life becoming more complex, managers are increasingly feeling the need for a deeper perspective. Having understood the value of any concept, they are impatient for techniques. For them, Wakhlu offers methods for meditation.

Management education and training have stressed skills, including behavioural skills. There are also inputs available on attitudes. Even more fundamental are values. Wakhlu in this book discuss the source of all values. He stresses the need for 'good work'. As *Gita* says, yoga is dexterity in work. Wakhlu's call is also for total health. Indeed, it is only through a healthy mind in a healthy body that righteous work can be performed.

Beyond the body, Wakhlu proceeds to the natural next stage of self, namely the mind—becoming aware of the mind, how it works and using it for creative thinking. Many past and contemporary debates and discourses, now available also on TV channels, stress the need for a positive attitude as opposed to negative thinking and behaviour. The aim of meditation is not monkhood. It is to improve life and managerial effectiveness. The first link to others is communication—'The Art of Joyful Relating'. The Indian philosophical ideal is for each to experience joy, in one's total life space, from birth to death, through all the stages of the life-cycle. Wakhlu deals with the skills needed to experience this joy in relating—listening, assertion, conflict resolution and interpersonal problem-solving.

A common weakness of people and managers is in regard to the handling of time. There is need for clarity in life and work objectives, and action orientation, here and now, without unnecessary postponement. Industriousness is a desired quality of a human being, especially a leader. Children should be brought up with awareness of the value of each second, even each millisecond. Procrastination is a clear sign of sloth. Hyperactivity is excessive passion. In the global competitive environment, management tasks are becoming more demanding. Individuals and organizations need to keep learning. Wakhlu deals with 'three levels of learning'. Fundamental to all of them is the desire to learn. A common observation is that executives, administrators and other leaders are individually bright, but not so effective in interpersonal

relations, and even less so in groups. Here, the questions that arise are:
Instead of synergy, is there 'entropy'? To the external business and social
problems, does the group add internal human problems? Wakhlu advocates not only solving problems through teamwork, but also doing
it 'joyfully'. He goes further to indicate the possibility of 'dissolving
problems'.

Management theory has been circular in many areas. Leadership is
one of them. Since the Ohio studies in the mid-1940s to about 1970, there
was much interest in leadership. Then came the cerebral, analytical,
system-based manager. Since about 1990, there has been a renewed
interest in leadership. The issue, of course, is not either one or the other,
but both. Wakhlu brings out the traits of the 'good' leader, who can
unfold 'wholesomeness'. There is a special responsibility of the elite—
to be a role model of good conduct, and to set the standards.

No person can be an island, particularly a manager working as he or
she is in a dynamic environment. Wakhlu recommends 'networking' for
continuous mutual sharing and learning. Knowledge and action, make
a formidable combination. Add devotion. It may be unbeatable. Such
devotion need not be to a distant God, but to the people in the shape
of external and internal stakeholders of organizations. This book is a
useful guide to all such dedicated and aspiring managers.

We are on the threshold of the 21st century and the third millennium.
There are prospects for peace, development and eradication of poverty.
There are also hazards of environmental degradation, resource wars,
religious and other social conflicts. The ideas and 'action points' in this
book can be useful to guide individual responses. I have been advocating
a three-part global movement—economic growth, social justice, and
spiritual emancipation—for all of human kind. Each world citizen has
to integrate herself/himself in three dimensions—with one's own inner
being; with fellow-humans; and with the threatened ecology and environment around us. For each individual it has to be a continuous process
of learning about self and deploying that learning for the good of others,
the organization, society and, of course oneself. The book advocates a
holistic view of management. It blends spiritual ideas and practical
guidelines and it brings together knowledge streams normally kept
separate—the managerial and the spiritual. I do hope the readers will
not only find the book interesting and stimulating, but also respond to
it through inspired actions and sharing.

MRITYUNJAY B. ATHREYA

≋ *Preface* ≋

This book has been written over a period of nearly 10 years. It is an offering born out of my understanding of the needs of thousands of people whom I have come across during my work as a management consultant and educator. In a sense, this book is a sharing of my own journey of discovering the key principles that make for peaceful and prosperous working in teams and organizations. These very principles and ideas also make for more joyful living.

The growing economic and psychological stresses all over the world clearly point to the fact that our organized understanding of human systems—as embodied in management theory—is still far from providing solutions to certain recurring and basic human problems. Joyful living appears to be on the decline.

There is also a crying need, in almost all sectors, for higher quality, better teamwork, more enthusiasm and 'spirit' at work. Above all, we seek deep peace and satisfaction in our hearts. We need to understand ourselves and our true potential. Finally, we need to relate deeply to our work and to align it with the evolutionary flow of life. There is a strong need to develop new approaches to work and life.

For this to happen, we need to understand our true self—our sacred core. This is like reconnecting back to a perennial source of energy. We are again energised and brought alive with deeper insights to live life more wholesomely.

I have found that a holistic synthesis of modern management principles and the inspired perennial wisdom of the ages can be a practical and powerful way to come to grips with some of these problems. This book describes this synthesis and suggests a way forward. This book also addresses, what I see, as some of the highest opportunities for positive personal growth.

In the course of my professional studies at the Indian Institute of Technology, Delhi, from 1971 to 1976, I realized that technology was by itself not going to solve some of the basic human problems that I saw around me then. Living and working in Bombay from 1976 to 1978 exposed me to the stresses and strains of living in a large metropolis. I ran away from Bombay to the Indian Institute of Management, Ahmedabad, hoping to find some answers in the science and art of management. The questions and searching, however, remained. I found some answers in the field of values, human resource development and organizational development. My second job with the Tata Administrative Service took me to Jamshedpur where I also taught business policy and corporate planning at the Xavier Labour Relations Institute (XLRI). I kept learning the lessons of effective working and management development at Tata Engineering & Locomotive Co. Ltd (Telco) until 1985. My wife and I then started 'The Pragati Group' in Pune, at the other end of India, in 1986.

Since 1986, my team and I have been fortunate to serve more than 120 of some of India's leading companies, as well as non-governmental and government sector organizations. We have worked with over 20,000 people including senior IAS officers, teachers, students, managers and executives in industry, social workers, women, parents and our own selves! *We are amazed to find that the fundamental problems cropping up are the same in most groups.* This led us to the design of programmes which cover the topics presented in this book. The feedback and impact from these programmes has been very positive. People in these programmes have often asked me for a copy of the overhead projector (OHP) slides which I used. Many of them are contained within these pages.

Having read all this, you may be tempted to ask, 'Why another book? If so much has already been said and written about communication, thinking, action, etc., then why one more tome?'

There are three main reasons for writing this book:

1. While there is already an enormous amount of information on areas such as communication, values, thinking, learning and spiritual traditions, there are few books that hold it all together in a unified single framework which can guide action. The problem is not a lack of information or ideas, *but a lack of synthesizing vast amounts of information and presenting it in an integrated form for practical use.* This book aims at giving new insights into the process of managing human

systems. It is designed to equip practising managers, academicians and students of management with fresh conceptual frameworks to resolve some of the problems in today's theories of organizational and human behaviour. It draws ideas from authentic ancient wisdom and presents a totally new paradigm of management thought. In this book I have integrated ideas from many different fields. I have always enjoyed making connections and gaining insight into the 'big picture'. Doing this during the course of my work (including writing this book) has been a source of great joy and peace.

2.   Second, while many attempts have been made to integrate the perennial wisdom of life with our day-to-day working, these have often been couched in terms which only the Indian/Hindu mind can understand. Without detracting from the value of this work, I believe that *there is a way to express these truths in a manner which transcends any single culture*. I believe that there is a core human tradition which goes beyond any single cultural mindset. We do not need esoteric language or *shlokas* to explain laughter or pure water. I believe there is a pure stream of insight which can be expressed in simple and universal terms. That is what this book attempts to express.

The language in this book has been kept simple and the style readable. While many books have been referred to, I have consciously avoided a heavy academic style which tends to put off the busy manager. Each chapter ends with practical ideas for action related to the contents.

3.   Finally, *the perennial Truth needs new forms of expression from time to time . . . forms more suited to the current milieu.* This is somewhat like making keys that fit into the locks of today. Imagine opening an Aligarh lock with a Godrej key. It wouldn't work! The truth is always the same and will always remain so. The eternal values that worked at the time of Jesus Christ still do today. What does change, however, are the outer layers—cultures change, technology changes, and peoples' perceptions change. What therefore needs to be done, from time to time, is a re-interpretation or re-presentation of the same basic truths. These are given new forms which are more aligned with prevailing mind-sets.

This book is a *key* for today's organizations. It is a reminder for us of the Eternal Truth which governs our lives and how it can apply to the day-to-day bustle of work in organizations and our daily lives. It shares about how you can connect to the 'Heart' everyday and how this might benefit you. This could lead to fresh approaches for solving problems and to tackling situations with a deeper insight. This would also bring a powerful transformational energy and integration to the many problems facing us today. Above all, it would pave the way for inspired action.

One last point about the book. Readers may discover that I have randomly used the feminine and masculine pronouns throughout the book. If any usage jars you, pause for a moment to reflect on *why* this is so. However, let me say here that I have great and equal regard for all women and men. Any awkard usage of pronouns need not come in the way of our remembering that *all* people are valuable, *all* are divine and are therefore equally honoured.

As I write this in my study, I can see pictures of Osho, Ramana Maharishi, Swami Paramhansa Yogananda and the Mother looking benignly from a 'Life Positive' calendar. I feel that this book is my offering of gratitude to all of them and also to the many masters at whose feet I have learnt. It is an offering towards the unfolding of a world based on love rather than on fear, on the celebration of the human spirit rather than on self limitation. It is based on the firm conviction that all human-kind is deeply connected and that life is one integrated whole.

Our work at Pragati is inspired by the same vision. We share it with people of all age groups. Over the years, we have often heard people comment, *'I wish I had learnt these things at a younger age. My life would have been totally different.'*

This has prompted us to develop a programme for young people under our non-profit organization, Pragati Foundation. This project is called 'COOL' (Creating Our Own Life). It is aimed at developing the young people of India to be inspired, active and skilled contributors towards unfolding peace and prosperity in India and the world. The royalties from this book will go towards this project. By buying this book, you are contributing to a positive mission. My deep gratitude to you.

I pray that this book enables you to realize your divine Self which is the Heart of everything good in life, and to express yourself fully in inspired action for a better world.

ARUN WAKHLU

≈ *Acknowledgements* ≈

*I*f I were to sit down to map out all the contributors who have given and shared to make this book possible, I would end up mapping out, the whole universe! For example, the workers who helped produce the paper on which I am writing would be included. So would the hundreds of farmers who silently grow the food, which nourishes our bodies. I express my gratitude to all of Existence. I am experiencing a melting of the heart and deep peace as these words unfold.

The whole journey of my life begins with my parents Kshema and Omkar. I owe a deep debt of gratitude to them. My parents have not only brought me up with abundant love and care, but through their own shining example of courage, creativity and contribution have shown me the way for leading a full life. Omkar has not only been a loving father, mentor and guide, but also a co-creator of many interesting insights and frameworks including the one of Wholesome Development in 1993. It is great working with him.

Existence has blessed me with the opportunity to learn from many living spiritual masters of our times. Each one, in their own compassionate way, at the right time, have nudged me (and sometimes whacked me!) forward along my spiritual journey. A very special thanks to Maharishi Mahesh Yogi and Osho Rajneesh whose compassionate contribution to the expansion of Joy and Peace on planet earth is truly revolutionary. If there is anything good in this book, it is because of their blessings. If there is something that doesn't sit right, it is my own ego. I bow my head at their feet, and express my sincere thanks.

I also owe much to the teachers, authors and thinkers who have influenced my life. Some of them are featured in the References. Their stimulating thinking and writing has catalyzed my own.

I am especially indebted to my friends in the Moral Re-Armament (MRA) movement and the Osho Network, who have shared so much of their love and affection with me.

I want to offer my sincere thanks to the many individuals and organizations my colleagues at Pragati and I have been priviledged to work with. We have had the opportunity of testing, developing and refining the concepts and ideas presented in this book over the past decade. The interactions have been very stimulating. I would like to say a grateful 'thank you' to all our clients and their MDs, HR heads and members with whom we share joyful 'partnerships in progress'.

The speedy and skilful use of the computer by my assistant-cum-artist-illustrator, Kumar Kudalkar, has contributed a lot to the creation of this book. Kumar's patience with multiple drafts, artistic and computer skills (bordering on wizardry) have gone a long way towards the completion of this book. I offer him my sincere appreciation and thanks.

All my other colleagues at our organization Pragati—the 'learning, growing, celebrating and sharing community'—have given me much of their affection, feedback and love. It is great working with this team and I am deeply grateful to all of them for making Pragati what it is. To all of them, my love and gratitude. A special thank you to Kiran Gulrajani and Raymond Moses for their very useful contributions in the revision of this book.

I am indebted to my friend Ranjan Kaul at Response Books whose constant encouragement, feedback and admirable patience during the course of this project have been a source of inspiration. Thank you Ranjan.

My brother Bharat, with whom I have shared a beautiful childhood and many beautiful moments together, has helped me grow professionally and personally. To him I offer my love and thanks. My deep gratitude to all my dear friends and relatives who have nurtured me all these years.

My wife, Anu, has been a constant source of insight and loving support both as a life partner and as a colleague. Her considerable contribution during this entire project in the roles of scribe, editor, motivator and project manager is something I am deeply grateful for. She has organized the production of the manuscript with great dedication. Her cheerful help has made the whole process thoroughly '*flowful*'. In many respects, this is as much Anu's book as it is mine.

My daughters, Nitya and Pragnya, are a constant source of wit, creativity, humour and enthusiasm. Their loving wisdom keeps me challenged to 'walk my talk'. To them my love and blessings.

This list of acknowledgements would not be complete without mentioning Snowy and Cleo, our dogs. When I looked into their loving eyes, as I sat writing this book, I understood the essence of managing from the Heart.

And finally, I thank you dear beloved soul for reading this book and giving me an opportunity to share with you. You are divine and I love you.

ARUN WAKHLU

Introduction
The Big Picture

What lies before us and what lies behind us
are small matters compared to
what lies within us.
And when we bring what is within
out into the world,
miracles happen.
RALPH WALDO EMERSON

*I*magine a world where all people are at peace with themselves, and with each other, and living in an environment that is pure and green. Imagine a world where organizations exist for the total development of their own members. Where inspired working contributes to the well-being of planet earth and its inhabitants. People working in such organizations would:

- Work with an abundance of energy and enthusiasm
- Find work easy and fun
- Make work so deeply joyful and rewarding that it would feel more like play rather than 'work'

Such inspired work, done with joy in the heart, would be deeply liberating. It would be the creative engine for progress which, in turn, would unfold more joy. This freedom, progress and joy is what the people of the world today are thirsting for.

If you ask anybody what they truly want out of life, they will most probably say 'inner satisfaction', or 'peace' or 'happiness'. All people would like their lives to be happy ones. We are constantly looking for that blissful condition of deep peace and freedom which we have all experienced at some time or the other.

I have experienced glimpses of this beatitude while:

- Watching the explosion of colours and cloud shapes in the sky during sunset in the monsoons
- Working with a creative team to accomplish something tough and important
- Simply being with friends in a quiet and trusting dialogue

Can our whole life, both at work and play, be more creative, trusting and productive? Can it be a life of inner and outer abundance? Can we live each moment with deep insight leading to more inspired action?

The answer is a big 'YES!'. Let us see how this book can serve as an inspiration and a guide towards this goal.

The key to living life in this manner, starting right now, is to trust the Heart . . . that unencumbered loving centre which is the source of everything good in life.

The 'Heart' in this book refers to the very core of our being. It is the centre of the universe and also the sub-stratum on which everything exists. The great sage, Sri. Ramana Maharishi has said about the Heart, 'The Heart is not physical. It is spiritual . . . the Heart is the centre of all.'

This divine centre has been called by different names. Hindu sages called it *Brahman*, the Buddhists *Dhamma*, Sufis *Allah* and the Bible *I am*. Other labels that have been stuck onto the ultimate non-sticker are being, existence, sacred core, the real Self (with a capital 'S'), bliss, joy, pure awareness and spirit. No matter what name we give it, it is the same mysterious essence. While, on the one hand, it is not something we can grasp or see, it upholds and *is* everything real and imagined. The Heart is the whole. It is existence and life itself. It is pure spirit . . . the very source of true peace and unlimited abundance.

Managing from the Heart is essentially about unfolding this spirit at work and in life. The approach shared in this book is shaped by a deep conviction that the basic purpose of life, and therefore managing, is to be the very best we can be. It is to build and create from a centre of love, and through our own life to influence the unfolding of others. Everything we do can be an offering of love from the Heart. Something that integrates, makes whole and inspires. In its highest form, managing from the Heart is about *being whole*. It is a total oneness with life where, from the silent depths of the Heart, we contribute our own song to the unfolding music of the divine orchestra.

Different aspects of managing and living are closely linked. The very qualities that make one a good leader also help her to be a better mother. Good listening, for example, helps one with better people development, better customer service, better parenting, improved teamwork and also lowers stress. One stone, many birds! Similarly, learning to work and live from an inner condition of unboundedness and silent awareness impacts almost everything we do. The way we communicate, think, manage our time, plan and play with our children all depends on our inner state.

While the focus of this book has been on 'managers', management from the Heart is not something to be used only in organizations. Management, as I see it, needs to be seen as a universally useful and holistic process, which can be helpful not only to corporative executives, but to all people. It is an approach to life, which has applications at home, in the family, in the neighbourhood and in almost every human situation. I see management as a process of leading a full life, which harmonizes all spheres of activities. I can therefore use the contents of this book to guide me in my interactions with my child's teacher at her school. With equal ease, I can also use it to inspire my actions as a leader of a large organization.

In its final manifestation, managing from the Heart expresses itself as a life lived joyfully, moment to moment. Joy with its attendant positive qualities of peace, health, satisfaction, freedom and love begins to expand in our lives.

> And then he saw that Brahman was joy: For from pure joy springs all creation, by joy it is sustained, towards joy it proceeds and unto joy it all returns.
>
> TAITTIRYA UPANISHAD

As we connect to the Heart—the deep source of bliss within us—fear melts away. As the immobilizing power of fear weakens, we begin to think more creatively. Also, as we will see later in this book, the more we let go of our own ego and limitations, the more we connect with the rhythms and flows of Nature. Nature's power then becomes our own power, because there are no boundaries between nature and us. This is a very joyful way to live our life.

If a meter of the kind shown in the figure below were invented, the needle would move towards the right as our life unfolds. As we choose to grow more and work in tune with life as it is meant to be, the pointer moves towards energy, order, health and joy. The purpose of life is indeed an expansion of joy. It is to lead a full life of inner freedom and outer abundance. All this is based on a process of joyful learning.

Learning, freedom and joy are interlinked. The Sanskrit saying, 'Sa-Vidya, Ya-Vimuktaye' means 'true knowing is that which liberates'. As we

Tension	**The Joy Meter**	Peace
Misery		Joy
Disorder		Energy
Illness/Disease		Order
Dissatisfaction		Health/Ease
Stagnation		Satisfaction
Anger		Learning
Stress		Freedom
Fear		Love

grow in insight and awareness, which comes from true learning (not stuffing oneself with information), possibilities for inspired action and new experiences begin to open up. Our range of exercisable choices increases. We gain more self-mastery and ease in our work. Our relating with people becomes more creative. We manage our time better to really do the things we want. *All this leads to an expansion of joy and freedom.*

This is what *Managing from the Heart* is all about. In fact, our own inner sensing of where our joy meter is pointing is a clear indicator of whether we are managing from the Heart or not.

People in many organizations today report a loss of spirit and enthusiasm. This is born out of routine and uncreative patterns of working. In three well-known large companies in India, I asked people to rate their organization on a three-axis scale of Head, Heart and Hands. Each axis went from a low of zero to a high of ten.

Very broadly,

Head	characterized	clear *thinking* and decision-making; the use of tools and techniques
Hands	characterized	dynamic *action* towards clear goals
Heart	characterized	*spirit* and positive *feelings* like joy, love, peace and enthusiasm

People rated both the Head and Hands dimensions around 8–9 on the 10–point scale. The Heart dimension got a score of around 2! The ratings were almost identical in all the three organizations. People continuously talk about growing stress and a loss of soul and heart. Organizations the world over seem to be running out of spiritual energy when they need it the most.

When I ask people about whether they enjoy their work or not, the answer usually is 'sometimes'! Most of the time, people share feelings of sadness, frustration and helplessness when they talk of work. These feelings are symbolized by the chained person you see on the left of the following figure.

Work: Enslaving or Liberating?

In my work I ask people what the chains in the picture represent to them? Many see these chains as constraints. They mention the 'boss', 'lack of resources', 'the system' and above all, 'a lack of power' as the main chains of constraint. While this is true, we can also see that most of our chains come from our own minds. The person on the right is seen as having more energy, more enthusiasm and more freedom. He has options to choose from. He is more powerful. He also appears to be enjoying life more than his chained counterpart.

Can we free ourselves from these chains?

The chairman of a large Indian business group had this to say when I met him in early 1998:

We're dealing with a different business scenario now. This requires a different mind set and way of working. Maybe, I expect too much from my people. I find a lot of corporate inertia. Resistance to change is what we have to deal with. People feel we are market leaders, No. 1, so why bother to learn. This has to change. Even if they realize that the old ways of functioning are no longer relevant, very often they don't know how to bring about this change. I find people don't want to take responsibility, be proactive. It's very frustrating to see people just sit tight doing nothing even in the face of crisis. Is it apathy, or demotivation? Nothing works . . . even training programmes don't! Driving people, the carrot-and-stick approach, doesn't provide the answer either.

He summed up what is on the minds of many CEOs today in the current environment of new threats and new opportunities. Many 'tools and techniques' have been used to respond to these challenges. These have met with only limited success.

In a conference on 'Total Quality People for Total Quality Management' which I addressed recently, I asked people for their views on some of the problems associated with implementing total quality. They mentioned things such as:

- A *'Chalta Hai '* (things will go on anyway) attitude in which people just do not stretch to improve quality.
- A low sense of belongingness and ownership.
- Low energy for action.

While discussing the transition to higher levels of quality, some of the questions they raised were:

- 'How do we prepare people to actively take part in, contribute to and lead change?'
- 'How do we have a highly motivated and charged up team?'
- 'How can we reduce our stress and tension?'

The essence of what they said was: 'We can't find the time or energy for change. There is so much fire-fighting to do that we cannot do anything about improving quality.'

My work as a management consultant and trainer has shown me that the same kind of problems seem to exist everywhere. They are the most fundamental problems of existence in human organizations today. I give below a list of typical issues that have surfaced repeatedly:

Self-mastery

- Managing stress, leading a balanced life under tough conditions.
- Time management. Making time to work on long-term issues, for reflection, and for developing people and the organization. Also, spending more time with my family.
- Working with integrity and values for a more peaceful future.
- Meditation and total health.
- Maintaining equanimity under pressure. Not losing my temper.

Thinking

- Thinking creatively.
- Boundaryless thinking. Transcending the 'resource trap' and seeing abundance.
- Innovating systematically.

Interpersonal Effectiveness

- Developing interpersonal skills (especially listening and assertiveness).

- Building trust.
- Improving boss–subordinate relations.
- Resolving conflicts.

Team Work

- Working joyfully in a team.
- Facilitating group processes.
- Making participation a way of life. Participative planning.
- Working together with other departments, ministries, groups.
- Coordinating and interacting systematically. Systematic problem-solving.

Managerial and Leadership Effectiveness

- Influencing skills. Leadership and personal power (as against positional power).
- Managing the political sub-system skilfully. Managing the interface with politicians in a way that is self-empowering and value-based.
- Leading people, enhancing their commitment to a shared vision; improving their accountability. How to get people to work in an inspired way.
- Developing people.

Organizational Learning

- Organizational learning: learning how to make it happen.
- Managing and catalyzing whole system change.
- Organization development and institution-building.
- Creating result-oriented and inspiring cultures.

If the joy meter described earlier had two big sensors, as shown in the figure alongside, and you could fix these onto a person to get a reading, you would find different people with different readings. Some would show high levels of peace, enthusiasm, joy and learning. Others would not. Exactly the same would apply to readings on organizations. Some organizations would be vibrant and active in a healthy and balanced way. Others would be dull and stagnant. Now stretch your  imagination and connect these two sensors to planet earth as a whole.

Would we see an increasing level of peace and joy or growing tension and disorder? Most people I have met feel the latter. They think that the world is going downhill.

At the global level, we are faced with many daunting challenges. These could well mean the difference between the total annihilation of human beings or a green and peaceful planet earth.

Today, technological advances have undoubtedly helped us to increase our productivity. We have gadgets such as computers, fax machines, cellular phones, organizers, videoconferencing systems, televisions, pagers and cyber shopping malls. But have these gadgets really contributed towards higher levels of health and happiness? The growing interconnectedness of national economies has almost led to one single global economy. However, this has also brought in its own ability to transmit instabilities. The activities of a single derivatives trader in Singapore can send tremors to financial markets all over the world. At the touch of a few computer keys currency dealers and speculators can send the currencies of several countries into a tailspin. Established industries across national borders employing thousands of people in one country may have to be closed down because of the sale of imported goods from other nations. People do not seem to be getting more of what they really want—a stable means of earning a living, a decent place to live, healthy and pure food, excellent education and health care for their children, and a vibrant green environment close to where they live. Above all, peace seems to be eluding most of us. Thousands of people are caught on the never-ending treadmill of work harder, earn more, consume more and be less joyful! It almost seems that people exist for economies. Their peace is sacrificed on the altar of economic growth.

Consider this: The average per capita consumption of resources in the Western world is 100 times greater than it was at the beginning of the Industrial Revolution. During this same period, population has grown 10 times. Multiply these two curves together and you have a 1000-fold increase in growth, pollution, waste, bio-deterioration, stress and so on! If this is projected for a population of 11 billion people, and even if we allow for significant improvements in waste and pollution control, it is evident that human beings are in danger of overwhelming themselves and the planet. While the rise in per capita consumption in America in the last twenty years has been 45 per cent, the *decrease* in the quality of life as measured by the Index of Social Health has been 51 per cent. This situation is made worse by additional problems such as the growing drug menace, AIDS epidemics, deforestation, depletion of the ozone layer, and an unprecedented increase in civil disorder and violence.

At the root of these problems is a loss of understanding, integration and inspired action. We seem to be cut off from the well-spring of wisdom, wholeness and inspiration in our lives. It is as if human beings have lost the connection to the very Heart of life.

When we rely *only* on the mind to manage our affairs, life runs into many complications born out of the very nature of the mind. Divorced from spirit, we experience a loss of integration and wholeness. Our sight is partial and short term and so are our decisions. The energy and enthusiasm that a truly spiritual life entails are absent. So our actions are either uninspired or absent.

At the global level, managing without heart and spirit is largely responsible for the present crisis in the world. The absence in action of deeper values such as compassion, celebration, forgiveness and deep caring have contributed to the economic and environmental chaos around us. It is a consequence of spirit being overshadowed by clouds of delusion and falsehood.

To quote the enlightened master Osho, *'The way out is the way in'.* He refers to the Heart. Living and managing from the Heart manifests in three ways. It leads to an increase in:

1. Insight
2. Integration
3. Inspired action

An easy way to remember this is that the Heart is the real 'I', and all the three words above begin with 'In'! Let us explore these ideas and see the connections.

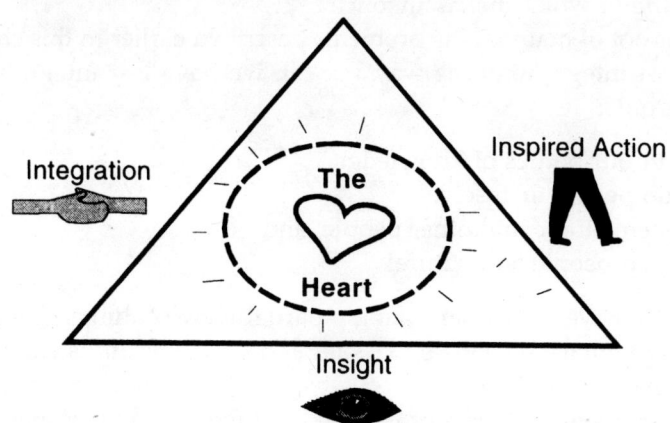

Insight

The Chambers dictionary defines insight as: 'The power of discerning and understanding things; imaginative penetration; practical knowledge; enlightenment; a view into anything; awareness; of one's own mental condition'. A Zen master described it as 'seeing with the eye behind the eyes'.

As we operate from the Heart, which is 'no-mind', we begin to see things as they are. The mind, with its tendency of judging and fragmenting, is transcended. A more complete view of things emerges.

Insight comes spontaneously from understanding the workings of our own mind. As we gain more insight into the layers of conditioning which cover our essence, we also gain the power to dissolve them. As we begin to see the causes and consequences of our thoughts, words and actions, we expand our capacity to make insightful choices. When we get insight into everything, including the deepest recesses of our own mind, true objectivity dawns. We then stand at the threshold of enlightenment. Some people have described it as *pure awareness and pure insight*. This is the ultimate understanding that all is one . . . the very Heart and essence of integration.

Integration

Managing from the Heart is born out of a wholistic view of the world. It also manifests as integration. Integration means connecting, being one, coming together and being in touch. The word comes from the Latin root *in-tangere* which means 'in touch'.

At the root of many of the problems described earlier in this chapter, is a loss of integration. The way I see it, we have lost integration on several fronts:

1. Within our bodies of knowledge,
2. Within people themselves,
3. Between people and other people, and
4. Between people and nature.

All these have led to our taking a partial view of things. They have led to fragmentary responses to issues and problems and a consequent loss of balance.

Let us start with our base of knowledge. Like the six blind men trying to define an elephant, specialists try to get a handle on life using their own limited frameworks.

Management theories and concepts proliferate at incredible speed. Every year, we have new thoughts emerging. These only go on fragmenting approaches. A look at management literature today shows many different tools and techniques which are often the same thing with different brand names. To quote Eccles and Nohria (1993) in their book *Beyond the Hype:*

> *In recent years, there has been an amazing amount of verbiage instructing managers on how to become 'leading-edge', 'excellent', or 'innovative'—yet little of it attends to the practical questions of how to actually get things done in organizations.*

Moreover, the connections between different bodies of knowledge is rarely shown.

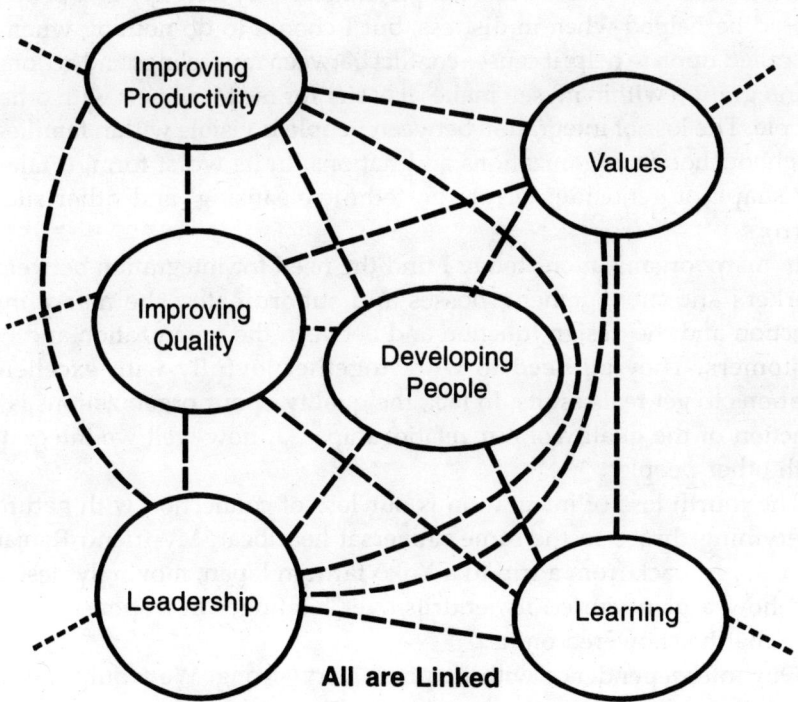

While management thinking is fragmented, the problems that nature throws up are not! For example, while all the above issues are linked, we are often given only partial frameworks. The connections between them are not fully discussed. The effect of this is that an enormous amount of energy is dissipated in dealing with the mental boundaries between these 'subjects' and in trying to make connections.

I have come across managers who groan about doing work on total quality management, Kaizen, human resource development, balanced company scorecard and policy deployment with the comment: 'When are we going to find time to do some real work?' If managers could see the basic interconnectedness of different areas of knowledge and also see their underlying unity, life could be a lot more productive and peaceful for them.

The loss of peace is also caused by a loss of integration within themselves. To lead joyful and creative lives, we need to work as one unified whole. This means that there must be integration between my thoughts, communication and actions. It also means that I must have all aspects of what I call 'me'—my body, mind, feelings, heart, skills, thinking, etc.—working together in great love and harmony. There must be no conflict within me. For example, if I feel very strongly that people should be helped when in distress, but I choose to do nothing when I am called upon to help, it causes conflict between my feelings and actions.

Integration within myself makes it easier for me to connect with other people. The loss of integration between people is visible within families, neighbourhoods, organizations and nations. In its worst form, it takes the shape of genocide, terrorism, 'ethnic cleansing' and other such horrors.

In many organizations today I find the need for integration between workers and management, bosses and subordinates, the marketing function and the design function and between the organization and its customers. They all need to work together joyfully with excellent relations to get real results. In fact, the quality of our organizations is a function of the quality of our relationships . . . how well we integrate with other people.

The fourth loss of integration is our loss of connection with nature. Everything throbs to the same universal heartbeat. My friend Ranjan Nehru, just back from a trip to a Yoko farm in Japan, movingly described how a plant curled its tendrils over his finger in response to the love that he showered on it.

Our interdependence with nature is very strong. We would not be able to live long without water, air, sunshine and plants.

We have just lost awareness of this deep connectedness. Losing awareness of this interdependence leads to a loss of harmony and alignment. We often act as if there was no environment. Or, as if we can go on robbing our children of fresh air and water with impunity. They deserve a healthy and joyful future.

People need to learn that true joy and productivity can come only when we are working in harmony and alignment with Nature. A violation of this law leads to waste, pollution, environmental hazards and degradation. These take our joy meter towards the negative. Industries, which produce chemical pollutants and spew them callously into our streams, ponds and air are not working in harmony with the environment. The destruction of as many as 17 million hectares of rain forests (an area about the size of Japan) each year seems to apparently have nothing to do with us in India. However, the green house effect and other global impacts of deforestation, such as the rising levels of the oceans, would one day affect not only India, but also every living creature on this planet. The winds and ocean currents do not carry passports.

Managing from the Heart helps us to heal these 'dis-connects'. It helps us to join things together with the power of love and understanding. It is the cure for, what the great twentieth century physicist David Bohm calls, 'the virus of fragmentation'.

Inspired Action

Do you remember moments in your life when you were doing things with passion, joy and energy? When you were totally present to the action at hand? Such moments have a magical quality to them. They are infused with spirit.

The dictionary defines 'spirit' as 'soul'. The word comes from the Latin root *Spiritus* which means 'breath'. *Spirare* means 'to breathe' or give life. For us, spirit is the same as Heart. Inspiration is something that comes from a pure connection with the Heart. Inspired action is simply action arising from this pure connection. As we connect with the Heart in our lives, spirit unfolds. This leads to an expansion of joy, awareness and inspired action. Our life becomes truly spiritual.

Spiritual is simply spirited. It is about living life with inner abundance. Despite its positive source, the word has been widely misunderstood. People often associate the word 'spiritual' with something mystical, other-worldly, life-negating or with dogmatic religion. Most consider it too fuzzy 'to be of any practical use'.

In one of the most popular articles published in the *Noetic Sciences Review,* Rachel Naomi Remen (1988) defines what spirituality is and what it is not. She describes it as:

• Profoundly non-judgemental and non-separative
• Unchanging

- Trusting the great flow or pattern manifested in all life, including our own
- The deepest sense of belonging and participation

Spiritual is also joyful. This is distinctly different from the ups and downs of 'happiness and sadness'. The joy of spirit is uncaused and eternal.

Action from this inner space of joy is inspired and inspiring. It brings abundant blessings to the actor, and also to those who are touched by the impacts of the action. In all probability, the successful leaders of the twenty-first century will be deeply spiritual people committed to inspired action.

The three manifestations of managing from the Heart are deeply connected to each other. Insight, Integration and Inspired Action intertwine together to make the solid cable of managing from the Heart as shown in the figure. At their core is spirit. As our insight grows, we see and experience more integration. Boundaries begin to melt. The beautiful interdependence of life and the sheer vision of intrinsic oneness spontaneously lead to inspired action. This action, in turn, generates new insights and a further expansion of spirit. Life then becomes a joyful dance of discovering our true essence.

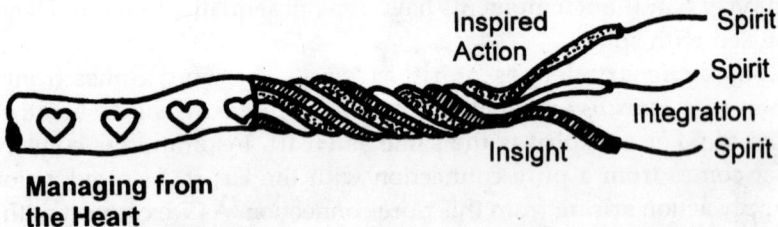

Managing from the Heart

This is the same as unfolding spirit. Hence the subtitle of this book, *Unfolding Spirit in People and Organizations.* Spirit begins with individuals. Then spreads to others around. The organization begins to get inspired. Spirited organizations, full of joyful people, can have a positive global influence.

So we can look at managing from the Heart at three levels:

1. Individual

2. Organizational

3. Global

Most changes that we are seeking on the outside have to begin with people. When individuals change, relating is more joyful and productive. As people relate and work better together, organizations start functioning more effectively. They become like living organisms.

As teams and organizations begin to unfold their full potential, their actions send positive ripples outwards into the rest of society. Families begin to benefit from peaceful mothers and fathers, customers delight in excellent high-quality products and services and they, in turn, provide *their* customers with excellent outputs. The environment benefits as awareness and creativity grow.

> If there is light in the soul,
> There will be beauty in the person.
> If there is beauty in the person,
> There will be harmony in the house.
> If there is harmony in the house,
> There will be order in the nation.
> If there is order in the nation,
> There will be peace in the world.
>
> CHINESE PROVERB

I believe that global change can begin with each one of us . . . with our own choices in thinking, communicating and acting.

The table on the next page captures the meaning of managing from the Heart at all the three levels just mentioned. In this table, we see the effects of enhanced Integration, Insight and Inspired Action at the individual, organizational and global levels.

By now, you would have got a good feel of what managing from the Heart is all about. The question of how to practically make it happen in one's own life is probably on your mind. The rest of the book, dear reader, shares with you the 'how to' part of managing from the Heart. A mental road-map of the way forward is given in the figure. This represents the model of 'How to Manage from the Heart'. We have been using it in our work for the past twelve years.

The origin and end of this journey is the Heart . . . the sacred oneness of being, our innermost self, the source of life and love. It is the core and goal of the approach presented in this book. Everything connects to it and it *is* everything. Even when we are not aware of it, it is present. Chapter 2 of the book describes the indescribable mystery of the Heart and shares the practical art of meditation. In it we also look at the benefits of regular meditation at the individual, organizational and global levels.

The next layer of the model from the inside is 'Joyful Living'. Only when I am living from eternal values (integrated with the Heart), doing work I love (integrated with my inner calling), and leading a healthy and balanced life-style, can my life be truly joyful. A joyful life celebrating each moment, sharing out of love and living with ease in the body-mind is also a full life. Chapter 3 on 'Joyful Living—Values, Good Work and Total Health', explores these dimensions.

Process→ ↓Level	Integration	Insight	Inspired Action
Global	• One World • Synergizing the use of resources • Electronic networking	• Seeing the unity of Mother Earth • Seeing the wholeness and interdependence of all creatures • Generating insight globally	• Working actively across nations for a greener planet Earth • International initiatives on pressing human problems • Sharing resources freely wherever they are needed
Organizational	• Integrating with the community and industry • Connecting with other departments • Connecting with customers, suppliers • Connecting to other people	• Shared vision and shared values • Understanding the needs and expectations of my internal and external customers • Giving and receiving feedback • Seeing the power of our collective unique potential • Getting insights into the market place and industry	• Actively caring for and sharing with others • Innovation and creation • Loving service • Minimum waste and effectiveness in action • Unleashing collective power in the service of life
Individual	• Integrity: walking my talk • Committing myself to my inner calling and values • Integrating with nature • Connecting my body–mind–spirit	• Understanding my body-mind • Listening to my inner calling and seeing my own potential • Understanding who I am • Understanding the laws of nature • Getting insight into the Heart	• Working with passion and responsibility • Giving the world the best I have • Sharing from my deepest strengths and talents • Being total in my actions and working from love

Having got some basic ideas on how to lead a joyful life, we then look at the three important and related life processes of:

• Thinking
• Communicating
• Acting

Can you imagine life without these three? They are central to everything we do.

Chapter 4 gives us insight into 'Thinking . . . Our Most Stretchable Resource'. In it, we look at the mind and how it can take us away from wholeness if we are not conscious of its workings. We will also learn about how to use our head in creative, accountable and positive ways.

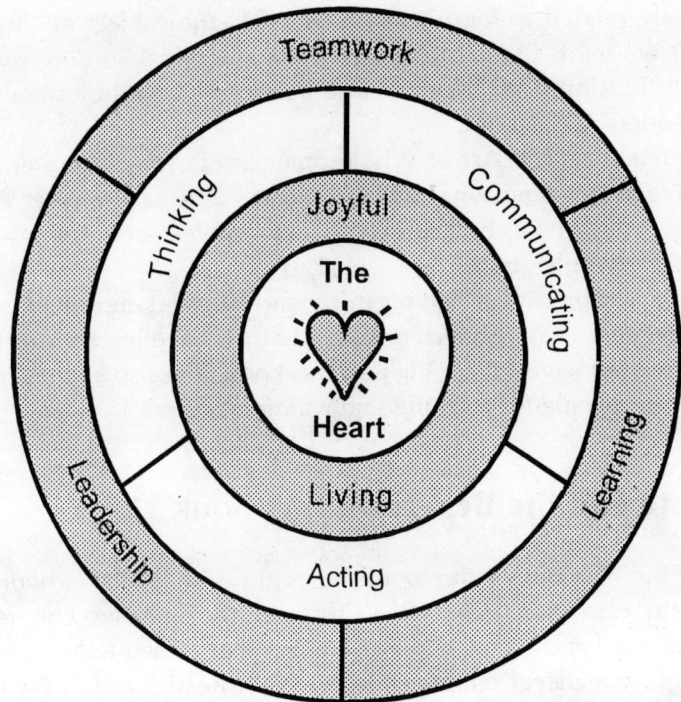

How to Manage from the Heart

'Communicating—The Art of Joyful Relating', is discussed in Chapter 5. We learn about the power of effective communication, and how processes such as active listening and assertiveness can significantly enhance our insight. We also discover how they can help integrate us with other people.

Thinking and communicating would be sterile without acting. Having equipped ourself with the capacity to see clearly and to share an inspiring vision, we then move to 'Acting—Skills for Managing Time and Life' in Chapter 6. This chapter is about the art of making things happen. It is about the nitty-gritty of living your life in alignment with the deepest values close to the Heart.

The next layer is about applying all that we have learnt to learning, teamwork and leadership. All these build on the processes developed in the earlier chapters. In Chapter 7 we learn how learning gives us the evolutionary edge. We understand what learning is, why it is important in today's environment, and what the three levels of learning are. We also look at 'learning organizations' and how we can enhance learning at all levels.

Closely related to learning is teamwork, the subject of Chapter 8. With it we learn the art of working together and solving problems joyfully. Putting it all together in a balanced and wholesome way is what leadership is about.

'Leadership—The Art of Wholesomeness' is what Chapter 9 deals with. We understand what wholesomeness and balance are. We then see how being whole and leading others to wholesomeness is what good leadership is truly about.

Finally, Chapter 10 on 'Staying in Touch—Networking and Integration' shares ways to stay connected with what we have learnt, and to keep reminding ourselves of the ideas in this book. It is also about staying in touch with people for learning and acting together.

How to Get the Best from this Book

To get the best out of this book, to begin with, see this book like a bridge to your own Heart. Read through the first two chapters, the 'Introduction' and then Chapter 2 on the Heart. Then follow your bliss and go to whichever chapter interests you. Read through the chapter and reflect on the 'Ideas for Playful Action' given at the end. Select some of these for experimenting with. Try them out joyfully and review your experience from time to time. As you flip through the pages of this book, see what resonates with the peace in your heart. Sense what makes you calm and peaceful. Look for ideas and insights that add more value to your life. Record them in your own *Personal Learning Journal* with a section on 'Ideas for Playful Action'. This journal could be a thick spiral bound notebook in which you could record your feelings, thoughts, insights and ideas for playful action as you go through the book.

As you take concrete action on these ideas, you will experience a freeing of spirit and an expansion of your innate potential. Revisit Chapter 2 on the core and the goal. It connects you to the 'heart of the matter'.

As we master the art of managing from the Heart, interdependence and fullness will unfold. This is how Nature really is. As this fullness unfolds, our capacity to respond to life with joy increases. Joy is love, and love is God, or the Heart. Loving is the highest expression of learning, and responding creatively to life's challenges is the highest expression of love.

According to Mikhail Naimy (1971), the only lesson to learn is love:

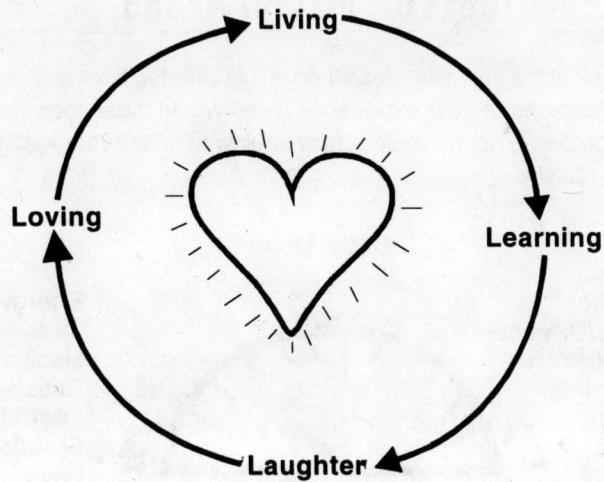

You live that you may learn to love,
You love that you may learn to live.
No other lesson is required of Man.

This is the true meaning of managing from the Heart—living, learning and loving together. To make good things happen and enjoy each moment of life. Getting a lot done and having a lot of fun!

With these pages, I invite you on a journey to the Heart of light and love. I welcome you to a further expansion of joy in your life.

Ideas for Playful Action

1. Take a look at the joy meter described in this chapter. If we took readings for different aspects of your experience, what would these look like? Please put a large dot (•) on the scales shown below to reflect your readings at this point in your life:

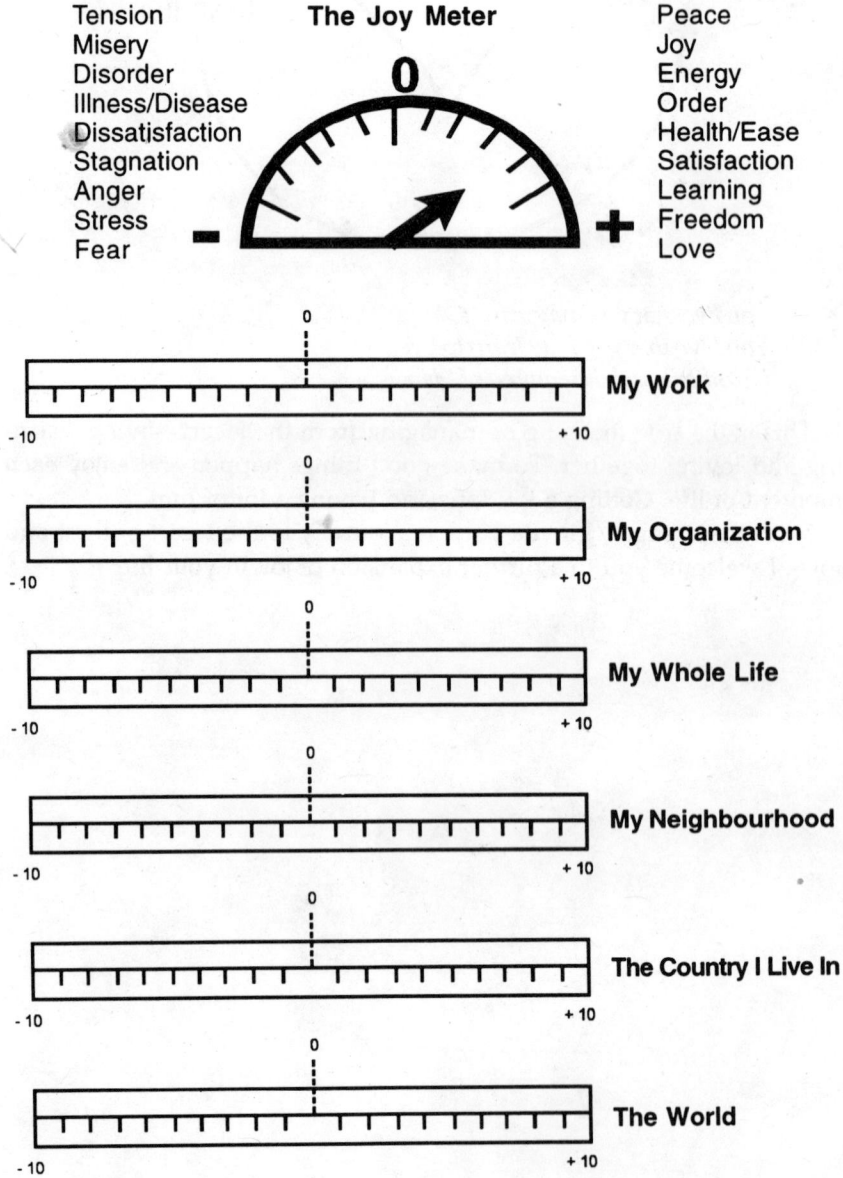

Tension	**The Joy Meter**	Peace
Misery		Joy
Disorder	**0**	Energy
Illness/Disease		Order
Dissatisfaction		Health/Ease
Stagnation		Satisfaction
Anger		Learning
Stress	**−** **+**	Freedom
Fear		Love

My Work

− 10   0   + 10

My Organization

− 10   0   + 10

My Whole Life

− 10   0   + 10

My Neighbourhood

− 10   0   + 10

The Country I Live In

− 10   0   + 10

The World

− 10   0   + 10

2. Reflect on your own life and think of areas which make you uncomfortable. See these as opportunities for growth. List them below:

   - Individual
   - Organizational
   - Global

3. Which areas of your life could do with more:

   - Insight?
   - Integration?
   - Inspired Action?

   Use the table in this chapter to jog your ideas. What steps can you take to make these happen?

4. Sit silently seeking the guidance of your innermost guide . . . your Heart. Ask the question: 'What do I need to do to be whole?' Write down your answers using quick non-stop writing for a few minutes.

5. Study the model of 'How to Manage from the Heart' given in this chapter. Identify the areas you need to put more attention on.

6. Take a decision to accept life as it is and to start enjoying it here and now. What are some things you can start doing/stop doing? List them down and set up some time to make them happen.

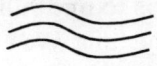

2

The Heart

The Core and the Goal

If I am to know God directly,
I must become completely God,
and God I,
so that this God and this I
become one I
MEISTER ECKHART

The purpose of our life is to find fulfilment. In the pursuit of this goal, we are busy all the time. We are either running after things or running away from things. From morning to night, and even during the night, the mind–body is active trying to find fulfilment. Each one of us has our own notion of what it will take to fulfil us. On this perpetual treadmill seeking the fulfilment of our dreams, we achieve some objectives and then new ones take over. What we all want is the feeling of lasting satisfaction which can come when our wants and deep desires are met.

There are some universal wants that we all have, such as:

- Good health
- The freedom to pursue our own inner calling and to express ourselves
- A sense of community
- A clean and green environment
- A world full of harmony and peace
- Inner satisfaction
- Outer abundance

All these can be summed up in wanting a *joyful life*, now and forever . . . for ourselves and for the coming generations.

Our basic longings are deeply connected to our notions of who we are. If I *see* myself as being powerful, I will act in a confident and empowered way. My craving for power will not be high. On the other hand, if I see myself as a limited entity with little power, I will try my best to gain control over other people. I may also seek external trappings of power to complete my inner sense of deficiency. All of us have different patterns of deficiency and desire born out of different notions of who we are.

Most of us have a limited notion of who we really are. We imagine that we are the body, or the role we are playing, or a member of a particular religion. Each of these limited notions has a sense of deficiency or a lack of something associated with it. For example, getting identified with the body gives us the feeling of being limited in space and time. This body has to die one day while I would like to stay on forever. So I try to prolong my life and collect things to be more joyful. I write my name on walls and trees to 'live on after I die'.

Getting identified with the mind shows me how limited my knowledge (read contents of memory) is. I therefore keep collecting bits of information, quotes, stories and newspaper cuttings to 'expand my knowledge' and to 'increase my mental wealth'.

In other words, my sense of incompleteness or limitation becomes a driving force in my life. To fill this gap and to seek the fullness of completion becomes the purpose of my life. One's identity, thus, defines ones purpose. It serves like a silent springboard for our goals. This springboard of identity can be located at different levels of Existence. Just as an ocean has different levels, Existence—or the whole of life—also exists in different layers. In the ocean, we have rough and choppy waves on the surface. At its deepest level it is still. Life is somewhat similar. One way of looking at life as a whole is to see it as a continuum, going from:

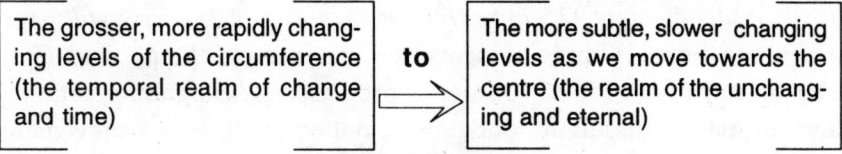

The grosser, more rapidly changing levels of the circumference (the temporal realm of change and time)	**to**	The more subtle, slower changing levels as we move towards the centre (the realm of the unchanging and eternal)

The Centre represents the Silence of Being . . . the very Heart of Life. This is depicted symbolically in the figure given on the next page.

Different people 'park' their notions of 'I' at different levels of Existence. Some have a predominantly physical idea of who they are. This would correspond to I_1 in the following figure.

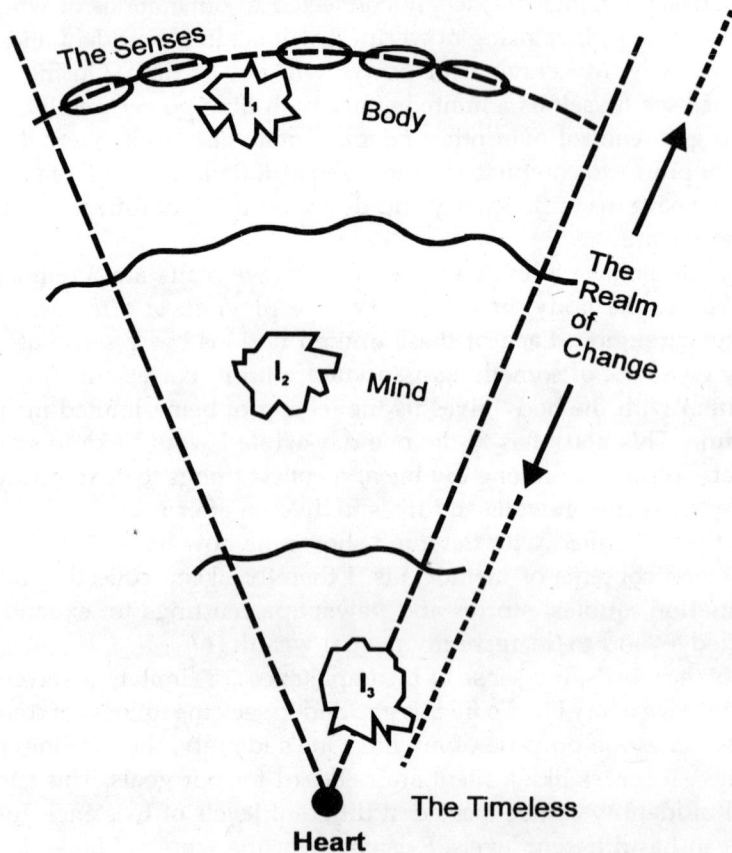

The Changing World

The Senses

Body

I_1

The
Realm
of
Change

I_2 Mind

I_3

The Timeless

Heart

Where We Locate Our 'I'

Others would have a more mental or intellectual notion of who they are (I_2). Still others may identify with the divine Spirit, but may *still* have a separate (limited) image of themselves, for example, 'I am a soul' (I_3). The journey of our life is a journey of progressively expanding, refining and ultimately dissolving our limited notion of 'I'. It is a movement towards total oneness with life as a whole.

In this journey, the greatest teacher or *Guru* is life itself!

The direction in which it is pushing us is the direction of wholesomeness. From limited, partial and false notions of ourselves, we move through the promptings of life's experiences towards a true, complete, and whole realization of our true self. We are all born and go through a whole series of experiences. Each experience teaches us something. It provides us with the fuel we need to grow and unfold. Each setback or suffering is a gentle nudge from life. It teaches us to look at our ways and make the necessary changes towards a more balanced and loving life.

The expansion of happiness is the purpose of life, and evolution is the process through which it is fulfilled . . . the expansion of happiness carries with it the expansion of intelligence, power, creativity and everything that may be said to be of significance to Life.

MAHARISHI MAHESH YOGI

One's life becomes an unfolding drama of progressive completion. One moves from lower levels of fulfilment to higher levels . . . much like the ripening of a fruit on a tree.

Each level of understanding of 'who I am' has a level of joy and peace associated with it. The more expanded my notion of self, the more peaceful I become. When I learn to slowly let go of all false notions of the unreal or limited I, and reach out into the fullness and glory of the Heart (my real Self), I experience an expansion of blissfulness and joy. The joy meter described in Chapter 1 progressively moves towards the right. Life's purpose can then be seen as a dance of unfolding evolution . . . a progressive movement towards completeness, wholeness and oneness.

A human being is part of the whole called by us 'Universe', a part limited in time and space. He experiences himself, his thoughts and feelings as something separated from the rest—a kind of optical delusion of his consciousness. This delusion is a kind of prison for us, restricting us to our personal desires and to affection for a few people nearest to us. Our task must be to free ourselves from this prison by widening our circle of compassion to embrace all living creatures and the whole of nature in its beauty.

The following table shows the progressive journey of our notion of 'I' from the *realm of change* to the *realm of the timeless*. Finally, it dissolves in one beautiful and mysterious embrace that integrates and unifies the timeless and temporal dimensions of life into one.

ALBERT EINSTEIN

This state of being or wholeness is the goal of evolution. It is what we have called the Heart in this book. It is a rather funny goal because it is already attained! What we are seeking is already found. It is like a lost pair of spectacles which was all along perched on our nose while we were frantically looking for it all over the house. Or, like the musk deer, who hunts for the source of its own musk in all corners of the forest. Life is a process of learning towards this lost insight. It is a progressive journey of return to our own origin. As Osho says of the Heart:

You are the way and you are the goal,
and there is no distance between you and the goal.
You are the seeker and you are the sought;
there is no distance between the seeker and the sought;
You are the worshipper and You are the worshipped.
You are the disciple and you are the Master.
You are the means and you are the end.
This is the Great Way.

OSHO

How the 'I' Unfolds

	Stage 1	Stage 2	Stage 3
■ Where the 'I' is Located	Body	Mind	Existence, Life
■ What One Sees as **Identity**	'I am limited in space and time. I am deficient'	'The Divine am I, Eternal am I, pure am I . . .'	All one! Mystery?
■ What One Sees as **Purpose**	'I have to acquire, get, complete. . .' 'I have to get rid off . . .' 'I have to hold onto . . .'	'Doing the will of the creator'	Leela .... Divine Play!

All of life's experiences are prodding us towards this understanding of unity or of discovering our own true self. This is a state of deep harmony and health in its truest sense. It is a very peaceful and blissful experience where there is nothing to do and no doer. Yet all that needs to happen happens of its own accord. This bliss and divine freedom is the goal of all goals. It is the very end towards which all our striving, wittingly or unwittingly, is leading us. Whether we like it or not, all that we do is a search for our divine self.

Describing the Indescribable

The central core of managing from the Heart is this innermost self. It is both the means of our unfolding, and also the goal. It is like the pivot of a wheel, which balances and upholds the movement of the wheel and yet remains completely still. It is an important reference for our lives and the very goal of our evolution.

In what follows, I will share several ways of looking at this process. What I will describe in these paragraphs is at best a mystery and often beyond the comprehension of the logical mind. So I'll need your patience and sensitivity.

Our mind works with words. The Heart is beyond words. Yet, there are words that are a fragrance of the ultimate. These words can be seen like a spring-board to dive into the understanding of the Heart. Buddha compared this process to using a thorn to pull out another thorn, and then throwing away both the thorns. These words are not the truth, but are like windows which open out onto the sky of truth. This sky is not out there somewhere. It is your own blissful, free and divine core.

> It is not for the sake of the husband that the husband is dear, but for the sake of the Self that the husband is dear. Not for the sake of the sons, are the sons dear, but for the sake of the Self that the sons are dear. Not for the sake of the wealth that the wealth is dear, but for the sake of the Self that the wealth is dear. It is not for the sake of anything that anything is dear, but for the sake of the Self that everything is dear. Dear Maitreyi, the Self should be realized, should be heard, should be reflected upon and meditated upon.
>
> SAGE YAJNAVALKYA TO HIS WIFE MAITREYI

The analogies described below can be seen as fingers pointing to the mystery. You can see where the finger is pointing, and let go of the finger!

While ice and waves represent different forms of water, everything is still water. One wave on an ocean might be bigger than another one, but both *are* the ocean. Similarly, while ice floating on water apparently looks separate from water, it finally dissolves and becomes water.

Pure awareness or unbounded consciousness is like water in the above example. Pure awareness is the ultimate witness. Whatever we see or touch or feel is the *observed* or the seen. That which is aware of it, or sees it, is the *observer* or the *seer*. Anything that I can see or observe (including my thoughts, feelings, bodily sensations, memories) are all in the realm of the seen. The seer is pure awareness. This leads us to some interesting insights.

The awareness within us, which witnesses all our states and changing conditions, cannot be seen itself. Whatever I can observe or conceptualize is, therefore, not me. Any image, idea or notion that I have of myself is only a limited mental construct. There is a deeper awareness, which is my innermost Self, witnessing it. The real witnessing self, therefore, is

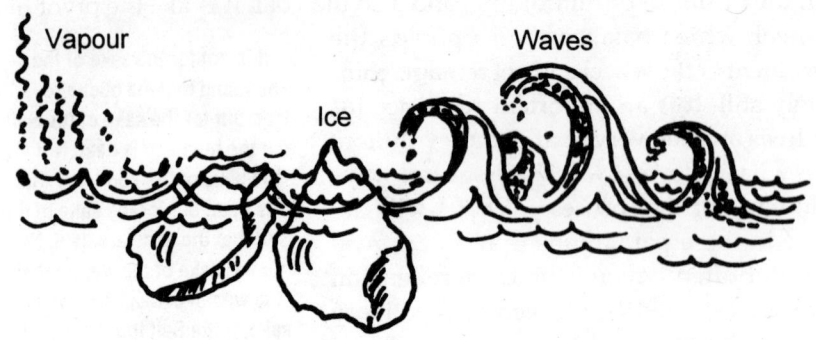

Vapour

Waves

Ice

Apparently Separate
But All are Water

Forms of Spirit: All are One and the One is All

beyond all conceptions or definitions. If we could define it, it would be something we observe and not the witnessing self. So, we cannot answer the question *'Who am I?'* with a clear definition. Any definition is an observable concept and not the innermost witness.

This lands us into mysterious territory again! Not being able to define myself means I have no boundaries. If I have no boundary, then the unbounded whole is I. Since there can be only one whole, my self and yourself is the same. What we today think of as our limited selves are but small waves on the one ocean of Being which is all this. This is *poorna, wholeness* or *Heart* or whatever other name we give it. This is pure unbounded love. No separation is experienced anywhere. It is the mystical oneness and grace described by the masters of yore.

It is, as the *Upanishads* say, *'Seeing all beings in one's own self and one's own self in all beings.'* This timeless love also includes everything that changes. Paradox and mystery once more! In the earlier paragraph,

> **The Ultimate Truth**
>
> It moves. It moves not. It is in the distant. It is in the near. It is within all. It is outside all.
>
> ISHA UPANISHAD

we had seen the centre to be unchanging and timeless. And now we see it as including the whole realm of change also. It is both and neither. It is empty because there is nothing there, and yet it is so full. Everything, from the smallest blade of grass to the greatest galaxy is contained in its infinite love.

So what can one say? 'Empty–fullness' perhaps. Similarly, we can think of love as infinitely attached, because it flows to everything. Yet, it is also the epitome of detachment. Nothing sticks to it. It is blissfully pure and silent. And yet the music of life, with all its notes is part of it.

If you look at a white page as background for writing, it is empty. If you look at the shapes on it you see content or the foreground. Like that, in life, we are usually so busy focussing our attention on things (the foreground) that we miss attention on awareness itself (the background).

Take a look at these shapes. What do you see? Now focus attention on the white background. Holding the page at a distance may help. What appears now? If you haven't got it, turn to the end of this chapter for the insight.

The table below will give you a feel of the differences in behaviour arising from being the real self, which is our central core, and identifying with our limited self which is our ego:

Limited Self (Partial)	vs	**Real Self** (Whole)
Ego, Mind		Mystery, No-Mind
Fear		Love
Stressed and Unbalanced		Healthy and Balanced
Dis-ease		Ease
Bound		Free
Rigid		Fluid
Artificial		Real
Deficient		Full
Fixed		Flexible
Greedy		Giving
Habitual		Creative
Focused on thoughts		Present to feelings
Judging		Accepting
Attached		Detached
Circumference		Centre
Agitated		Peaceful
Dual		One

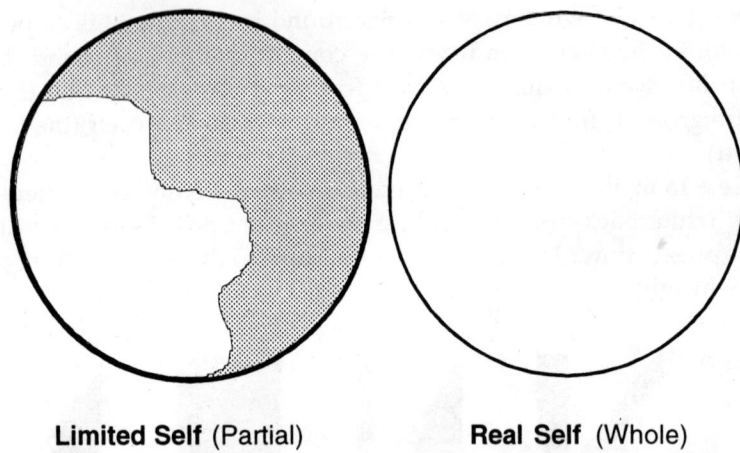

Limited Self (Partial)   **Real Self** (Whole)

The real self encompasses and accepts the left-hand side.

> *It is good to look outside because outside is God's creation; it is good to look inside because inside is sitting the creator. Both are good. Eyes are meant to blink; they are not meant to remain open forever and they are not meant to be closed forever. They are meant to blink—open and close, open and close. That is the rhythm—out and in, out and in. Look outside—the beautiful creation; look inside—the beautiful God. And by and by you will see that the in and out meet and mingle and are one.*
> OSHO

    Having got some insight into the behaviour arising from the real self, you might be wondering how to make this a way of life. While the ideas discussed here are central to joyful living, one still needs a practical pathway towards living one's life with *Being* as a continuous foundation. How do we practically live from the Heart in our own lives?

    Meditation is the pathless path to doing this.

Meditation . . . Connecting with the Heart

In this chapter, so far, we have seen how an erroneous perception of who we are keeps us away from realizing our full potential. This erroneous perception arises from getting trapped in the mind.

    Human behaviour has its mainspring in the human mind. All that we think, say or do is shaped by what we hold in our minds. This includes our values, beliefs, assumptions about ourselves; about the world and other people; our habitual patterns (or ruts) of thinking, our memories and associations from the past, and our anxieties about the future. All these form, as it were, a massive filter through which we interact with the world. This is a subtle but powerful web which constrains and binds our thoughts, communications and actions into a narrow range. The result is what we see all around us today. People having more material wealth than they need but feeling trapped, or empty. Anger, frustration and incorrect perceptions on the job. A sense of helplessness in the face of challenges even though so much can be done. A loss of the ability to innovate and to come up with new ideas, and a general sense of dissatisfaction, or at best, indifference. Needless to say, these problems are attended by one or more of the physical symptoms that are related to stress. Coming back to the first statement—the potential that we were talking about is the potential to live life freely, productively, creatively— a life full of peace and compassion, and inspired service accompanied by a deep sense of inner satisfaction and poise. What keeps us from living out this potential? The webs, ruts and traps that bind us in our minds!

Meditation is the route to come out of the prison of our own limitations.

What is Meditation?

Meditation is a simple, easy and effortless method which takes awareness beyond our mind to a space which is totally and completely free. It is a gentle movement towards the mind's ground-state of unbounded awareness. Meditation is going beyond thought to the very source of all thought. It is the seeing of what is and going beyond it.

Meditation is a process of transcending the barriers of our false I by witnessing it. As we have discussed, we cannot be something that we watch. When in meditation I watch my body and the sensations in it, when I witness the movements of my mind and feelings, then, by and by, it dawns on me that there is a deeper reality beyond the changes of the body–mind and the outer world. In the figure on page 44 meditation means moving closer to the centre of the figure. As I do this, I begin to let go into a space of deep peace, silence and rest. In fact, at the very centre nothing moves because nothing is there.

Meditation has therefore always been described as the deepest level of rest. A wit has rightly called it 'the last resort!'. In meditation, we are totally present to the moment. We are now here and yet nowhere!

The heart of meditation is witnessing and being aware. I am sitting in this chair looking at a statue of Lord Buddha. The statue is there and this body–mind is here. Yet there is one more dimension. The inner witness is watching this body–mind seeing Buddha's statue, listening to the sound of traffic on the street outside and watching the flow of words onto paper. This witness is meditation. Since there is no tangible witness to lay one's hand on, one doesn't really know if one is there or not there. That is why meditation is also a mystery beyond comprehension.

In a nutshell, meditation is:

- Being the real or whole self, the Heart
- Being Love
- Being 'now–here'
- Total 'let-go' and deep rest
- A mystery beyond comprehension
- A play to revel in

You may have heard that the word Zen has its origins in the word *dhyana* which is the Sanskrit for 'meditation'. When *dhyana* was taken to China by masters like Bodhidharma, it was called *Cha,an* there. On proceeding further to Japan, it turned into Zen, which in Japanese also means 'good' or 'mindful'.

Meditation Myths Debunked

There are many misconceptions about meditation. The statements below are meant to debunk them:

1. Meditation is not forcing the mind to be thoughtless. It involves 'no-doing'. Any attempt to force the mind into any state is not meditation.

2. Meditation is not a state of mind. All states and experiences are modifications of the mind. Meditation is the witnessing 'no-mind' which is beyond all states and all changes. All states of the mind come and go. They are transient. Meditation is beyond any change and is eternally there. It neither rises nor sets. It is important to remember this. Many people associate meditation with a blank, dark emptiness of the mind, or with a state of *'light joyfulness'.* This is not meditation. These are only transient experiences that come and go. Meditation is the seer, which witnesses all states.

3. Meditation is not concentration on any single point or theme. It is very commonly assumed that if you want to meditate, you have to 'concentrate the mind' onto one thing. This is not the aim of meditation although it may be an initial approach. Meditation is openness to all possibility. It is a silent acceptance of everything that is. It therefore does not exclude some things and prefers others.

4. *Meditation is not 'religion'*. Many religions of the world have some form of meditation as their core. For example, Hinduism has customs of using certain *mantras* or sounds as vehicles for meditation. Similarly, Buddhist traditions use techniques such as *Vipassana*, which literally means 'insight'. However, meditation in its purest form is a simple process of going beyond the mind and revelling in spirit. The spirit is universal and one. It is beyond the confines of ritual and organized religion. In fact, it is the very sky to which all the windows of religion open out.

5. *Meditation is not glorified sleeping*. Many people feel that, just because both are done with closed eyes, sleep and meditation are the same thing! Many beginners fall asleep when they first meditate. This reinforces the idea that meditation is a form of deeply refreshing sleep. This misconception is born out of not understanding the difference between sleep, the waking state and meditation. The table below captures the difference.

	Not Restful	Restful
Not Alert	Dream Sleep	Deep Sleep
Alert	Waking State	MEDITATION

During the waking state, we are alert to what is happening around us, but are not rested. When we are asleep, we are not alert to what is happening around us and may be rested or not rested depending upon how deep our sleep is. It also depends on our level of emotional turbulence and dreaming. Meditation, however, is restful alertness. It is a stateless substratum on which the states of wakefulness, dream and deep sleep rise and set. The substratum itself neither rises nor sets.

6. *Meditation is not a daily ritual.* While you may start off by scheduling some time for meditation everyday, it will slowly expand from
something you *do* for half an hour everyday to your whole life. A cup of
tea sipped with awareness, remembering who you are, is meditation.
Walking with total attention to your body and the surrounding stimuli
is meditation. Sleeping at night and watching your body–mind sleep
while you are fully awake is meditation. It is no longer something you
do in the morning, but something you become and are. It is life itself.

7. *Meditation is not listening to the 'inner voice'.* It is also not praying.
Both these processes are very useful. However, since in both cases there
is a sense of doing, they are not meditation, which is 'non-doing'. Also,
both processes have an underlying sense of expectation that either God
will speak or God will listen. Meditation is beyond all expectations.

Some Methods for Meditation

Just as a circle has many routes from its circumference to its centre,
there are many approaches or pathways to reach the self. All of them
take you to the same place . . . your very own self, the ocean on which
all changes are like waves. In fact, the word *'medi'* in Latin means 'middle'
and it points to our centre. It may interest you to know that the word
'medicine' also has the same root. It is about connecting with our Heart,
the ultimate healer, and leading a balanced life by choosing the middle
path.

Different methods of meditation have a different appeal and their
own appropriateness for different people. There is no right or wrong
method. Since we are all different, a method that suits my needs may
not suit yours. Just as there are different specialities in a hospital, each
one catering to a certain kind of a problem, there are many different
routes to the Heart through meditation.

Initially, unbounded awareness remains for a short time. The regular
practice of meditation, however, establishes it over time as a permanent, never-changing basis for everything in one's life.

Some of the well-known methods currently practised in India are
Vipassana, Dynamic Meditation and other methods by Osho Rajneesh,
Transcendental Meditation, *Siddha Samadhi Yoga, Sahaj Yoga* and *Kriya
Yoga.* While the outer processes may be different in each case, as one
approaches the inner core of being, all methods will have the same three
underlying features:

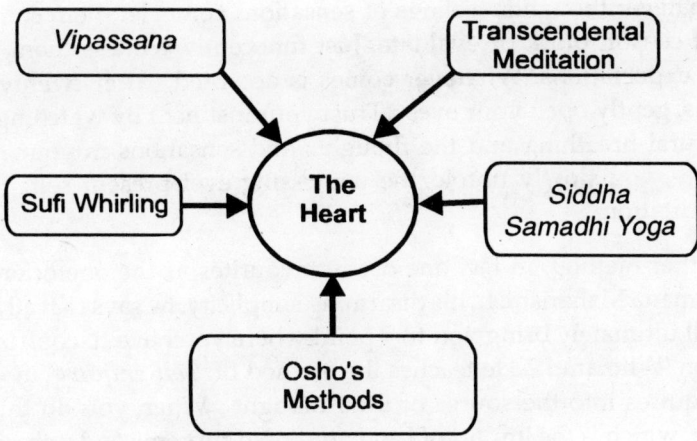

Many Paths . . . One Goal!

1. *No doing.* No concentration. No forcing. No analysis. No effort. No fighting. No regulation or control. No day-dreaming or imagining. No verbalization and no artificial creation. Just a state of relaxed and easy 'let-go' and silent being. Some people call this 'total surrender'.

2. *No judging.* No judgements. No evaluations. No expectations or comparisons or desires. Letting go of even the desire for freedom. Dropping the past and the future. Totally accepting whatever is in a choiceless way. No running away from anything or running after anything. Just being here.

3. *Being present to what is.* Being 'here–now', totally present to what is, innocently witnessing the process.

You can find many teachers and methods of meditation in your own city, if you actively look for them. Trust the peace of your Heart to guide you to the right one for you.

Two Methods to Play With

One simple method to get started is called Annapanna, which literally means 'incoming–outgoing breath'. Here's how you can do it:

1. Sit comfortably with your back straight. Be in an easy posture.
2. Close your eyes gently. Let go. Relax.
3. Witness the rise and fall of your belly as you breathe in and breathe out. Do not force, concentrate or evaluate.

4. Whatever thoughts, feelings or sensations come, let them come. Do not censor, block or evaluate. Just innocently witness them. Have no expectations. Whatever comes is accepted. After twenty minutes, gently open your eyes. (Trust your instinct.) By watching your natural breathing and the thoughts and sensations in your mind–body, you slowly unfold the witnessing ever-present self. This is meditation.

Another method, in fact one of my favourites, is the one offered by Shri Ramana Maharishi. In his disarming simplicity, he says that all methods will ultimately bring you to a point where you have to confront the question 'Who am I'? He teaches the method of *self-enquiry* in which one enquires into the source of the I-thought . When you do this, the real self, which is the import of I and your own supreme and unbounded being, is realized. You discover that which you always were and will be. You drown all false notions of who you are in the vast and mysterious ocean of knowing.

As Shri Ramana himself once remarked:

> *Do not meditate–Be!*
> *Do not think that you are–Be!*
> *Don't think of Being–You are!*

He taught that our attention during meditation needs to be continuously on the 'experiencer' rather than on the experience.

Self-enquiry, according to Shri Ramana should not be regarded as a meditation practice that takes place at certain hours and in certain positions, It needs to carry on irrespective of what one is doing. He saw no contradiction between our regular actions and a meditative foundation for life.

Benefits of Meditation

Meditation is an end in itself. It is its own goalless goal. It is not something we do to get benefits. However, many benefits do happen as we meditate regularly. These however, should not become the reason why we meditate because that very expectation takes you away from the spirit of meditation (No-mind). Statements like: *'I've been meditating for six months now and nothing is happening!'* or *'God give me patience and I want it right now,'* come from the mind! The expectation of benefit from meditation itself becomes a hindrance in its most natural flow.

Having said this, some of the benefits of meditation are described below. These are based on extensive research. The benefits of regular meditation can be looked at three levels: individual, organisational and global.

Each higher level of benefits is a manifestation of the preceding earlier level. For example, as my own personal sense of well-being and inner freedom unfolds, this has a positive impact on my interactions with other people. As people begin to work better with one another, the organization as a whole begins to benefit. It becomes more creative and flexible and works more like an organism with a unified spirit and Heart, rather than like a machine. As organizations (especially business organizations) begin to operate with greater awareness and more joyfully, their impact on life as a whole begins to improve.

Looking at it in another way, the world is made up of people. It is their thinking, communicating and acting, which collectively impacts life on this planet. As peace and health begin to unfold in individual lives, the effects begin to unfold at the gross level. In fact, the whole thrust of the 'New Management' movement is based upon managing from our most profound inner awareness and in connection with the consciousness of others and with nature. This is made possible by people who meditate and who have begun to live more peaceful and harmonious lives.

A look at the effects described above shows that they all contribute towards a more wholesome life at the individual and collective level. It does not mean that problems will disappear overnight or that difficulties will not arise anymore. They will only be seen in a new light and will be responded to more creatively. Life will be more 'abundant' as people discover their own and others' inner resources. Behaviour driven by a sense of deficiency will be less prevalent.

Benefits of Meditation at the Individual Level

1. Regular meditation has a positive effect on one's *physical health*. Research has shown that regular meditation improves physiological processes like metabolism, blood circulation and resting. Chronic illnesses like asthma and high blood pressure have been cured through regular meditation. Dean Ornish (1990), in his popular book *Reversing Heart Disease,* shows how exercise, a vegetarian diet and regular meditation can unblock clogged arteries in the heart.

2. One's own sense of *worth* and *self-respect* improve significantly. One experiences a deep 'okayness' which is not dependent on any external conditions. The understanding that one is pure unbounded

awareness melts away all limitation and fear. Discovering one's true self leads to a dramatic shift in the paradigm we hold of life. Life becomes more playful and less serious. This contributes further to our effectiveness and also to a deep acceptance of life as it comes. The net result is a growing sense of the innate perfection of life. This significantly reduces our stress.

3. *Creativity unfolds* as we let go of the mind. We continue to use the mind, but more like a useful slave. It no longer is the master. Originality, flexibility and fluency of ideas, all unfold with regular meditation. At the same time our comprehension and the ability to focus also improves. More humour and laughter become a part of our life.

4. *Job satisfaction, productivity and performance* have all been found to increase through regular meditation. This is the outcome of all the above factors as well as increased energy and vitality, decreased anxiety and hostility, and significantly better teamwork.

My own personal experience with regular meditation for over two decades now shows that it connects me with a source of peace and freedom which has nothing to do with outer events. A sense of equanimity and peace have become permanent features of my life.

Organizational Benefits of Meditation

Just as each person has his own level of consciousness, all people working in an organization produce a collective or organizational consciousness. If the individuals making an organization are joyful, enthusiastic, creative and in harmony with nature, the corporate consciousness will reflect this collective wisdom. Not surprisingly, the business will run profitably as well as joyfully. We will find prosperity with peace.

Many organizations are introducing their managers to meditation. This is not surprising. General Motors, for example, spends more money on the healthcare of its workers than it does on the steel for its cars. In this era of organizational transformation, we have found personal transformation to be the stepping stone to collective change. And in our approach, meditation is at the heart of this transformation.

As people begin to reflect the effects of meditation in their life, the following changes and benefits occur at the organizational level:

1. *Productivity and innovation.* As individuals are less cluttered with habits and conditioning, there is more availability of energy for work and life. Creativity comes from a new depth within the individual and new solutions emerge from what seems like totally impossible situa-

tions. The work climate, the quality of work and the aesthetics of work all improve. There is more enjoyment at work and also an increased output.

2. *Strategy and flexibility.* As more people gain insight, the organization can quickly adapt to changes, both internal and external. Forms, roles and priorities change naturally. Despite economic changes, these organizations are more stable and grow while others may have to close shop.

3. *Teamworking.* As people become clearer and more objective, there is less internal conflict and more integration. Interaction is more meaningful and is based on trust and mutual respect. Decisions are made from a wider perspective along with looking at relevant data with full understanding. People relate to each other as human beings and not merely as roles. In fact, roles are just a way of organizing work. There is high play in the organization. People see the funny side of things and are less serious.

4. *Leadership.* Inspired action becomes a way of life in such organizations. Leaders are developed naturally by all. People with more presence, clarity and objectivity are chosen for responsible roles. Leadership is based on presence and expertise rather than on power, popularity, money or position.

5. *Motivation, responsibility and growth.* The rewards become a balanced mix of internal and the external ones rather than only the external. People do not work for material rewards alone, but because they value themselves and want to contribute and enjoy themselves. They also appreciate more freedom and responsibility. Responsibility is defined as the ability to respond appropriately to a given situation. Work becomes a place for enhancing awareness, understanding and personal evolution.

Benefits at the Global Level

'If there has to be peace in this world, let it begin with me.' The whole world is impacted by peoples' choices. What we do, both at the individual as well as the organizational levels, changes the world a little bit. As we become clearer about the 'know why' of things, as our perspectives widen and understanding grows, our thoughts, words and actions create more joyful ripples on earth. This leads to:

- more individual well-being and evolution,
- more harmonious relations between people and between nations, and
- a balanced and caring relationship with Mother Nature.

This is the goal of global well being . . . It is the overarching purpose of life on this planet.

Ideas for Playful Action

1. Stop for a moment and just witness what is happening. Listen to the sounds around you, experience the sensations in your body, feel the taste on your tongue and . . . look for the witness which is watching all this.

2. Try to bring in more mindfulness into your daily actions. This can be done by consciously slowing down the pace of things you normally do, such as, eating your food, writing a letter, walking down the stairs. Do all these at half the speed you normally do.

3. Try out one of the two methods of meditation mentioned in this chapter and record your experiences.

4. Write down your idea of 'I' on a sheet of paper. Then answer, '*who wrote this piece*?' Then answer, '*who is asking this question*?'

Witness the search and BE!

The insight:

≋ 3 ≋

Joyful Living
Values, Good Work and Total Health

God is Love; His plan for creation can
be rooted only in love.
Does not that simple thought,
rather than erudite reasonings,
offer solace to the human heart?
PARAMAHANSA YOGANANDA

The highest good in human beings is their *own self*. This is the love, awareness and bliss of our innermost divine being. Everything worthwhile in life is an expression of this divinity. All that we value is a hidden quest for this divine source.

In Chapter 2, we saw how we can regularly connect with this source. Our steady evolution will one day awaken us to our innate oneness with life. The foundation of living life joyfully is regular meditation. The first story is leading a value-based life, doing work which empowers, and leading an energetic life of total health.

In this chapter, we will learn how to make our Heart the foundation for a value-based life. How some organizations see their values is touched upon next. This is followed by the process of working joyfully as an important aspect of leading a value-based life. Finally, I will share with you some practical tips on how to make our own life healthy and full of energy.

Values

Everything we do is based consciously or unconsciously on our beliefs, attitudes and values. *Values are our conceptions of what is good and desirable. They are our notions of what ought to be.* They are based on assumptions about how the world works. Our idea of what the right thing to do in a situation, comes from our values. They are like our own internal model of reality, somewhat like the operating system of a computer. They affect almost all aspects of our lives and especially the choices we make. They even affect our ways of perceiving the world.

Values are directly connected to our vision of life. When I know the destination that I have to reach, I can choose the correct path when I come to a crossroad. When our values are clearly known because our goal in life is known, we have a sound basis for making the correct choices in different situations. Without a clear sense of purpose and values, we are rather lost and confused. For example, whether to spend an evening at a casino or to spend it in quiet reflection on my work will depend on my values. Similarly, the choice of one's career and the kind of organization one chooses to work in, is also a function of what one considers valuable. That, in turn, is dependent on the contents of our mind.

Most minds are a bundle of conditioning inherited from our parents, our society and our surroundings. Our notions of good and bad, right and wrong are like software handed down from others. The underlying assumptions are rarely questioned. They remain in the subconscious mind and act like red and green lights in moving traffic. They tell us from inside what we should, or should not, do. They are our inner static road-maps to guide us through the territory of life.

If life were static and very much the same at all times and in places for all people, the problem of following our values would be no problem at all. We would have our inner software to evaluate the static situations in our life. All we would have to do to answer the question '*What ought I to do in this situation*?' would be to refer to our internal rule book, which would promptly give us the answer.

But life is not stationary. The only thing permanent is change. One man's nectar is another man's poison. My shoes, which are so comfortable on my feet, will give you blisters because your feet are different. My needs for development, at this point in my journey of life, are different from yours. What is good in one part of the world, may not be so in another. What is good at one point in history may not be so anymore. So, what do we do?

Do we consider the baggage of our do's and dont's as a lot of moralistic hogwash to be discarded because it is irrelevant and impractical in today's society? Do we cling to it the way a drowning man would clutch a life-saving buoy? Or do we use the inner compass beyond our mind to guide us safely through life's turbulent journey?

Most young managers today tend to take the former view. They talk about freedom from the lifeless structures imposed on them by others. They talk of rebellion and authenticity, shunning the hypocrisy that has characterized earlier generations. They speak with passion of leading a more creative and contributory life where *'they are doing their own thing'*, *'letting others be and trusting others to let them be'*. These voices are an expression of a longing for freedom and a creative and full life. Ask any of these youngsters what they truly want out of life and they will tell you that they want good work, happiness, good health, and peace. Who doesn't?

Isn't this what values are all about anyway? Aren't all our notions of 'ought' and 'ought not' supposed to help us choose so that we can maximize our chances of leading a wholesome life? So, where is the trouble then?

In what follows, we take a fresh look at values.

The ultimate source of all values is our own *real self*. When we probe deeper into why we value things, we will see that the reason is the Heart. For example, when we value friendship, we are valuing our own inner ocean of connectedness on which we are but transient waves, superficially separated but deeply connected all the same. When we value a beautiful work of art, we are actually valuing the deep silence that occurs in the moment of rapturous wonder as we see a thing of great beauty. To get a direct feel of this connection, lets play with this small exercise:

List down a few things you really want in life. Put them in blobs like these below:

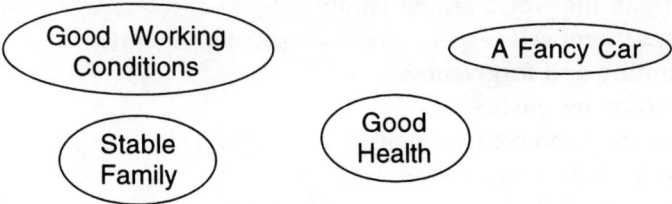

Now for each of these things ask, 'Why do I want this?' Try to get to the very essence of the 'real' reason you want that thing. Put the answer in another blob below the first one. Now for the second blob, again ask the question, 'Why do I want *this*?' Keep going on like this, asking the why question at least five times. You may find that the answer begins to converge onto a few common blobs as you go deeper in. It will probably all begin to look like a tree of this kind:

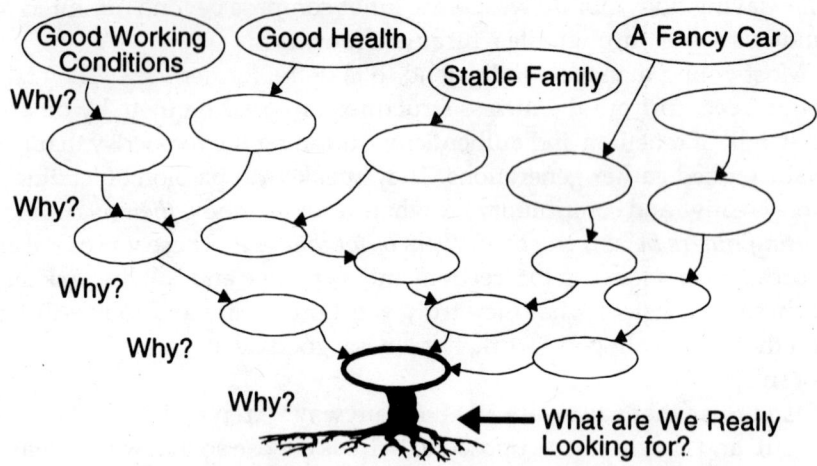

What is at the root of this tree? What are we really looking for?

The Brahamakumaris, a spiritual group residing in Mount Abu have distilled a list of about forty values into a condensed list of 'Twelve Wonder Values' (Hassija 1995a). Their view is that if these twelve values are adopted in all professions and in all age groups, it would make our world a better place. These are given below.

Twelve Wonder Values

Take a look at the twelve values listed below:

1. Spiritual love and goodwill; concern and cooperation for the well-being of the world as one family
2. Respect and self-respect, based on spiritual identity
3. Humility and forgiveness
4. Honesty and justice
5. Simplicity and contentment
6. Purity; cleanliness
7. Effort for excellence; enthusiasm
8. Positive thinking and self-control
9. Tolerance; non-violence; harmony
10. Trusteeship and detachment
11. Truthfulness
12. Equanimity and peace

If you examine them carefully, it will become clear that each one of these values depends upon a still deeper reference. For example, simplicity and contentment (5) are born out of being full inside. They are also born out of being one with nature, which is not only simple, but also supremely abundant.

Similarly, equanimity and peace (12) refer to the experience of balance and inner silence which comes from being ourselves. Equanimity comes from transcending the mind with its likes and dislikes. It comes from the innocent, non-judging acceptance of pure awareness. Again, it is the divine Heart which is the reference. The same is true for honesty and justice (4) which arise from looking at the *whole* situation objectively—a standpoint which can be ours only when we see things directly as they are from the fullness of 'no-mind'. A similar reasoning can be applied to all the other remaining values.

So, *if we find our silent Heart, we have found the source of all values.* We have come home fulfilling our deepest longings. We have finally woken up, shedding all our illusions and limitations behind. We have found our inner barometer of bliss, our inner compass of eternal principle, which can act as an unfailing guide in every situation in life. We have found the secret of living in freedom and creativity in the here and now. Coming back to the practical aspects of living a value-based life, we have two choices. One, we can assess each situation through the mind and try to get a perfect solution to a complex problem involving hundreds of variables, known and unknown. Alternatively, we can just rely on the source and goal of all values to spontaneously guide us in each moment.

Relying entirely on the mind blocks insight. Imagine a blind man following instructions given to him to come out of a house, cross the road and enter a building on the other side. He has no idea about the structure of the house or of the traffic on the road. Because of his lack of vision, he has to rely completely on the instructions given to him. This analogy illustrates how some people 'follow values'. The other view of values is to move out of the house with the eyes open, fully aware of one's surroundings and of the changing conditions, taking decisions moment to moment based on a correct understanding of the situation. The second view represents an approach to living a value-based life which is like moving through unknown territory with open eyes and a guiding compass. It is based on instantaneous feedback telling us whether what we are doing is effective or not. The test of this effectiveness is not in the future. Nor is it lying somewhere in the dead past. *It is a direct inner sensing of the degree of peace, calm and freedom, which one finds with every impulse or situation.* It is a direct discernment, here and now, of whether something feels peaceful and free or not. Considering that life happens only in the now, it is simply a way of saying that *I will choose to live each moment blissfully*. It is saying YES to life, and living one's life with full awareness.

You must have guessed my preference by now! Following this way is quite easy, if one is meditating regularly. Just as a person who has tasted sugar can tell if something is sweet or not, one who has centred himself in the divine can sense immediately whether something is wholesome or not.

Meditating regularly keeps us in touch with our innermost divine core, the real self, which serves as a guide for our actions and decisions.

This approach sees life in the here and now as the only goal. What can be more valuable than a moment joyfully lived? A moment which unfolds peace and is not dependent on an inner policeman or an inner rule book, but the highest good lived right now. *The point many people miss is that doing something good, caring and creative is intrinsically joyful and satisfying. The valuable reward is instantaneous!*

Core human values over the ages have intrinsically remained the same. This is because, as we have seen, they are based on timeless principles. Interpretations of these principles, as they apply to this time and place, can however vary.

There are therefore two aspects of values. One is *Shruti*, originating from a direct and immediate experience of reality and the whole truth. This aspect is timeless. It represents the unchanging Heart and the eternal values of life. The other aspect is *Smriti*. This embodies the interpretations of the eternal values as they apply to a particular time and place in history. They form the traditions of that era. *Smriti* can change and often needs to. It is changed by people who are in touch with the underlying stratum of pure awareness and also who have a clear understanding of the needs of a particular time.

It has often happened that certain traditions that were vital and relevant at a particular point in time became obsolete in another age. They became like dead empty shells of what was once a living process. Such traditions are then set aside and new ones created with a clear understanding of our highest good.

Effective people need to listen to their Heart and create their own culture and traditions best suited to them. This process needs to go on all the time because if we 'cling' to a ritual or method for too long, it loses Heart and spirit. It becomes dead. The divine core will always guide you to the right choices for you, if you listen. Looking out to what others are doing may not help much in matters of values. Don't forget that you are unique. Trust your own Heart.

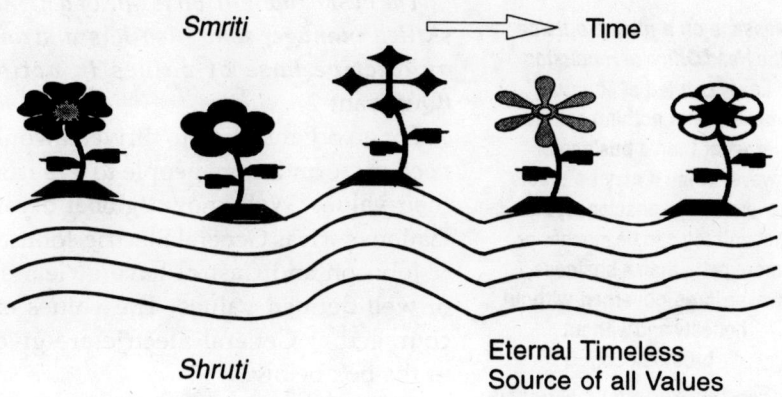

Changing Manifestations of the Timeless Truth

In Quadrant 1, are managers who are weak on skills and have negative values. Quadrant 3 describes managers who are high on skills and have negative values. The characters Duryodhana of the *Mahabharata*, and also Ravana of the *Ramayana* would both fall into Quadrant 3. Such

Skills vs Values

A clear understanding of the values that are current and relevant to one's life needs to go hand in hand with skills in order for managers to be effective.

Chakraborty (1991) talks about a simple framework on how managers need to be good at both skills and values.

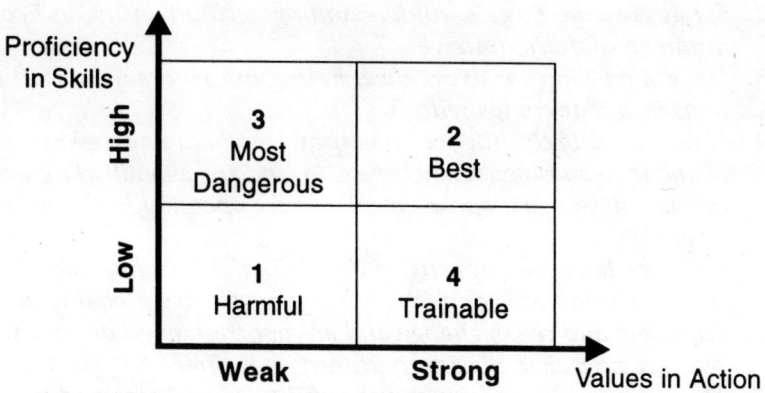

In Quadrant 1, are managers who are weak on skills and have negative values. Quadrant 3 describes managers who are high on skills and have negative values. The characters Duryodhana of the *Mahabharata*, and also Ravana of the *Ramayana* would both fall into Quadrant 3. Such

managers can be dangerous because they actively create negative impacts. Managers who are weak on skills but have good values are ineffective. They can be trained to improve their skills.

The best combination is one of a highly skilled manager who also has a strong and active base of values in action (Quadrant 2).

For an organization to thrive, it would need more and more people to live from their values. Well-known global organizations such as General Electric, Johnson & Johnson and Castrol have a clear set of well-defined values. The values encouraged at General Electric are given in the box below.

Message on a plaque outside the Head Office of Hindustan Lever Limited at Mumbai:
I believe that nothing can be greater than a business, however small it may be that is governed by conscience; and that nothing can be meaner or more petty than a business, however large governed without honesty and without brotherhood.

THE FIRST VISCOUNT LEVERHULME

Management Values of General Electric

General Electric leaders, always with unyielding integrity:

1. *Create a clear, simple, reality-based, customer-focused vision and are able to communicate it straightforwardly to all constituencies.*
2. *Set aggressive targets, understanding accountability and commitment, and are decisive.*
3. *Have a passion for excellence, hating bureaucracy and all the nonsense that comes with it.*
4. *Have the self-confidence to empower others and behave in a boundaryless fashion. They believe in, and are committed to, workout as a means of empowerment and are open to ideas from anywhere.*
5. *Have, or have the capacity to develop, global brains and global sensitivity and are comfortable building diverse global teams.*
6. *Stimulate and relish change and are not frightened or paralyzed by it, seeing change as opportunity, not threat.*
7. *Have enormous energy and the ability to energize and invigorate others. They understand speed as a competitive advantage and see the total organizational benefits that can be derived from a focus on speed.*

In General Electric, a man who 'makes the numbers' or, in other words, meets the business targets, but who does not follow the values of the organization is asked to leave the company. This is the price the organization, pays to build a culture of trust and excellence, with clear values as a foundation. These values guide everything people do. They act like an invisible glue that holds the organization together.

Given below are some of my observations about values in my work as a consultant to many organizations:

- Some vibrant people naturally live out all the values of the organization. They do not have to keep referring to the official list to remind them of these values.
- Other people only go through the motions (of following values). These often include leaders who have the values of their organization framed up on their office walls.
- Many organizations have found a significant improvement in their integration and inspired action as they unfolded their values starting inside out from each person's own personal insights.
- Where this process was supported with regular meditation, the values have remained vital and vibrant.
- When value-based management goes hand in hand with helping people find, and do, their most natural work, spirit unfolds further in the organization. I call this 'good work'.

Good Work

One important dimension of leading a life based on values is doing *good work*. It is the process that happens when we discover our unique strengths and capabilities and joyfully use them to serve other peoples' needs. It also happens when we learn the art of loving whatever work we do.

It is working with a spirit of love and total commitment, making work a constant challenging adventure rather than routine drudgery. Some workers in a company where I consulted many years ago described their work as *'two punches and one lunch'*, the punches referring to punching the time card 'in' and 'out' when they arrived and left. The company's lunch, with its 500-calorie desserts, was the high point of the day.

> The meaning of man's work is the satisfaction of the instinct for adventure that God has implanted in his heart
>
> PAUL TOURNIER

Most people do not love their work. They do not find it a wonderful daily challenge or adventure. For them fun and adventure begins in the evenings or on weekends. That is when they can passionately spend energy on evening classes, theatre, discussions on history, sports, or on creating something with their hands. When they come back to work on Monday, work seems dull and boring once again.

We spend around one-third of our lives at work. This is more than one-tenth of a million hours! Research has shown that not being happy at work can give a person migraines, ulcers, depression or obesity. If work does not help us to grow spiritually and materially, we are wasting our precious life on it.

All this points to the need for people to make 'good work' the main focus of what they do, instead of making it a peripheral activity. This will significantly enhance the unfolding of spirit in organizations. It can do wonders to the world's progress and health.

People can restore their true value by exhalting work and understanding its true significance in life. When we see work as a means of sharing the very best we can and contributing meaningfully to life; and furthermore, when this sharing is born out of our inner conviction and calling, work becomes a spirited and creative adventure. It brings out the full potential of people.

This total working with love leads to an expansion of spirit and joyfulness. Our insight grows. We become more silent inside. Our limited 'I' expands as we reach out to other people through our loving service.

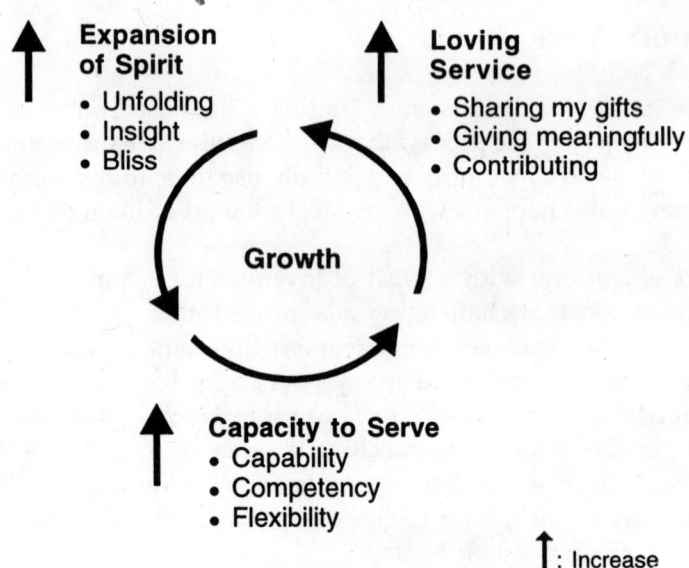

The expansion of spirit, in turn, leads to an increase in our capacity to serve. Our competency, skill and capabilities grow. This leads to still better sharing and contribution. This is work as a process of growing and continuous evolution. It calls for being in touch with one's own purpose and vocation in life.

There is a calling, which lies hidden in our Hearts. It creates a desire for a particular work in each one of us. Discovering one's calling and pursuing it in an inspired way is one of the foundations of a joyful life. The vitality of our lives depends on our capacity to work with love in our hearts.

> Without work, all life goes rotten. But when work is soulless, life stifles and dies.
>
> ALBERT CAMUS

Just as a garden has different flowers, life is full of different people. Each person has their unique patterns of motivated skills, talents and strengths. Some are like tulips, some like dahlias and still others like roses. Each one has been designed by nature to fully bloom in its own unique way. If we try to distort this process by trying to make a tulip into a rose, we will lose a tulip and will not gain a rose.

Our unique personal mission, or the 'good work' we are meant to do, integrates our deepest longing to express ourselves with something that needs to be done. In the figure below, this is represented by the shaded space M lying at the intersection of the two circles.

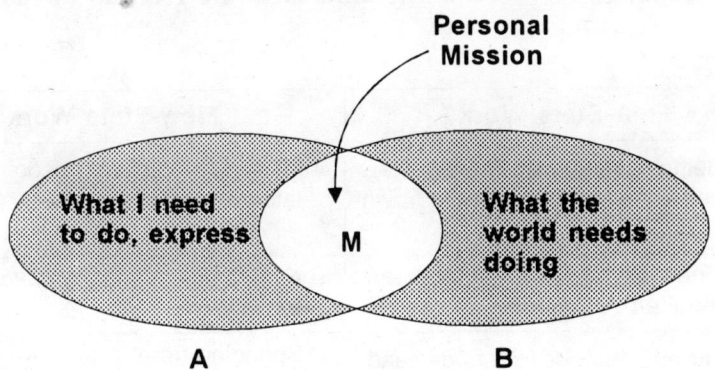

If there is something that I long to do and am good at doing, but which does not meet anybody's needs (Space A in the figure), it will not be a viable mission. Similarly, if I am contributing to others' needs, but am not operating out of my own motivated skills (Space B), then again this is not the right mission for me. My right mission is something that happens, when my own loving and sharing from the Heart contributes to someone else's needs (space in M).

I need to get in touch with my unique strengths and also with what I enjoy doing. I then need to scan the environment for areas where my skills can make a contribution. Seeing this connection between my capabilities and others' needs, I need to act with love in my Heart. Delaying or postponing the fullest expression of the very best in me is harmful to me and the world. It deprives existence from creative expression, and it deprives me of an opportunity to grow.

How much we grow and what the quality of my work will be depends upon the motive with which we work. I have come across people who know what they love doing, and are aware of their calling, but do not pursue the work because it does not pay anything. In a materialistic age, where one criterion for success is the money earned, it is quite easy to get distracted away from one's inner direction.

> If you work without love, you are working like a slave. When you work with love, you work like an emperor. Your work is your joy, your work is your dance. Your work is your poetry. And when you work with love you bind yourself to yourself, and to another, and to God. Work based in love brings you closer to yourself and closer to others and finally, closer to God himself.
>
> OSHO RAJNEESH

The difference between work which is driven from the outside (what others' expect, others' notions of success, what they want me to do etc.) and work which is flowing from inside (in touch with my calling, an expression of love and inner fullness) is immense. The whole attitude and feelings towards work and life are different. The differences are given in the table below:

Fear-State Work	Flow-State Work
• Being miserable and servile. Perpetuating the misery of my own limitation.	• Masterfully unfolding freedom. Relating joyfully to the ecstasy of life.
• *Fear:* False Evidence Appearing Real	• *Flow:* Fullness and Love Overflowing in Work
• Driven by outside (others' demand, comparisons, others' values)	• Springing from inside (own mission, values, vision)
• Focus on what can *I get*	• Focus on what can *I give*
• Being judged by external yardsticks. Not feeling okay.	• Unconditionally okay as one is. Seeing who I am with respect. Perfection as unfolding evolution.
• *Basic Questions* —'Where can I get the best deal?'	• *Basic Questions* —'Where's my own bliss?'

(Contd.)

(*Contd.*)

—'Who pays me the most?'	—'What's the best that I can give?'
• Work based on operating from the false I, and its inherent sense of deficiency and limitation. One is caught up in setting goals for the future . . . trading our energy, creativity and time for some imagined idea of future happiness.	• Work based on operating from the real self. It is a fullness expressing playfully for ńo specific goal. The bliss of being is *poorna* or complete here and now, independent of outer happenings.
• No true lasting joy is possible. At best, it is conditional or caused.	• Joy flows naturally. It is an unbroken, underlying and uncaused substratum.
• Give only to get something in return. 'The more I get, the more I have. The more I have, the more I am.'	• Give your energy freely in rhythm with life here and now. 'The more we give, the more we connect. The more we connect, the richer we are.'
• Work is a pain. It is slavery, drudgery and a great bore.	• Work is play. It is love expressing and evolving.
• It keeps me separate from my core, from other people and from nature.	• It connects and integrates me with my Heart, with other people and their problems, and with the totality of life.

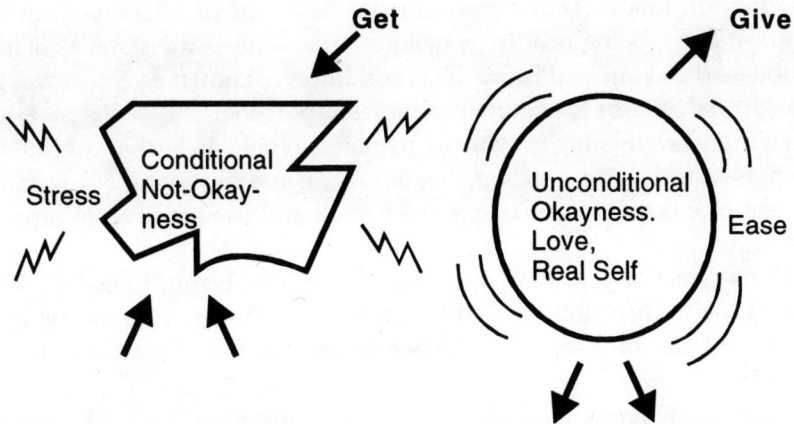

Get **Give**

Stress Conditional Not-Okay-ness

Unconditional Okayness. Love, Real Self Ease

Driven by what others need, desire, expect, want me to be. Learning the skills needed by them.

Seeing who I am with respect. Seeing my patterns of unfolding expression. Seeing my unique nature and function in Existence.

Finding one's calling and working in the 'flow' state is indeed a blessing. However, 'good work' is not something

Happy is he who has found his work and let him ask no other blessedness.

THOMAS CARLYLE

that will happen in your life accidentally. It will call for a very conscious effort, not only once but several times over in our lifetime. This is because we change, and so do our career choices and preferences.

Organizations can do a lot to facilitate these transitions. To start with, people can be given more importance. We need to take more interest in their own unfolding pattern of expression in the adventure of their lives. We need to share more, dialogue more about our own journeys, and our common adventure as an organization. This will bring out the initiative, creative energy, intelligence, enthusiasm and belongingness that we so long for in today's organizations. Enabling people to discover their creative adventure of 'good work' in their daily lives is to help them live a fuller and healthier life. It is one of the most important routes to total health.

Total Health

The World Health Organization defines health as a 'state of complete physical, mental, and social well-being', not merely the absence of disease or infirmity. It is the manifestation of a fully functioning natural system with total ease and freedom and in a state of total peace. In its simplest form, being healthy is being at ease. This is the same as being established in your real being. This condition is known as *Syamstith* in Sanskrit or *Swasth* for short. It denotes a personal and social state of balance and well-being in which a person is whole. In such a condition, the person feels strong, active, creative, wise and deserving of love and respect. She is totally free to express herself and use her diverse capacities fully.

To be effective as a manager and as a human being, I need to take care of my body–mind, so that it is fully functioning. This means that my thoughts, words and actions need to be pure and aligned with natural laws.

I need to actively make choices that are conducive to total health. A simple way of remembering these choices for sustaining health is the *'5F' Framework* which I have adapted from the Sadhu Vaswani Mission, Pune (Sajandas 1986):

1. *Flow-state work: Fullness and love overflowing in work.* Research

has shown that doing work that is fully in tune with our inner calling or vocation is a significant factor affecting our health. When we are expressing ourselves and using our talents and gifts to share with other people, our body–mind system is actually experiencing a state of deep joy. Our body chemistry reflects this inner satisfaction and has a healing and soothing effect on all other aspects of our life.

> The more a man lays stress on false possessions, and the less sensitivity he has for what is essential, the less satisfying is his life.
> CARL JUNG

Work is where we spend half our waking life. Make sure that your work is aligned with your talents, strengths and the silent calling of your divine nature. Ensure that there is spirit and heart at work and that you are doing what you love, and loving what you do. Make work a celebration.

This is a lot easier when we realize that we have only one life to live. Making work a means to other ends like earning more money, gaining power, getting our next promotion and more perks, leads to a missing of the intrinsic healing value of good flow-state work.

Besides choosing the right work, here are a few tips to help make your work more loving and flowful:

- In the morning, before going to work, thank existence for giving you an opportunity to share. The 'attitude of gratitude' is highly medicinal.

> We are prone to judge success by the index of our salaries or the size of our automobiles rather than by the quality of our service and relationship to mankind.
> MARTIN LUTHER KING JR.

- Prepare mindfully for your work. Take a few minutes to think through your important tasks and list them down. (More about this in Chapter 6). Shower, brush, eat and breathe mindfully.
- Say 'bye' to people with full consciousness.
- As you go to work, walk mindfully. Smile at people. If driving, breathe deeply and stay present. When you stop, be still and enjoy the silence for a few minutes.
- When you walk into your workplace, smile and greet people cheerfully.
- During the course of work, be conscious of bodily sensations. Listen to your body and give it the breaks and stretches that it needs from time to time. Remember that your body is not only your most important tool, but also your most valued 'internal customer'!
- Use breaks to truly relax. Get some fresh air and take a few deep breaths. Sit quietly and witness your breathing. Have your lunch with people you enjoy being with. Change your environment at lunch.

Remember to skip your lunch once in a while. Eating a little less can prolong our lives.

- In your work focus on the most important things at hand. Do them one at a time. Create and maintain a neat and orderly workplace. Bring in a few nice posters, paintings, photographs, plants and make it homely. Create an environment that you are attracted to sit and work in.

- Express your love for your work by doing high-quality work and taking care of all dimensions.

- Care for your organization and its resources because these are your own. Remember there is only one whole.

- Above all, remember that love can be expressed in your working relationships. Bring something valuable to each person: a kind word, appreciation, mentoring, encouraging, listening, empathizing, giving, trusting, harmonizing and peacemaking. All this is a way of saying 'I care' for myself and others. It is wonderful for your feelings, your health and the well-being of your people and organization.

2. *Feelings.* The more we keep our feelings joyful and empowering, the healthier we will be. Our feelings flow from our thoughts and beliefs. These, in turn, are the choices we make. We create our own thoughts, feelings and action. So, I can choose thoughts that lead to feelings that are positive, joyful and empowering.

Laughter and humour are known to have cured Norman Cousins (1991) of a life-threatening illness. You can read more about this in his famous book, *Anatomy of an Illness*. A positive mind which expects the best also helps to keep the body chemistry in good form. Thoughts of compassion, friendliness, love and forgiveness can actually improve our immune response. Dr Dean Ornish talks of reversing heart disease through these processes in his book by the same name. Opening the heart to other people and life's positive flow heals the body–mind.

3. *Fitness.* One way to prevent heart disease in the first place is by keeping the body fit through regular exercise. My experience with thousands of managers in learning situations is that there is a very high need for people to make time for regular exercise. The five per cent or so who do, regularly report that they are more positive and energetic at work, have better relationships with people, and work more productively. Keeping our sedantary body from exercising leads to an accumulation of toxins, which give us a feeling of low energy and fatigue.

So, make time for regular moderate exercise. Brisk walks, dancing, skipping, cycling, cleaning up the house, gardening, trekking, taking your dog for a run and playing enthusiastically with the children can all work wonders for your body and sense of well-being. Work up a sweat and do some activity in which faster breathing is required. Keep your increased heart beat to within 60 per cent of your normal rate while exercising. *Yoga asanas,* especially the set called *'Surya namaskars',* are highly beneficial and strongly recommended. You do not need fancy equipment or jazzy gyms to stay fit.

4. *Food.* Your body is what you eat. Pure, fresh balanced vegetarian food is more likely to keep your immune system working in a better way than if you eat non-vegetarian or impure food. Research has shown a significant impact of food on your health. Many people swear by raw food. Just a note of caution—don't get stuck in food fads. Remember, health = freedom!

A few more tips on the food front:

- Avoid the three white poisons in your diet as much as possible: salt, sugar and refined flour. Also, cut down on dairy products, meat, caffeine, processed food and alcohol. If you can reduce your intake of these, you will have fewer toxins for your body to eliminate and thereby more natural energy available to you.
- Increase your intake of:
  - Good quality water. The body is 75 per cent water and energy increases when we drink more of it.
  - Vitamins and minerals through fruits, vegetables, sprouts, raw salads.
  - More whole wheat and unrefined cereals.
- Bring in variety in your diet. Make it truly wholesome. Try out new recipes. According to the science of *Ayurveda,* a balanced diet must contain all the five tastes namely: sweet, sour, salty, bitter, astringent.
- Follow the old adage *Breakfast like a king, lunch like a prince and supper like a pauper.* A little supper helps you to not only sleep well in the night but also helps in the process of renewal and healing of your body. I love missing an evening meal once in a while. The mornings after this are fresh and energetic.
- Give your body rest from food once in a while. Experiment with a diet of fruit juices, or fruit once in a while. It helps to purify the body.
- Herbal teas, like one made from leaves of *Tulsi* and Lemon grass with some Ginger and lemon can make an excellent *pick-me-up* after work.

5. *Faith.* One view of 'faith' is Foresaking All I Trust Her (FAITH), where her refers to all of existence or Mother Nature. When I learn to 'let-go' and align myself with the intrinsic creative intelligence of life through meditation and prayer, my body–mind is more likely to be at ease.

Affirmations such as, *'This too shall pass'*, *'The world is perfect as it is'* and *'All is a gift from the Divine'*, help to keep us healthy.

The regular practice of meditation and silent prayer puts us in touch with our own inner resources. A lovely prayer to strengthen our faith is the prayer of Saint Francis given below:

> *Lord, make me an instrument of thy peace.*
> *Where there is hatred let me sow love;*
> *Where there is injury, pardon;*
> *Where there is doubt, faith;*
> *Where there is darkness, light;*
> *Where there is sadness, joy.*
> *O Divine master, grant that I may not so much seek*
> *To be consoled as to console,*
> *To be understood as to understand,*
> *To be loved as to love,*
> *For it is in giving that we receive;*
> *It is in pardoning that we are pardoned;*
> *It is in dying to self that we are born to eternal life.*

As we take steps to purify our selves, by trusting the Heart for guidance, following our true calling and leading healthier lives, we become more integrated within ourselves and with our surroundings. This is a condition of dynamic joyfulness which is contagious. Your own thoughts, communication and actions then begin to create ripples of healing around you. You become a force of light and love unfolding joy and spreading peace.

Ideas for Playful Action

Values

1. One way to find out about what we value is to list down all the things that we want in life. For each of these, look a little deeper by asking yourself the question, *'Why do I want this?'*. Write down the answers for each thing. Then probe deeper by asking yourself the *'why'* behind all the answers. This will take you closer to your underlying pattern of values.

2. If you would like to get greater insight into a decision about something you are planning to do, try playing with this checklist:

- Am I doing this to please others, live up to their image of me or for my own highest good? Am I accomplishing this purpose to receive recognition or a pat on the back? Or is it because it is something I want to do and brings me joy?
- What would I do if I were alone? If I did not have anyone in my life who would gain or lose from what I did, what would be my choices? What would I do for *myself*? What would bring me peace and joy?
- How does what I want to do serve the planet? What is the *real* reason I'm doing this?
- How does it serve me? Is it truly helping me and others?
- Do I truly and really want to do this? (Check with your divine self.)
- Is doing this going to give me peace and joy? Does it feel right to the Heart?
- Is doing this contributing to my long-term goals?
- Would it make a difference six months from now? To what?
- Does doing this take me to a higher spiritual ground or does it not?

Listen to the soul and take action on its whispers. Believe in yourself and the goodness of the universe.

3. What are some of things you would do if you said 'YES' to life right now? List them down. Pick one and do it!

4. Think of all the rituals and traditions you follow in your life. List them down. Now ask yourself which of these have soul and meaning for you. Why? Re-invent, re-vitalize, re-form and re-new some of the other (dead) traditions by going back to the essence of what they were all about.

Good Work
5. Describe your ideal work situation. Visualize yourself in that work situation. (Don't worry about whether you are trained, educated or whether it is possible or not. Just let your imagination run freely.)

   - What would you be doing . . .
   - What skills will you be using . . .
   - Your work environment . . .
   - The money you will be earning . . .

   How much is the gap between your current work situation and what you describe above. Can you think of any small steps you could take to bring you closer to your ideal work situation?

6. If you were given a magic wand by which you could create four other lives for yourself, what fun work would you choose to do in each of them?
   Write down whatever comes. Do not censor!
   Now pick up one of these dream occupations and do something in that

direction for a few days, For example, if you wrote, 'Teaching children', in your list, maybe you could take a few sessions in your neighbourhood school. Or if you wrote, 'Be a painter', start painting.

Total Health

7. Using the '5F' Framework for total health, identify areas for change in your own life. Make an action plan for implementing this. Promise yourself that you will keep yourself fit and healthy for life.

8. Our body–mind has a built-in wisdom, which keeps us pointed towards health. If we listen to its promptings, it will tell us silently what changes we need to make to remove toxins and restore balance in our body–mind.

    Take some time to sit down and listen to your inner body wisdom. Record your insights on paper and take some inspired action on them.

$$\approx 4 \approx$$

Thinking
Our Most Stretchable Resource

No great improvements in the lot of mankind
are possible until a great change takes
place in the fundamental constitution of their
modes of thought.
JOHN STUART MILL

*I*n our journey of understanding managing from the Heart, we started off by looking at the inner core (Chapter 2). We then saw how this could be made the foundation for a more joyful life, paying attention to the routes of value-based living, good work and total health (Chapter 3). We now move further ahead into the three-fold circle of:

- Thinking (Chapter 4)
- Communicating (Chapter 5)
- Acting (Chapter 6)

These are the basic building blocks of almost everything we do. In this chapter we look at 'thinking'.

The saying,'*As a man thinketh in his heart, so is he*', encompasses every condition and circumstance our man's life and being. The mind, or the sum total of our thinking and thoughts, underlies everything we do. From the conscious act of writing a letter to the 'spontaneous' stopping by at a colleague's desk, everything is governed by the thoughts we hold in our mind. Every feeling and act of man springs from the hidden seeds of thought that he nurtures in his mind. Whatever man does is an

Mind is the forerunner of all activity; mind is the highest of all sensory powers. All relative concepts have their origin in the mind. Mind is the precursor of all perceptions; Mind is the most subtle of all elements in the phenomenal universe. All objectified consciousness has its origin in the mind. One who speaks or acts with a pure mind, happiness abides with him as his own shadow.

GAUTAMA BUDDHA

external manifestation of how he thinks, how he perceives himself, how he perceives the world and his pattern of deeper drives and inclinations.

As Emerson has said, 'The ancestor of every action is a thought.' Swami Sivananda said the same thing differently: *Sow a thought and reap an action, sow action and reap habits, sow habits and reap character, sow character and reap destiny.'*

It is our thinking that is constantly shaping our life, moment to moment.

Importance of Good Thinking

Organizational reality is also shaped by the thinking of people. Organizations are nothing more than ever-changing, dynamic, systems of interacting minds. People, money, time, resources, goals and everything else that go into making an organization, all begin in the minds of people. Great organizations started off as seeds of thought. Similarly, organizational excellence also has its genesis in good thinking. Excellent teamwork, for example, can be traced back, to the mind patterns, values, beliefs and assumptions held by people in an organization. This linkage is illustrated below:

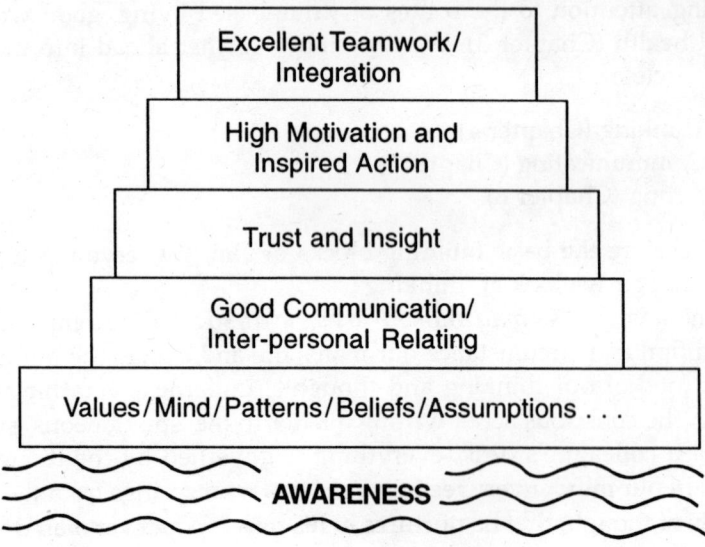

By the same token, at the root of many problems faced by people at work is the working of the mind. A mind that is not ordered, peaceful and creative will not be able to produce more beneficial responses to situations.

It is common to find people in organizations, bringing in their negative attitude and erroneous thinking into situations requiring change. For example, protecting turf, obstructing change because of personal insecurity, defensive behaviour, perceptual blinds, rigid and judgemental thinking, all come in the way of joyful learning. In today's environment how much an organization learns determines its chances of survival.

When the head of a British oil company was recently asked by his managers from 37 countries about the characteristics necessary for success in their global company he simply said: '*Brains . . . you need brains.*' This is also true for good leadership, a process which is really based on brain power. Insight, imagination, analytical skills and being comfortable with feelings remain the cornerstones of good leadership. All these need excellence in the use of the mind.

Not only is good thinking vital for managerial excellence, it represents an amazingly vast resource. Consider this mind-boggling statistic from *The Mind Map Book* by Tony Buzan (1993: 29–30):

> *The typical human brain has a total of 10–12 billion neurons. Each of these neurons has a possibility of connection with other neurons represented by one with 28 zeros after it! (10^{28}). What this means is that the total number of possible combinations and permutations in a single human brain, if written out, would be one followed by 10.5 million km of zeros! No human being yet exists who can use all the potential of the brain. For all practical purposes, it is useful to think of the brain as having unlimited potential. However, we all know that we do not use even a fraction of this incredible potential. Just imagine what would happen if this power was unleashed.*

It should now be clear why it has been said that the mind is the manager's most important tool and also his most *stretchable* (and often most unused) resource.

Being Aware of the Mind

Despite its importance, the mind still remains a mysterious no-man's land for many. Its underlying patterns are mostly hidden from our awareness. They are like the large portion of an iceberg, hiding unseen below the surface.

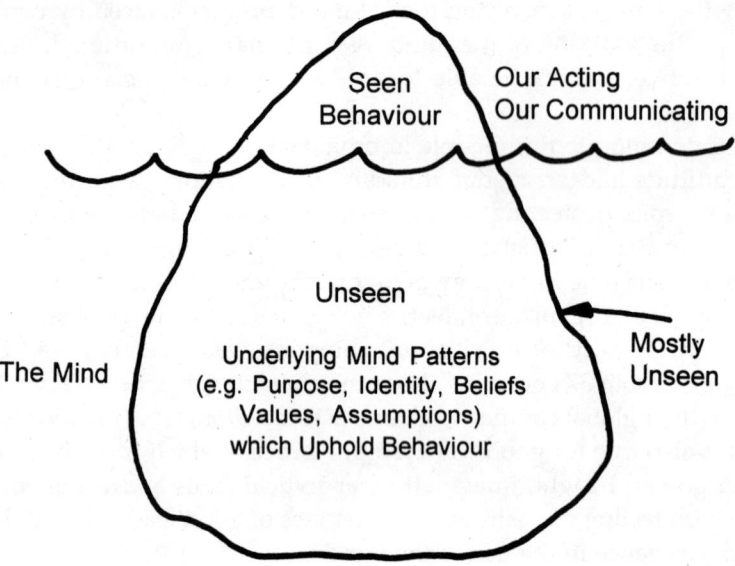

The workings of our mind often remain neglected in the daily bustle of routine work. Our identification with the mind and its deep layers of conditioning is so complete that the idea of using the mind skilfully, like an instrument, from a clear space beyond the mind, is either not perceived or is rejected as being too bizarre! Consciously harnessing the full potential of thinking in new ways, learning to cross mental boundaries, taking a holistic view of problems and responding to life with a positive unstressed cheerfulness are treated as things that would happen on their own. The truth, however, is that these do not happen naturally unless a conscious awareness of the mind grows.

> The world we have made as a result of the levels of thinking we have done thus far creates problems we cannot solve at the same level at which we created them.
>
> ALBERT EINSTEIN

Whatever we have seen about thinking so far raises the following questions:

Is it possible to consciously act in a way which is free of mind patterns, and life enhancing in all situations? Can we think in a way which expands our own, and others' sense of well-being and ease?

What is the difference between thinking which block one's own potentialities, and one which frees them?

Before we can respond to these questions, let us try to understand the mind a little more.

How the Mind Works

We know that there is a stream of thoughts, memories and ways of looking at life inherent in each person. The mind is the sum total of all our memories, images, desires, expectations, beliefs, feelings and other such mental processes. Thinking is therefore a sequence of images and events which constitutes our mind. If there are no thoughts and no memories, we can say that there is no mind.

The mind constantly stores information about our experiences, and converts it into 'maps of reality'. This includes our notions of purpose, identity, our beliefs, values, and assumptions. It is useful to think of these maps as patterns with different shapes. These patterns affect our perceptions and generate thoughts in definite ways:

1. *They affect what we notice*. We notice and pay more attention to things that are related to our desires . . . to what we want. Also, we sometimes unconsciously delete information or ideas that do not fit into our mind patterns. We overlook or tune out some things. For example, a boss may not listen to the negative feedback he gets from his subordinate because it does not fit with his image.

2. *Mind patterns distort reality*. Personal prejudices and assumptions twist our perceptions thereby giving different meanings to things. A rope begins to look like a snake.

> We don't see things as they are, we see things as we are.
> HOLY TALMUD

3. *They project and generalize*. Under their spell we reach global conclusions based on one or two experiences. If my first meeting with a person did not 'go off too well', I believe I can *never* 'get along' with him.

Mind patterns are the basis for the following processes:

- Choosing (for vs against)
- Dividing, splitting into categories
- Limiting our possibilities
- Forming, structuring, defining and excluding
- Creating separation, and non-connectedness
- Comparing, judging, evaluating
- Binding our freedom

The mind also imagines and weaves webs of fantasy. These draw the attention away from the 'here–now' to either the past, the future or to somewhere else.

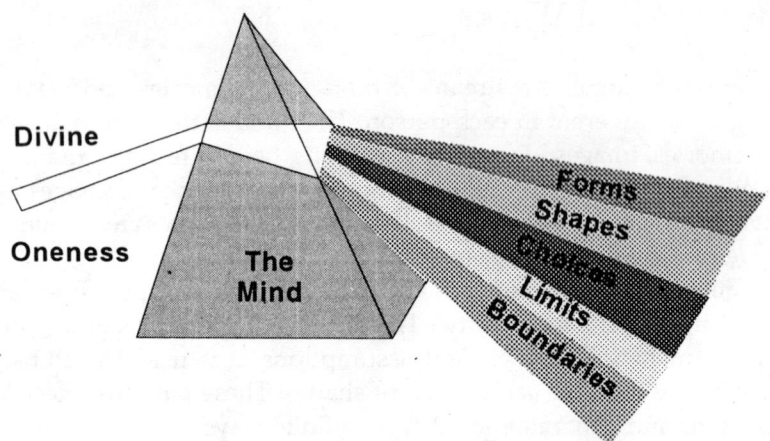

The mind with its patterns keep us caught in partial understanding, whereas the truth is the whole. Acting like a prism, it breaks up the divine light of oneness into many colours!

Before the reader gets the idea that mind patterns are all 'bad' (that would be partial, and not the truth) let me clarify a few points.

The mind, with its ability to do all that has been listed above, is an extremely useful device. Man owes his progress to its workings.

The problem is not the mind. It is the process of allowing the mind to become the master, driving all that we do. That is the danger. If I am driven by my likes and dislikes and react to situations, I allow myself to be controlled by them. If my feelings get hold of me and I am driven by them alone, I am in the grip of my mind. Similarly, if I do things for my own limited ends and for narrow purposes ignorant of the larger picture, I am a slave of my ego. A sure récipe for misery.

Now, look at the mind as a beautiful and useful slave. Let the inner hierarchy be clear. Let it be subservient to awareness, to that which is beyond the mind. Let pure unbounded being be the master of the mind.

If I can transcend the forms, structures and limitations of the mind and respond from an inner space of pure silent creative energy, then I am operating from self-mastery.

The difference between being a slave to the mind and being its master is largely a question of *awareness*. If I can be more aware of the fact that my mind is like the software of a computer, which can be re-programmed, I am free to choose whatever thoughts and beliefs I wish. I can also think of the mind as the clothes I wear. Just as I am not my shirt I am not the contents of my mind. These are only choices I have made. I can therefore, modify them. For example, I am neither a Hindu nor a

Muslim (these are only mind conditionings), nor am I an introvert nor an extrovert (these are my own choices). The freedom to *choose* my own mind state and feelings, my own beliefs and perceptions equips me with a tool, which can truly transform my life. Remember *awareness gives me choice*.

Besides being aware, what are the other practical tools I can use to make the best use of my thinking? A simple way to remember three powerful tools I can use is to imagine wearing a magic 'CAP' on my head at all times. This CAP is about thinking, which is:

Creative
Accountable
Positive

C—Creative
A—Aware and accountable
P—Positive

We will look at these three starting with awareness and accountability since this is the basic foundation for the other two.

Awareness and Accountability

As we have discussed, awareness of my mind is the starting point for mastery. With mastery comes accountability. The outlook associated with accountability is something like this:

Ultimately, you're the one who's responsible for yourself. You play a part in every situation in your life. What you are today, is a result of your choices. This is accountability. It is taking charge of your life . . . not blaming others, not blaming circumstances. It is nothing short of mastering your own fate . . . being the one person who decides how you are going to live, respond and feel in almost every situation that life presents you.

In a recent training programme for senior government officials, the participants raised the issue of helplessness. I encountered a large volcano of anger spewing forth when I suggested that they could do something to change the situation! *'There is nothing we can do until the rules under which we operate do not change, and politicians stop poking their noses in our work. We are totally helpless.'*

In another programme, a group of young entrepreneurs who were being trained to set up their own industries were asked, *'How many of you think that you will be able to succeed in your business without paying any bribes?'* Of the 25 participants present, not a single one responded in the affirmative.

School principals and teachers attending yet another training programme on making education more creative strongly felt that they could do absolutely nothing about the very heavy syllabus imposed by the government's education department. They complained about the tremendous pressure a class of 60 students puts on them. They said they were helpless to change this.

As a management consultant I encounter feelings of helplessness and powerlessness amongst many people in various organizations. Except for differences in the specific conditions in which people find themselves, the story is invariably the same:

☹ 'Nothing can be done to change the system.'
☹ 'We are powerless to do anything.'
☹ 'The politicians have all the power.'
☹ 'We are upset and angry, but again what can we do?'

> **We are all the time from our childhood trying to lay the blame (for things going wrong) upon something outside ourselves.**
>
> SWAMI VIVEKANANDA

This feeling of *powerlessness* in the face of things we would like to see changed appears to be a widespread problem in society today. To my mind, it is the single biggest cause of inertia and helplessness amongst many in India.

At the root of this helplessness is the tendency to blame. It is easy to put the blame for every situation on somebody else. I have seen people blame their bosses for their own misery. Others say that it is their inherited past that is responsible for their present condition. Many do not hesitate to blame their stars (especially Saturn!) for a dull and tough life.

The most common form of blame I have seen is people cribbing about the inefficiency of others. In training programmes, whether it is supervisors mentioning their superiors (*'Why don't you first get them into the course'*) or senior government officials (*'When are you going to train the politicians'*), the problems are always seen as being elsewhere. When you ask politicians in New Delhi about the condition of our nation, they do not hesitate to point towards the 'foreign hand'. One of my favourite pictures showing this condition is adapted from an ad of Krupp Industries (at that time Buckau Wolf) shown on the facing page.

Blaming does give some satisfaction. It puts us on a pedestal from where we can feel superior by putting down others. This, however, gives only temporary relief. It puts us in a momentarily comfortable

position—the comfort of inaction, continuation of the secure status quo and of not rocking the boat. But this comfort is only short-lived. It disappears when the negative pressure of unsolved problems raises the level of pain once again to the point where the blaming begins afresh. Blaming is like a painkiller. It alleviates suffering for a while, without treating the basic problem.

So how do we become more accountable? Here are two powerful ideas:

- *Take charge of your thoughts and feelings by choosing the right thought-seeds. Recognize that you are the creator of your own thoughts, words and actions.* The entire process of becoming the creator of what you are, rather than the result of what others have programmed for you, begins with your own willingness to look at your personal thinking habits, and choosing a way of thinking that helps you to be more effective. In this context, I find the analogy of seeds and harvesting very useful.

> If you hurt others, don't expect kindness in return. One who sows rotten seeds will get rotten fruit. God is great and compassionate but if you plant barley, don't expect a harvest of wheat.
>
> JALALLUDIN RUMI

If we continue to believe as we have always done, and we continue to act as we have always acted, we will

Shaping Our Future by Acting Now . . .

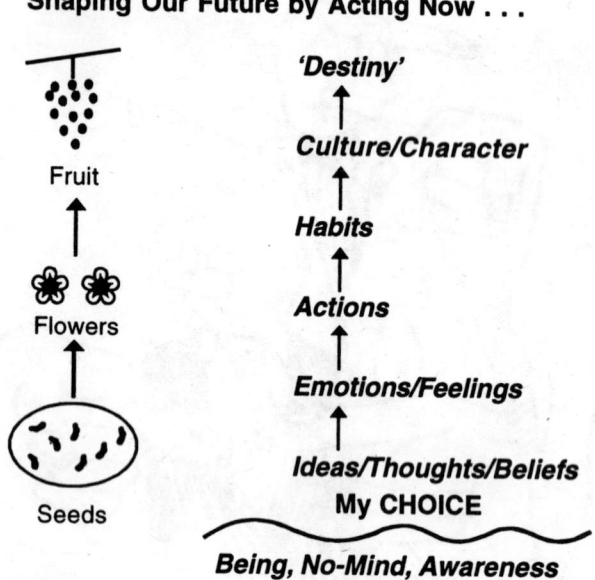

Fruit

Flowers

Seeds

'Destiny'

↑

Culture/Character

↑

Habits

↑

Actions

↑

Emotions/Feelings

↑

Ideas/Thoughts/Beliefs

My CHOICE

Being, No-Mind, Awareness

continue to experience what we have always experienced! In fact, one definition of insanity is doing the same thing over and over again and expecting different outcomes.

We are responsible for the thoughts we have in our mind at any given time. We have the capacity to think whatever we choose and thereby change our experience. *Once we understand that all our emotions and actions come directly from our thoughts, we will simultaneously understand that the way to attack any personal or psychological problem is to change the thoughts that support our negative emotions and self-defeating behaviour.*

Focusing attention on the factors within your control   Look for ways in which YOU can contribute in solving a problem. Focus your energy on what you can *do*. Whatever we put our attention on is our reality in that moment. Everything else is blocked out from our view. The mind can focus attention on only one thing at a time. It can hold only one perception in a given moment.

I came across an example of this recently. In the ground floor conference hall of Godrej and Boyce at Vikhroli, Mumbai, is a mysterious sculpture. When you look at it from the side it looks like a rabbit about to jump upwards. Looking at it differently, it suddenly looks like a fish about to take a dive. You can choose either view. If you see it is as a rabbit, the fish vanishes. See the fish and the rabbit is gone! Can you see

both of these perceptions at the same instant of time? No, you cannot hold both these perceptions together. You have to make a choice.

This is the same as the famous example of the glass which is half empty and half full. It all depends on how you *choose* to see it. *Attention,* or choosing what will receive our energy, is the fuel for growth. Whatever we choose to put our attention on in the moment, will expand and grow.

It will also define what our behaviours and the outcomes will be. Let us apply this to accountability.

In every situation there are some factors that I can influence and some factors that others do. Let us call these the 'I-factors' and 'They-factors'. When I focus my attention on the 'They-factors', I lose sight of the factors within my zone of awareness and influence. Consequently, I imagine (erroneously) that there is nothing I can do. The situation seems to be out of control. This leads to feelings of helplessness and inertia. I feel like a victim. On the contrary, when I decide to focus my attention on the 'I-factors', i.e. the factors within my own zone of influence, I choose to empower myself. Therefore, I feel more at ease and more in control.

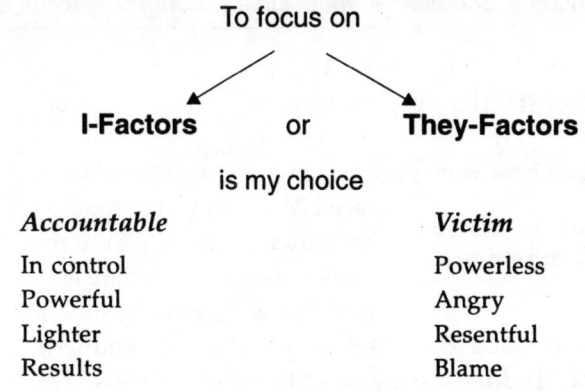

To focus on

I-Factors   or   **They-Factors**

is my choice

Accountable	*Victim*
In control	Powerless
Powerful	Angry
Lighter	Resentful
Results	Blame

Since the 'I-factors' are also the zone of action, focusing on them lights the way for action. If I invite further suggestions from other people about what I can do, a few more practical ideas can almost always be added to my own list. And remember, whatever you focus your attention on increases. A person who runs his life according to the principle of accountability, grows in strength with every constructive action. This is the same way that a muscle when regularly exercised, grows and is strengthened. If not used it becomes smaller.

Accountability keeps expanding in the following manner:

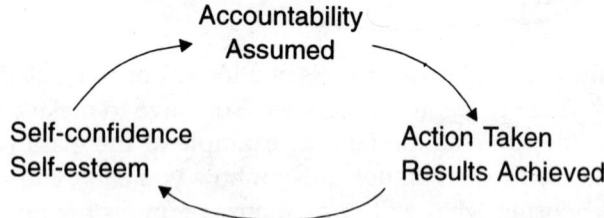

You will gain personal power and the ability to get results if you assume accountability in all situations.

This simple attitudinal shift in outlook can help people to 'empower themselves'. They discover resources that they did not see earlier, feel in control of their life, and act in new ways to solve problems. It not only improves productivity, but also helps in restoring self-confidence and self-respect of the people involved in the change.

Accountability is simply another way of saying that people are not the creatures of circumstance but the creators of circumstance. Situations do not affect us, it is the view we take of them that affects us. This view is our *choice*.

An easy way to remember accountability is this equation:

Circumstances = Situation + My Choice (Thoughts, Words and Action)

Creative Thinking

We have seen how our thoughts and perceptions get trapped into patterns. We also learnt how we can be more

Discontent is the first step in the progress of a man or nation.
OSCAR WILDE

accountable for our thoughts. Now let us explore how to consciously transcend mind patterns and generate new ideas.

Creative thinking is mental activity, which produces new ideas or new insights. It does this by de-patterning, or re-patterning, thoughts.

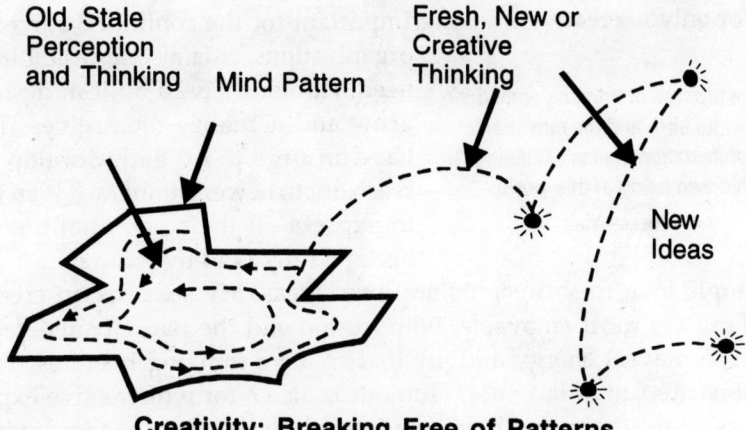

Old, Stale
Perception
and Thinking   Mind Pattern

Fresh, New or
Creative
Thinking

New
Ideas

Creativity: Breaking Free of Patterns

It means living in an unpatterned way, free of prejudice, approaching and responding to unknown situations with a responsive intelligence. It means letting go of the familiar, structured and 'knowledgeable' approaches to problems and life.

The well-known author, Arthur Koestler, defines it thus: *'Creatively is an act of liberation—the defeat of habit by originality.'*

Innovation is applied or fructified creativity. When a person creates something that is accepted by society as new, original, useful and beneficial, we say that the person has innovated. The emphasis in innovation is more on the adoption of new ideas. It focuses on their subsequent development into either a finished product or a useful practice. It is the organized creation of beneficial change.

New ideas mean progress. We owe our success to creativity. Everything worthwhile today is the result of new thoughts and ideas in the minds of people. Today's organizations are virtually thirsty for innovation. *'Innovate or fall behind'* is the war-cry for many businesses today. This is no surprise considering the immense benefits of applying creative thinking in organizations. Here are just a few:

- Systematically solving problems in new ways
- Making quantum breakthroughs in quality, productivity and performance
- Finding new business opportunities by creatively matching the capabilities of the organization with the needs of the marketplace
- Improving the technology of products and processes
- Inventing new ways of doing business
- Finding new ways to add value to customers

There is no limit to this list.

Not only is creative thinking important for the continued success of organizations, it is also a basic human need. Humans have a built-in desire to grow and actualize themselves. They have an urge to expand, develop and reach out to newer frontiers. It is an urge to express all their potentialities and become fully who they can be.

> It is the process of bringing something new into birth and the most basic manifestation of man's fulfilling his own being in this world.
>
> ROLLO MAY

People love fresh insights and new ideas. My sessions on creative thinking are most enjoyable, both for me and the participants. People love the playful energy and joy that creative thinking liberates. These sessions are full of laughter. Humour is also a form of creative expression. A logical story with an unexpected ending or a sudden twist of perception sends people into peals of laughter.

If you put all these benefits together, you get a self-reinforcing cycle of unfolding joy.

The picture below shows what this cycle would look like.

If creative thinking is so useful, why is it so scarce, you may ask.

According to one estimate, we use around 90 per cent of our creative potential at the age of two. By the age of seven, this has plummeted to 10 per cent. Notice that the child starts going to school between these ages! Finally, on an average adults use only 2 per cent of their creative potential. As we grow older, our mind seeks security. The limited I, or ego, tries to perpetuate and preserve itself.

> Creativity is an expression of one's uniqueness. To be creative, then is to be oneself.
>
> MICHAEL F. ANDREWS

Anything new is, therefore, threatening and unwelcome. This blocks creative thinking. One image that captures this process is the image of a rest house on a journey, which is given on the next page.

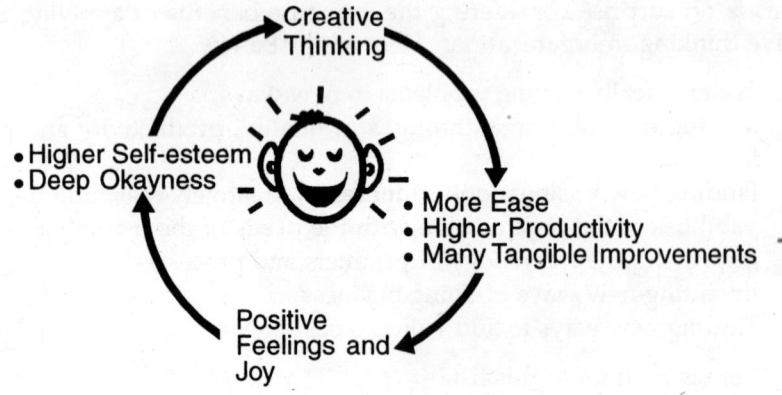

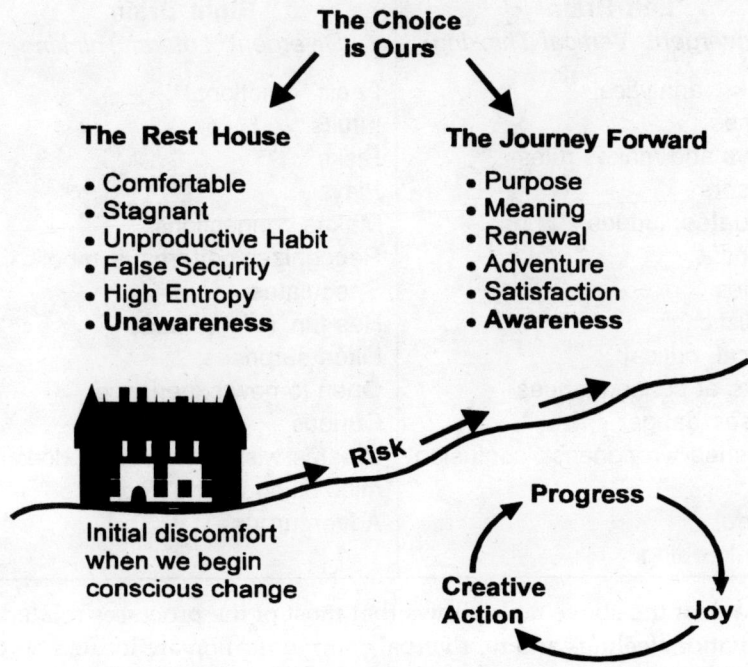

The 'rest house' gives us a false sense of comfort. We are comfortable with our pet theories, dearly held beliefs and other mental models. Like old shoes, these are safe and familiar. It takes courage to let go of them. Creative thinking requires taking risks.

Another block to creative thinking comes from an overuse of convergent thinking. There are two basic thinking processes that we use: convergent and divergent thinking.

While the latter is like exploring a huge geographical area for oil (using lateral, sideways movement, looking at several possibilities), the former is like drilling at one place for oil (vertical, probing deep at the same place, fixed). The first one is connected with creative thinking and the second with analytical thinking.

You are aware that our brain has two different hemispheres. Research on the functioning of the brain has shown that these two thinking processes occur in different hemispheres. The following table captures some more characteristics of the two thinking processes:

Left Brain (Convergent, Vertical Thinking)	Right Brain (Divergent, Lateral Thinking)
Thinks, analytical	Feels, emotional
Senses	Intuits
Obeys and makes rules	Risks
Censors	Plays
Evaluates, judges	Makes connections
Scientific	Recognizes patterns, symbolic
Guides	Speculates
Realistic	Has fun, is impetuous
Logical, critical	Likes surprises
Looks at consequences	Open to new experience
Senses danger	Curious
Punishes 'wrongness', 'confusion'	Dreams, wishes, fantasizes, doesn't mind being 'wrong', 'confused'
Fearful	Adventurous
Safe-keeping	

A look at the above table shows that most of the processes related to imagination, feelings and non-verbal communication are located on the right side of the brain. My own experience with groups of engineers and executives in industry shows that people prefer to use the left brain mode of thinking. They tend to be highly critical, and judgemental in their thinking, and feel lost when asked to express their feelings. After a moving experience or exercise, when I ask people about how they *feel*, the response is often, *'It was a very good experience.* When I again repeat my request to share their feelings, they say, *'We must all learn to work together.'* Sharing feelings are a strong no-no! It is not seen to be masculine.

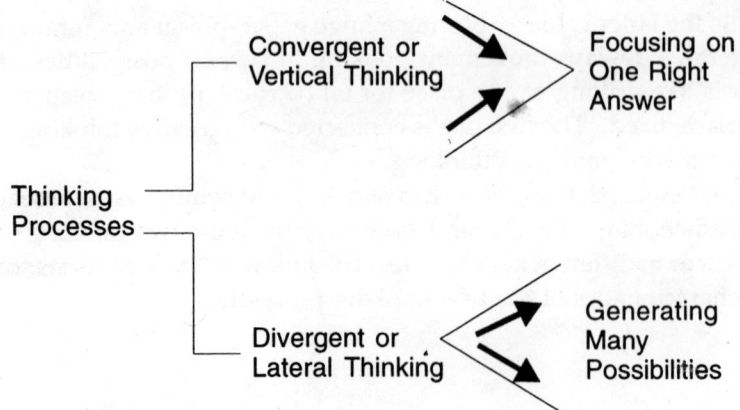

Maybe this low use of right-brain thinking has to do with our existing educational system. Most schools follow a strict regimen of stuffing children with right answers (convergent thinking) rather than teaching them the art of asking the right questions. Both hemispheres of the brain are equally important. They are like the two legs we have to walk with. Both have to be used in a balanced way for us to move ahead.

> **The quality of our future will depend upon the quality of our thinking.**
> EDWARD DE BONO

Enhancing Creative Thinking

Here are a few ways to enhance our capacity for creative thinking:

1. All attempts to generate fresh ideas need to follow one cardinal rule during the process of idea generation: *Suspend evaluation and judgement*. This is like switching off the evaluative and critical left hemisphere during the process of creative thinking.

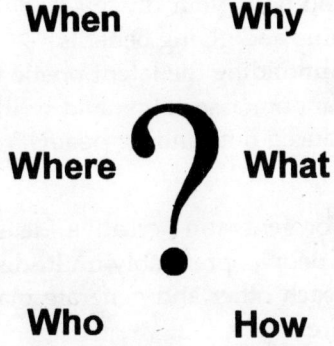

When   Why

Where   What

Who   How

2. The most useful and easiest to use tool for creative thinking is *questioning*. The proverbial six friendly men of Rudyard Kipling, the Five Ws and one H, are very effective in stretching the boundaries of our perception. They are the engines of generating new ideas.

Question all limits and beliefs. Question the assumptions behind your feelings and actions. Then question the assumptions behind your assumptions.

Questioning with awareness has the creative power to take you straight to the mystery of your own Heart. Playing with the question, 'Who am I?,' can open up windows of insight, which normally remain closed.

3. One of my favourite methods for creative thinking is *random association*. When you connect any idea randomly to something requiring new insights, fresh ideas emerge. For example, I want to generate new ideas on moving forward in my career. I see a bottle of water in front of me. I mentally connect the bottle to the issue of getting ahead in my career. Some ideas that this throws up are:

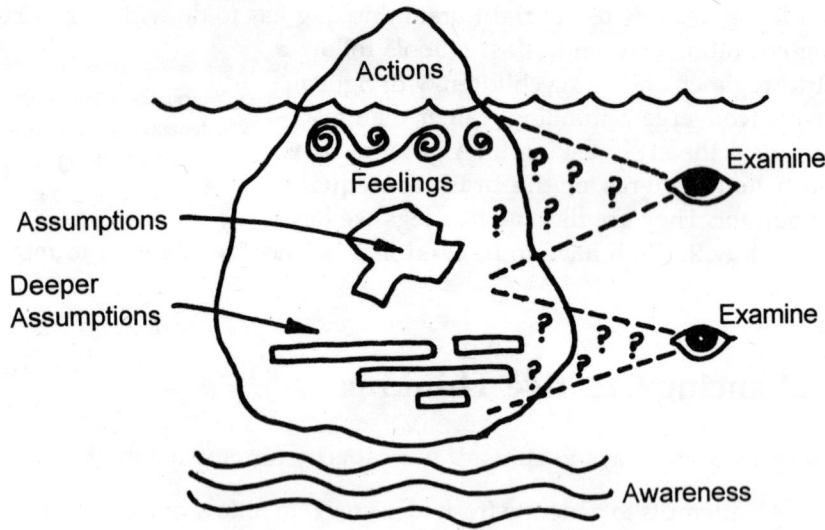

- Be more transparent
- Be more flexible like water, and adapt to the situation
- Be rigid like the glass, and firmly hold on to your dreams
- Quench peoples' thirst by adding value and giving benefits

This method has worked wonders in unfolding the latent poetic talent of many people. A combination of random association and writing continuously without stopping, has produced outstanding poems from first-time poets.

4. One of the most popular methods for generating creative ideas is *brainstorming*. This involves a group of people, preferably multi-disciplinary, working together to stimulate each other and generate many ideas. The four rules of brainstorming are:

- Suspend judgement—no criticism or evaluation of ideas
- Free-wheeling—the crazier the idea the better
- Quantity is more important than quality—the more ideas the better
- Cross-fertilize—combine and improve on the ideas of others; this is also known as 'piggy-backing'

After defining a problem and giving the basic background information, people work on giving ideas in response to a question like, *'In how many ways can we . . . . ?'* or *'What can be done to . . . . ?'* All ideas are put up on flip-charts, where everyone can see them.

The group then selects the best ideas, and then does reverse brainstorming on the question, *'In how many ways can this idea fail?'*

There are many other methods for systematically unblocking our creative faculties. Openness to possibilities and a spirit of adventure born out of inner freedom are fundamental. Also, quite central to leading a creative life is freedom from the need for approval from others.

There are many other tools to stimulate creative thinking. However, it needs to go beyond just using tools. Creativity needs to become a way of life. A few things that can help:

- Encourage creativity and put a value on it. Encourage a variety of experiences. Reading and exposure to other viewpoints can help this immensely.
- Be playful. Play with problem-solving quizzes, brain-teasers and your children.
- Look for the shapes of fantasy creatures in clouds. Fantasize impossible solutions to problems to radically alter familiar trains of thought. Draw analogies from nature. Use metaphors.
- Take care of your body–mind and meditate.

Regular meditation and awareness of the Heart is the master key for unlocking your creative potential. Connecting to the realm of peace and joy beyond the mind puts you in touch with a fountain of creative energy. This source, which can produce insights worth billions of rupees, costs nothing to tap! It is available free. It is almost like a magic shop. The great saint-poetess of Kashmir, Lalleshwari, described it thus:

> *The Lord sits Himself in the shop,*
> *Hordes clamour for this or that.*
> *There's no one to hold you back,*
> *The guards are nowhere in sight.*
> *Go ahead and take what your heart desires!*

You are the supreme source of all that you really want. Tap it and bring out the treasures.

Some of the greatest works of art, and the most valuable inspiration reported by artists, inventors, businessmen and leaders have come from a source beyond their minds. It is as if a deep well of wisdom has allowed them to draw water from it and bring it up to the surface. These insights and breakthroughs happened while they were in a state of deep relaxation and joyful awareness. Allowing the Heart to do its silent work through our life is the art of creative living at its best.

Positive Thinking

This is the third element in the CAP of good thinking. *Positive thinking is thinking that expands one's own as also the other person's sense of well-being, joy, satisfaction, strength, competence, creativity and achievement of results.* Conversely, negative thinking or thinking the worst, actually contracts, decreases or blocks good feelings and productive behaviour.

Positive thinking helps in *empowering oneself and others*. It gives us and others around us a feeling of goodness and power within. It gives us the power to do more, give more, share more, enjoy life more and achieve more. It helps to expand the boundaries of limitation. You see yourself as part of nature and the entire world. You are no longer only limited to your physical self.

Positive thoughts, positive communication and positive actions are happily infectious! Positive people spread cheer, goodness, joy and humour all around them. This joy and enthusiasm spreads from person to person, and organization to organization. And inspiration and enthusiasm is what makes individuals and organizations prosper and grow.

Becoming Positive

It is quite easy to become positive. All it takes is a change in your mindset and your way of thinking. Once we understand that true happiness and joy do not come from the outside world but from within, we are on course to a more positive and creative approach to life.

> Enthusiasm is at the bottom of all progress. With it, there is accomplishment. Without it, there are only alibis.
>
> HENRY FORD

Some pointers that can help:

1. *Choice.* The first and most important step in becoming more positive is to recognize that we have the power to choose and control our thoughts. We can choose to think inspiring thoughts, power thoughts, possibility thoughts and thoughts that strengthen us. We can choose to 'act', rather than 'react', to situations around us.

Powerful transformation happens when we become conscious of what is in our subconscious minds, releasing and letting go of old patterns, and taking in positive new ones.

When we begin to internalize beliefs such as:

• The universe is friendly and is helping our evolution

- Life is full and abundant . . . there is enough for everyone's needs
- We can all live in peace, joy and love
- The intrinsic core of all people is peace

we find that diverse subtle changes begin to appear in our 'outer' life. The general atmosphere around us begins to radiate more peace, warmth and playfulness.

As the mind is purified and aligned towards a higher purpose, the outer changes in one's life begin to manifest automatically.

The *power of choice* is the greatest gift that we have. It means that in any situation, we are not bound to think or behave in a certain fixed way only. No matter, how difficult or trying the situation may be, we still have the power of choice to guide our thinking. This is the special corner of freedom that no one can take away from us.

2. *Vision.* Before we build a house, we have to first make a drawing. Similarly, great organizations start off with a dream of something carved out by the creative imagination. It is only when we have decided what we want in life, and have a clear picture of it, that we are inspired to move forward towards achieving it. Having a clear and big vision is a statement of belief in our potential. It is also the starting point for living our life in the way we want.

While making your vision, think big! *Do not make the mistake of approaching the ocean of life with a teaspoon in your hands.* Life is amazingly flexible and willing to yield its treasures to people who see them. It helps to see the larger picture, to expand our boundaries (both mental and physical) and explore all that is possible. The moment we step out of our small world of desires and focus our vision on the larger possibilities, we develop a strong determination. Things start falling in place, and petty concerns drop off.

Obstacles have been described by someone as, 'those terrifying things we see when we take our eyes off our goals'. If we focus our attention on the big picture and look towards the calling of our Heart, the obstacles that seemed so formidable earlier now appear inconsequential. Problems become challenges that help us to learn and test our mettle.

Great men (and women) reduce mountains to molehills!

3. *Appreciate people and situations.* Before giving constructive criticism, first offer genuine appreciation. There are always plus points in all people. Appreciate people. Criticizing is so easy to do! It doesn't take much brain power to find fault. Everyone can do it.

Judgement is just-in-case thinking. It means working from fixed beliefs which I hold on to for security . . . just in case I come to a situation where I need the safety that fixed beliefs offer.

Putting down other people also gives me a false sense of okayness. It takes effort and maturity to build on people's plus points. Problems and difficulties can only be solved by appreciating others' strengths. Sincere appreciation, when genuinely used, brings out the very best in people. It creates a positive atmosphere that makes work more joyful.

Changing one thing for the better is worth more than proving a thousand things are wrong. Lighting one small candle is better than wrestling with the darkness!

4.   *Give vs get*. When I was a child of 13, my grandfather once told me that you must always go through life with your palms downwards. At that age I did not understand what he meant. It was only later that I discovered that this was his simple way of saying, *'Always be of service, and always try to make a positive difference in the world.'*

One thing I constantly share with young people is to always seek ways to add value and give benefits to others. Do this out of a sense of inner abundance and fullness. Life's rewards will always come back in the form of spiritual and material energy. As we are nourished by spiritual energy, we grow. This, in turn, expands our capacity to give more. *'The purpose of life is to be a growing, contributing, human being.'* The belief that I am special and that I am doing something unique to the world, is highly empowering. When we look at people and situations from the viewpoint of *'What will I get out of it,' 'How will it help me,'* we are focusing on ourselves and our deficiency. On the other hand, one of the greatest contributors to positivity is a spirit of giving, a spirit of service. This attitude makes one positive because it takes attention away from the deficient 'I'. It focuses attention on what I have. The process of giving helps in the expansion of boundaries and limitations that we normally associate with our 'limited' concept of ourselves.

Think of this paradox:

The more you give and serve, the more abundant becomes your energy, joy, sense of power and well-being, and the amount and quality of the work you get done. The attitude you give will be reflected in the attitude others show you.

The saying, *'Give the world the best you have and the best will come back to you,'* is absolutely true. If you are positive and have a giving and sharing attitude, the same will be reflected to you by others. The universe operates through this dynamic flow of giving and receiving. One of the best ways to receive something is to give that which we seek. This way the joyful circulation of the universe keeps moving. Come to think of it, it is not difficult to bring small gifts or small acts of sharing to different situations. A warm smile, a word of appreciation, love and caring does not cost much. Yet it creates a freshness and joy whenever it is shared.

5. *Believe in people.* To influence people, be generous in your positive belief in them. Treat people as if they were what they ought to be and you help them to become what they are capable of being. Your positive expectations and thoughts about other people will make them that way. The 'Pygmalion effect' or the 'self-fulfilling prophecy' is a phenomenon according to which people actually live up to your expectations of them. They become what you expect them to become. Your image of them actually shapes their behaviour.

Managers who have high self-esteem, and who believe in their own capacity to coach and guide others, demand more from themselves and their team members. They actually create the conditions in which this comes true. This is because what we believe of others is consciously or unconsciously transmitted to them through our behaviour.

So, hold good images of people. It will help you and them achieve more and be happier.

A practical approach to this is to always remember the Heart. Remember that people have the peace, silence and goodness of the divine at their core. We are all waves on the same ocean and therefore hold the potentiality of the whole ocean in ourselves. When this is remembered, not only do we operate from the abundance of the whole, but also set the other person free to do so. This spontaneously creates the conditions for unfolding the very best in people and the situation.

This is also the foundation of good customer service. It is said that the weaver-saint Kabir would address his customers as 'Ram'. He would lovingly tell them, *'I have woven this cloth very carefully for you, Ram. Please take good care of it.'*

> **Who sees all beings in his own Self and his own Self in all beings loses all fear.**
> UPANISHADS

Imagine what would happen if we all consciously remembered the divinity in ourselves and other people. Our complete behaviour towards each other and ourselves would be very much more caring and gracious.

6. *Thinking well of yourself.* Count your blessings—they are many! You have an array of unique strengths and talents that is special to you as a person. Above all, you have the power to tap the tremendous source of love, joy, achievement, energy and well-being within your control.

This can be done by simple gestures like freely accepting and giving compliments.

These actions enable us to feel good about ourselves and to also recognize the beauty in others. Always speak well of yourself. It is perfectly fine to pat yourself on the back and to celebrate and acknowledge your strengths.

In my work, I have found it useful to invite people to think of their behaviour and thoughts as being distinctly different from themselves, just like the clothes they wear. It is easier to change something that is separate from ourselves, and to forgive ourselves when we make mistakes. Picture yourself the way you would like to be while at the same time fully accepting yourself the way you are.

Look after your body and listen to its signals. Treat your body well. Exercise and nourish it well. Always expect the best for yourself because life will tend to gravitate towards your dominant thoughts.

You have the power to give and transform. You also have the power to change the meaning of anything. The moment you can do that, you give yourself the freedom to choose thoughts and associations that empower you and other people.

7. *Harnessing the power of positive words.* Our words influence how we think and feel, and also what we do. Thoughts, feelings and actions all influence each other. We can sometimes change our feelings by changing our words. For example, when I say, *'I am happy,'* I am acknowledging and affirming my innate happiness and creating that state in my mind. The associated feelings and actions also get connected to the statement. However, if I say a weak, *'I am trying to be happy,'* I am acknowledging my own sadness and also the fact that I am not in control. The word 'try' implies that I may, or may not, be able to do something. Substituting the words *'I will'* makes for a far more direct and positive state of mind.

In my work with managers, I have found that it is always helpful to speak of some positive condition that we want, rather than saying that we 'want to get rid of' some negative condition. It is always worthwhile to focus on the light rather than fighting the dark. Similarly, when telling your child to clean up the room it is more productive to say, *'Please tidy up your room'* rather than *'Clear up this mess.'*

Always choose thoughts and words that can bring happiness and success to yourself and others. Remember, what you send out into the universe comes back to you like an echo.

8. *Attitude of gratitude.* Whatever we pay our attention to is attracted to us. We also tend to manifest in our lives the very things we visualize.

Our image of ourself shapes not only how we see life, but also the processes and outcomes of living. When we are grateful for things, life usually sends us more of the same. People who have the most beautiful relationships are those who value them. People who lead active and fulfilling lives are always grateful for what Existence is showering on them. They are always celebrating life.

My own experience with the 'attitude of gratitude' has been through two exercises that I usually use in my programmes.

One is the simple process of listing down all the things that people need to be grateful for. After a long session of complaining about the organization and its management, when people list down the things that they are truly grateful for, the perspective suddenly shifts. They begin to realize that, income-wise, they are in the top two per cent of India's population. They become aware of many things that they have taken for granted, for example, their eyes, good health, and so on, which helps them look at their current situation positively.

The other exercise I often do at the end of a programme is to ask the group, 'How many people should we thank for this beautiful learning experience we went through together?' The answer usually starts off with a small number such as twenty or thirty but soon goes onto expand into thousands. This happens when we see connections, such as being grateful to the people who made the cloth of the shirt we are wearing, or the farmers who grew our food, or the people who made the tables and chairs, and so on.

These exercises make us humble and feel one with the rest of the universe.

9. *The law of two feet.* This principle is inspired by Harrison *Owen's Open Space (1994)*. It is simply taking responsibility and standing up for what you truly care about. Or, in other words,'walking your talk', and following what has heart and meaning for you. It is doing something because it means ssomething to you, and not because someone is asking you to do. This is the foundation of commitment: *Be true to yourself and do not imitate.* Whatever comes from yourself, and from your deepest inner potential, will ring true. It will also always be original, fresh and alive.

The law of two feet is about integrity and integration. It means that my thoughts, words and action are all aligned. When I am true to myself and my inner promptings, and I listen to my own Heart, I express myself totally. This has a high ability to influence other people.

The Law of Two Feet

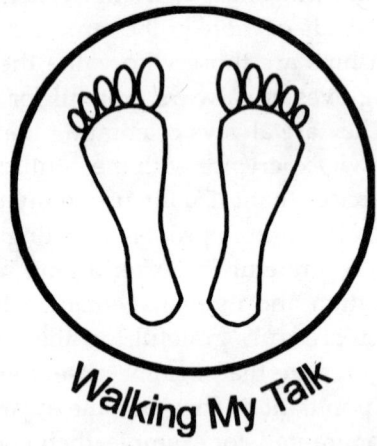

Authenticity/Integrity
Standing up for what
I believe in
Responsibility
Taking ownership for
making a difference
Commitment
Making it happen come
what may

Walking My Talk

10. *Being in the here and now.* This means be present and awake to what is happening in this moment. The past is dead and gone, and the future is only a dream. All that we really have, and can ever have, is this moment. So be a witness to things in this moment and never forget to remember that which sees—namely your innermost self.

Most negativity comes from either guilt and worry (about past matters which are dead and gone) or from anxiety about the future (which is yet to be born). After his serious accident on the track, the famous car racer Nicki Lauda had trouble getting back to racing. The memory of his accident haunted him and kept him away from the race track. It was only after his counsellor advised him to focus all his attention onto the wheels and track in front that he got out of his fear. When I first heard this story, I was reminded of what an Australian actress once shared with me about overcoming stage fright. She said, *'Go for the action now. Focus completely on being total in the here and now.'*

Plunging totally into the *now*, the only place where action can happen, keeps us positive. The memories of the past and anxieties about the future do not exist when we are in the present. All patterned action comes from the past. It is because of memory that we repeat past actions. Creative action, on the other hand, is free action: It is pure unblocked creative energy acting in the here and now. Because there are no patterns coming from clinging to the past or from desire for a future—it is totally creative.

This moment is fresh and pure. Being present, and living in touch with this moment, keeps us open to the vast abundance and silence of the whole. While things may happen all around you, this silent witness

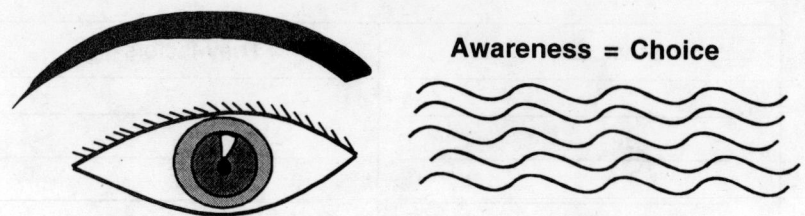

Awareness = Choice

watches peacefully and unchangingly at the centre. This mysterious being in the 'here–now' is not only the foundation of positive and creative thinking, but also the very essence of managing from the Heart.

Ideas for Playful Action

1. *Accountability Exercise*

   Think of a situation in your life that is not working out as well as you had hoped. You are disappointed with the outcome for some reason. Use this situation as the raw material for the exercise.

   - Briefly describe the situation here:

   _____

   _____

   _____

   _____

   - Describe your feeling about the situation:

   _____

   _____

   _____

   _____

- List three **'I'** inputs and three **'they'** inputs:

I-factors	They-factors
1. _____ _____ _____	1. _____ _____ _____
2. _____ _____ _____	2. _____ _____ _____
3. _____ _____ _____	3. _____ _____ _____

Get a friend or partner to give you some more new ideas for the 'I-factors'. A different perspective always yields fresh ideas.

Focus your attention on the 'they-factors'. How does it make you feel? Now shift your focus to the 'I-factors'. How do you feel now?

- What could I have done to prevent the situation?

_____

_____

_____

_____

- What can I do now?

_____

_____

_____

_____

- What are some of the positive aspects of the situation?

_____

_____

_____

_____

2. Identify a few problem areas where you feel stuck and which require fresh action. Use some of tools in this chapter to generate new ideas.

3. Spend five minutes writing down whatever thoughts come to your mind. Can you observe the stream of your thought? Does this not imply that your 'awareness' is different from your 'mind'?

4. 'An affirmation is a strong, positive statement that something is already so,' says Shakti Gawain (1988). Write a few affirmations for yourself. Put them up where you can see and repeat them out loud a few times in the day.

5. Make a list of things you need to be grateful to life for. Keep this in your diary for changing those low moments.

≋ 5 ≋

Communicating
The Art of Joyful Relating

*Relationship is surely the
mirror in which you discover
yourself.*
J. KRISHNAMURTHI

*L*ife is full of interaction. Our survival as small babies, much of our learning as adults, and almost everything we consider valuable in life is a result of a series of interactions with people.

Try this small thought experiment. Imagine there is a huge lever somewhere in the universe that controls all communication processes on earth. Something like the main electricity switch in your house. This lever is presently in the 'on' position. It is suddenly grasped by someone from somewhere and pulled to the 'off' position. All communication processes on earth suddenly stop.

Think about what might happen if such a communication blackout ever were to occur. Mothers will not hear their babies wail. Lovers will not be able to whisper sweet nothings in each other's ears. All forms of writing—letters, books, memos—will vanish into thin air. People will stop talking to each other. All forms of sign language will cease to exist. Organizations, where people share a common vision and join hands to achieve goals together, will dissolve. Life in all its glory will come to a grinding, deadly, halt.

This little thought experiment gives you a feel of the incredible importance of communication in our lives. In fact, communication is to life what oxygen is to our bodies. It has been estimated that around 80 per cent of your time as a manager is spent in some form of communication. Your personal success, not only in the managerial role, but also as a parent, spouse and team mate, all rely largely on your ability to make things happen. This, in turn, depends upon how you communicate with others.

The right words used in the right way and at the right time generate the required actions. They make things happen. I've often been excited by the image painted in my mind through the good use of someone's words. I can also remember the energy and enthusiasm with which I aligned myself to action because the communication related with my own deeper impulses.

Some of the best leaders, and most effective people I've come across, have always had one thing in common—they were all excellent communicators. Whether it was the inspiring speeches and writing of Rohinton D. Aga of Thermax, or the passionate entreaties of Hatim A. Tyabji, former CEO of Verifone, they all used communication skilfully to persuade, inform and inspire. They were people who engaged the hearts and minds of their listeners with their outstanding communication skills. They were highly skilled in creating a climate of trust and understanding and in expanding the awareness of their audience in dramatic ways. We often associate powerful communication with politics and great leaders such as Mahatma Gandhi, John F. Kennedy and Nelson Mandela—people whose words have profoundly shaped the way we see ourselves and the world.

Take this extract from Nelson Mandela's inaugural speech when he took over as President of South Africa:

> *Our deepest fear is not*
> *that we are inadequate.*
> *Our deepest fear is that we are powerful*
> *beyond measure.*
> *It is our light, not our darkness, that most frightens us.*
> *We ask ourselves, Who am I to be brilliant,*
> *gorgeous, talented and fabulous ?*
> *Actually, who are you not to be ?*
> *You are a child of God. Your playing small*
> *doesn't serve the world..*
> *There's nothing enlightened about*
> *shrinking so that other people*
> *won't feel insecure around you.*
> *We are born to make manifest the glory*
> *of God that is within us.*
> *It's not just in some of us; it's in everyone.*
> *And as we let our own light shine,*

we unconsciously give other people
permission to do the same.
As we are liberated from our own fears,
our presence automatically
liberates others.

The sincerity and authenticity of these words cannot but touch your heart. Here is an example of a great communicator.

Excellence in organizations draws its creative energy from outstanding communication. The section titled 'We Believe in Open Communication', in the book on *The Verifone Philosophy* defines communication as *'the exchange of thoughts, messages or information'.* Verifone, which is an organization headquartered in Redwood City, California, USA, believes that responsible communication and open dialogue throughout the company can and will create a culture of excellence.

> Only by having faith in
> ourselves can we be faithful
> to others.
> ERICH FROMM

Communication is at the core of working from the Heart. The reading on your joy meter depends significantly on how well you communicate. Free-flowing and open communication is the foundation of a full and creative life.

Communication as a Process

Communication is the process of unfolding understanding and meaning. It is about achieving a communion of understanding—a coming together in mind. If understanding has not occurred, communication has not happened. I'm reminded of the enthusiastic tourist in a foreign country who drew a mushroom, like this

to indicate his need to the waiter for mushroom soup. The waiter nodded his head, rushed off, and returned with an umbrella!! These two certainly did not come together in mind. So while ideas and feelings were expressed, communication did not happen.

Communication is the process by which we share facts, ideas, messages, information, feelings and attitudes. More specifically, it is the process of sending and receiving information to achieve a particular goal. That goal may be to inform, to sell, to motivate or to change certain behaviour. Whatever its purpose, every communication involves at least two entities or people—a sender and a receiver. One person or entity alone cannot communicate. You might well ask: *'What about a person who is talking to himself?'* In that case also there is one part of his mind talking to the other.

Most of us are familiar with the five-step process occurring between a sender and a receiver when they communicate:

1. The sender generates an idea in the mind.
2. The idea is then converted into words, pictures, sounds, symbols, actions. This is called 'encoding the idea'.
3. The encoded idea is transmitted to the receiver.
4. The receiver receives the encoded message through the senses and perceives it in the mind.
5. The receiver then decodes or converts the message back into a meaningful idea in his/her own mind.

This five-stepped sequence is illustrated below:

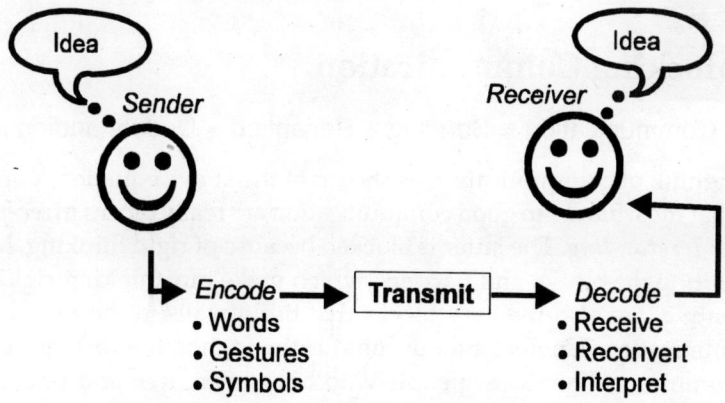

Transmission + Understanding = Communication

As an example of how this works, let us stop for a moment and look at what is happening now. There is an idea in my mind about the steps involved in the process of communication. (*The sender, that is me, has an idea*). I'm converting this into words and a diagram on paper (*encoding*). The idea is transmitted or conveyed to you (*the receiver*) through the medium of this book. You receive the message through your eyes, and finally, convert it back into an idea of the process of communication in your mind. It is finally in the receivers' mind that the process of communication is completed with the event of understanding.

Another way of looking at the process of communication is that, it is a process of *expanding the boundaries of awareness*. When I receive information, my own boundary of awareness and knowledge expands. I find this a particularly useful way to look at communication. Communication, then, becomes a way of changing what you and I *see*. It alters our view of things. I see something which I was not seeing earlier after I listen to you. When I express myself, I can show you things that you did not see earlier. When I speak to another and express myself, I am expanding the boundaries of knowledge and awareness of the other person.

After good communication, the boundaries of awareness would have expanded on both sides. We would both be seeing things differently. Our view of life changes. Remember, our view of life affects our way of life. Good communication is a powerful force, which brings us closer to seeing the truth and understanding the whole picture. It is a practical tool for unfolding insight and creating inspiration. Despite the importance of good communication, it is often blocked between people who need to work and live together.

Unblocking Communication

Communication = Sending + Reception + Understanding

If you think of communication as shown in the above equation, you will find that most *blocks* to good communication are really blocks in *reception and understanding*. The latter is blocked because of rigid thinking. Many of the thought-blocks and barriers, which make our thinking rigid and uncreative, are also the very blocks that build walls in the flow of our communication. Unblocking our mind is the foundation for unblocking our communication. Most people who have open, free and unblocked minds are also good communicators.

Here are a few tips on free-flowing communication:

1. The receiver is *listening actively*. She waits until the sender has completed the message before speaking.
2. There is *eye contact* in face-to-face interactions. This means that the people who are communicating look at each other directly in the eye.
3. The communication uses all the *senses*. It appeals to the eyes, ears and feelings of the listener.
4. The receiver has a good *knowledge* of the subject and is well *prepared*.
5. Both use *language* that they can understand.
6. The differences among the communicators (e.g. status, age, cultural, professional) are bridged by *mutual sensitivity* to each others' frame

of perception and thinking. There is a matching of language and thinking styles which builds the necessary rapport.

7. The atmosphere is comfortable, and there are no distractions or interruptions. Both the sender and receiver have made *time* for the communication.
8. The thought processes of both the sender and receiver are *open, creative and flexible*. They have a positive attitude and are deeply accepting of themselves and the other person. They respect each other and are caring and considerate of each others' needs.
9. Both are *honest and integrated*. There is total connection between what they are, what they believe, what they say, and what they do.
10. Both operate from a state of *total awareness and objectivity*. They can look at their own minds and the process of communication as it unfolds. This awareness gives them the possibility of correcting any problems that may crop up in the process of communication.

I have found free unblocked communication to be an almost mystical experience. In moments of open communication, I have experienced a deep sense of togetherness and understanding. It is almost like the sender and receiver are one, and are standing under all that is sought to be

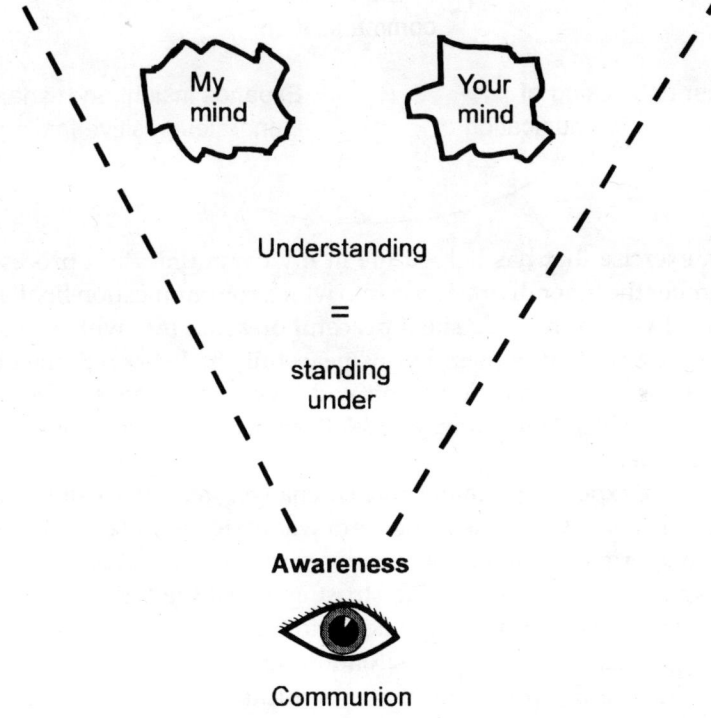

exchanged. It is like becoming one sky watching clouds of information and ideas go by. It is a dissolution of boundaries in the true sense of unity—a very liberating experience indeed!

As two people begin to understand each other's' viewpoints, they actually begin to 'stand under' their respective minds. They connect with a space of pure awareness, which is intrinsically boundaryless and one. This state of 'inner communion' or profound oneness is not only the source but also the goal of good communication.

When I speak or write from the depths of my silent understanding, words flow easily, spontaneously creating the magic of insight in the other person's mind. True communication is experienced as a deeply relaxing and ever expanding process. The discharge of pent-up emotions, the expressions of our viewpoints and good dialogue expands peace and awareness all around.

Good unblocked communication sets up a positive cycle which builds up higher levels of energy and understanding. Free-flowing communication feeds on itself and creates the energy to further unblock any barriers that may exist. Like an avalanche that starts with a small snowball, good communication swiftly creates a positive movement in both understanding and feelings. This positive cycle is represented below:

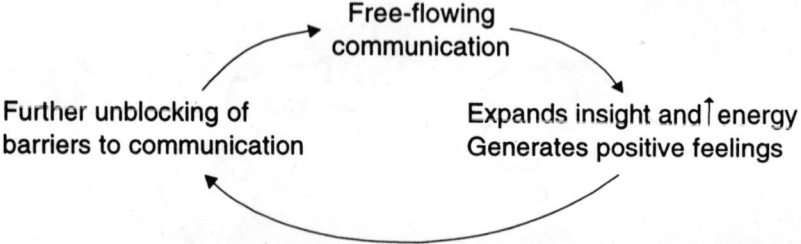

An exercise that has helped me in my communication process is to remember the inner divine Heart into which communication finally flows in the other person. It is a silent peaceful presence into which I am sharing. My own silent witness listens peacefully as I share. Remembering this, makes communication a soft and loving experience. It becomes a process by which I am made '*whole*'. It connects us both to the Heart and to each other.

We have experienced many magical changes that come from improved communication. Our consulting team was assigned to facilitate renewal and transformation in an organization some time in 1995. There was an atmosphere of suspicion and mistrust amongst the top managers. Fear and confusion had spread right down to the ranks. The senior managers barely spoke to each other. The situation was dramatically altered merely by facilitating the free flow of communication between people in the organization, starting with the top management team. It took only good communication to build bridges between people to come closer and relate to each other as a team. They felt much closer to each other.

Verbal and Non-verbal Communication

Feelings play an important part in our communication. Whether we are sending a message or receiving it, we need to be alert to the *feeling* component of what is being conveyed. Think for a moment of your favourite leaders at work. How do they speak? What is the tone and quality of their speech? How do they carry themselves? Do they smile a lot or go around with a frown? Are they enthusiastic and energetic speakers?

The use of words is only a small part of our total capability to express ourselves. *What* we say is often not half as important as *how* we say it. All of us are constantly communicating some kind of message in a subtle manner. Our bodies communicate constantly. We are often not aware of these messages. They are sent unconsciously.

Non-verbal (or non-word) communication includes all forms of communication other than the actual words and their meanings. These include gestures, movements, body posture, body stance, body movements and actions, touch, vocal cues like pitch, volume, speed and tone of our voice, breathing, eye contact, eye movements and the size of the pupils, facial expressions and changing colour of the skin, physical environment and body space, clothing and dress, status symbols and the objects we own, our timing and choice of language, and the words we use. All these express our feelings, emotions and attitudes. They tell about how people feel about themselves, about others, and about various situations.

Sometimes, our gestures and facial expressions match what we are saying; at other times they are incongruent.

If verbal and non-verbal meanings contradict each other, the non-verbal action is more likely to depict our true feelings.

According to some researchers, our feelings, emotions and attitudes are communicated non-verbally 93 per cent of the time. Only seven per cent of the time will people verbalize their feelings.

The break-up is shown in the figure on the following page.

This brings us to the importance of consciously observing our non-verbal communication. It opens up possibilities for more *integrated communication*, where our thoughts, feelings and actions are one. Improved understanding and awareness of non-verbal communication can greatly enhance our interrelating joyfully with others. Since joyful relating, which exudes well-being, is an important part of the skill of working together, we need to be sensitive to non-verbal communication.

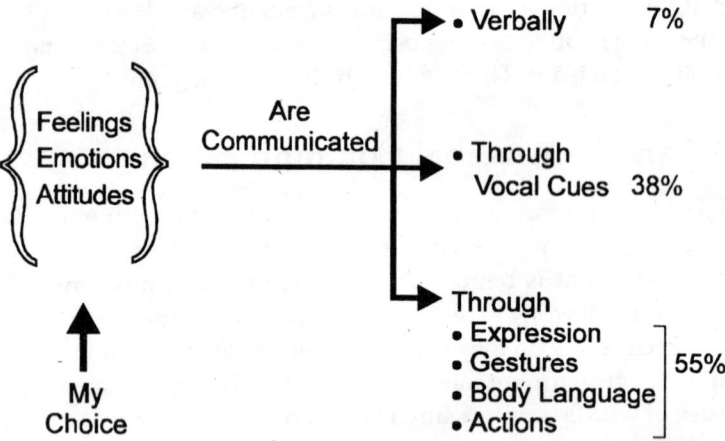

As a receiver of communication, I need to observe what others are expressing and then interpret these observations accurately. Listening or understanding the totality of what a person is expressing, therefore, requires the use of our eyes and our ears to pick up the vocal cues. Understanding another person's feelings can be a powerful gift you can give that person.

If life (including business) is for people, it is important to be sensitive to the other persons' feelings. The angry customer or the agitated team mate are both looking for *understanding*, before anything else. However, what I have often observed is that people do not even look carefully at the other person, let alone understand him. Managers carry on reading reports while they mumble to their subordinates that they are listening. There is little reception on the important channel of feelings. Since feelings are not understood, nor are the forces that drive motivation.

On the side of expression, our feelings of self-confidence are best transmitted by our non-verbal communication. Emerson has said, *'What you are speaks so loudly, that I cannot hear what you say.'* Your capacity to influence others depends on your mastery of body language and what your body is expressing. A slouched and collapsed posture, for example, is the habitual posture of a person who has a poor sense of personal 'okayness'. The posture of a person with his chest sticking out and chin tilted a little upwards indicates that the person is seeking attention. Our actions speak louder than words. Having looked at the importance of non-verbal communication in how we relate to other people, let us now look at the different modes in which we communicate.

Modes of Communication

As has been mentioned earlier, nearly eighty per cent of the time of a typical manager is spent on some form of communication. The break up ·is:

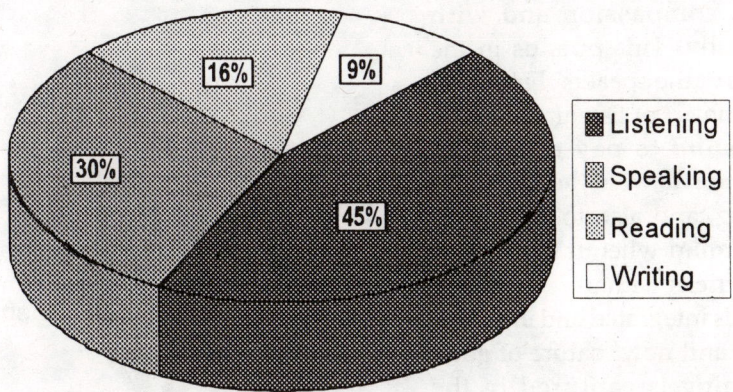

If you remember how we started learning communication in school, the order was exactly the opposite of its relative importance in our work life! We started with writing and then reading. Only a lucky few were formally taught the art of good speaking. Our educational system even now does not consider listening important enough to be taught formally. This is despite the fact that active listening (or the capacity to fully understand another human being) has been rated as the most important managerial skill.

Listening and Total Receptivity

Listening is the process of using our ears, eyes and brains to seek out the meanings and feelings in what a speaker is expressing. Its aim is to be totally receptive and to understand completely what is being said. It is the process of being so open to the expressions of other persons that you see what the others are seeing, feel what they are feeling, and experience what they have to share. Our ability to influence others significantly depends upon how much we have listened to them.

Listening is not hearing. It is hearing + understanding. Listening is also not acceptance. A common mistake that people make is to assume that, if they have listened to someone, they have to accept what the person is saying. This need not be so. *Listening is simply understanding.* Whether

I accept or do not accept what the other is saying is another matter. It is based on my free choice. This thought can be very liberating.

To listen totally, we use our *eyes* to pick up non-verbal signals. Also, maintaining eye contact, gives the other person the clear signal that we are listening. Our *ears* are also used to pick up not only the words, but also the tone and volume of the voice. We use our Heart to listen with care, compassion and with empathy. This puts us in the shoes of the speaker. Finally, in the fine art of listening, we use our *mind* to pay undivided attention to what the speaker is saying, and also to watch our own mind when it is prone to play tricks with us.

This integrated and intensely 'here and now' nature of good listening is captured in the Chinese symbol for good listening given alongside.

The practice of good listening is a near spiritual experience. We are totally present not only to the other but also to our own mind. We stand together as one witness while observing our thoughts, feelings and actions.

Listening expands my boundary of *awareness*.

Whatever was not known to me about the other before listening, becomes known to me after listening. I can initiate this process of expansion of my own boundaries of awareness through active listening.

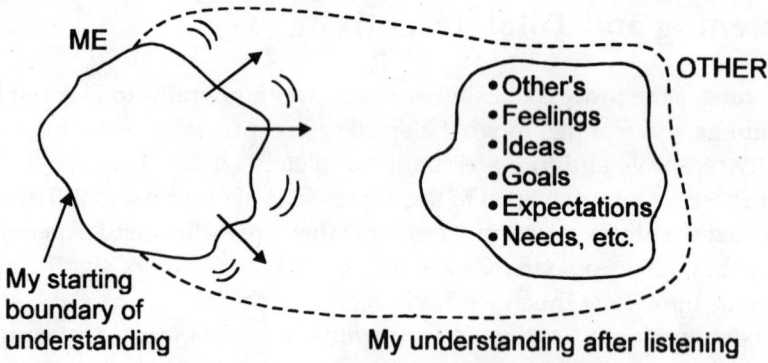

Listening Expands My Understanding

Let us now see what blocks active listening.

Blocks to Listening

1. *The prejudiced mind.* Most blocks to listening are connected with the mind. Remember what we discussed about the way our mind works in Chapter 4. We tend to colour what we hear by our own past experience. We imagine things that are not there because of our expectations. We delete information that does not fit in with our own fixed notions and prejudices. Information is distorted to match our own mind patterns. All this does not allow us to gain insight into the whole picture.

There is the proverbial story of a perverted king who would invite travellers passing by his castle to spend the night as his guests. The happy (and unwary) travellers would be led to a sleeping chamber with a bed. If a traveller was found to be shorter than the bed, he would be stretched till his length matched the bed. If his height was greater, his feet would be lopped off to fit him exactly to the size of the bed.

The prejudiced mind is like the king's bed. It distorts others' words and feelings to fit into the framework of our judgements, opinions and past experiences. A manager who has made up his mind about a team member being deadwood may fail to notice his strengths and potentials while listening to him.

Closely linked to this block is the tendency to evaluate.

2. *Evaluation.* We often jump to conclusions about what the other person is saying. We compare the present moment with some past standard or reference. This takes the form of *shoulds* and *musts*. Many of these come from the left hemisphere of the brain—the side which tends to evaluate and compare based on previous experience. I have seen this common block in many meetings, especially when someone comes up with a totally new idea. The small fledgling bird of a creative idea is instantly shot down by a flurry of evaluative arrows.

'*It can't be done.*'
'*Be more practical.*'
'*Don't waste our time with crazy ideas.*'

When the next new idea is shared, the person who launched the first bird is the first one to shoot his arrow at the next bird. The next person who had a creative idea to share keeps mum because people are too busy shooting arrows to listen to him.

3. *Preoccupation with my needs.* Focusing on my own needs means that I am more concerned with what *I* want in a situation rather than with what the other person feels and needs. This block takes the form of telling others what to do (we unconsciously want to show others that we

know more). It also manifests as arguing or rebutting, where the emphasis is on proving that *I am right*, rather than on, understanding *what is right*. It is common to find people waiting impatiently to say their own piece without paying attention to what the other is expressing.

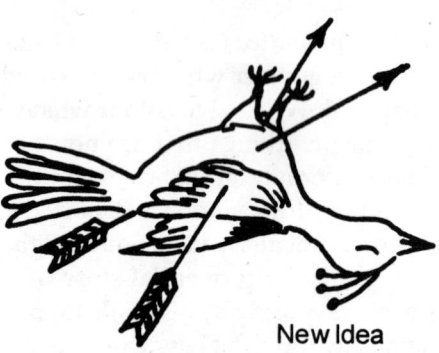

Premature Evaluation

New Idea

People often tend to talk about their own related concerns and stories, rather than understanding the other. I once saw a young subordinate go to his manager with a pressing concern. He ended up receiving a relentless verbal barrage from his boss on how the situation should have been handled. The subordinate came out frustrated mumbling, *'I never got a chance to open my mouth. He just went on talking!'* Imagine how he must have felt.

A barrier that many people choose to get irritated about is interruptions by the listener. This is a widespread problem and one that can be quickly rectified. People finish others' sentences for them without the courtesy of allowing them to finish speaking.

Sometimes one's own need for information and one's curiosity to find out more, leads to a tendency to probe excessively. At the back of this probing, which is asking questions, is a theory which is sought to be proved or disproved. The probing can take the form of a grand inquisition, especially if the question *'why'* is used inappropriately.

It requires considerable awareness and presence to take care of others' needs in communication. To me this is at the heart of relating well with others.

4. Not being fully present. Imagine a situation where you strongly feel the need to talk to someone about something you feel deeply about. You approach the person but he does not bother to even look at you! He looks outside the window or paces to and fro while you are talking. Chances are that you would feel highly irritated by such behaviour.

This is one of the most common complaints about poor listening. One is never sure whether the other person is truly listening or not. Even if a person is looking at the speaker, his mind may not be present to what the person is saying. He may be day-dreaming or privately thinking about what to tell the other person. His mind may even take off from one word or phrase and completely digress from the speaker's stream of thought.

This last barrier arises from a simple fact about our understanding. Our mind can absorb information at the rate of 800 words per minute. The typical rate at which people speak is in the range of 150–200 words per minute. So about three-fourths of the minds' information-processing capacity is free. *Good listeners use this excess capacity well.* They use this extra capacity effectively to make mental connections and to link up what another person is saying to what they know.

5. *Emotional filters.* This is an invisible barrier that allows only those things that are pleasant and desirable to enter the mind. We tend to block out things that threaten our thinking or are unpleasant or plain scary. Our emotional state at any time can also colour our listening. An angry person may see red even in the most harmless of statements. Similarly, an agitated mind may distort the meaning of what is shared.

An example of this is what happens in the annual performance review discussions. The subordinate is typically nervous and fearful. He reacts sensitively to even the slightest hint of negative feedback. He is anxious and worried about his final ratings and the impact this will have on his annual increment. This affects his listening.

How our emotions affect our perception is captured in an incident in the *Ramayana.* In the story, Hanuman insists that the colour of the lilies he saw in a pond in the Ashok Vatika (where Sita was held captive by Ravana) was red. Sita gently tries to convince him that the lilies were white. The difference, as you would have guessed, was in the eyes of Hanuman. He was very angry and his eyes were bloodshot when he saw the lilies. What was white, appeared red to him. Haven't we all, at one time or the other, seen a ghost where there was only a tree?

6. *Distractions,* such as glare, telephone calls, interruptions by visitors, or physical discomforts like a toothache or an uncomfortable chair can take the attention away from listening. Besides these outer physical distractions, one can also be mentally distracted. Like the bus to be caught at five'o'clock or that misplaced diary that has yet to be found. People I have met often grumble about managers who always look out of the window to see if anything more interesting is happening outside. They are irritated by managers who cannot put on hold their incoming calls for a short while. The cellular phone has made matters worse!

7. *Underlying assumptions about listening.* Several barriers to listening are born of the assumption that listening is not really that important. Many people erroneously believe that listening takes up too much time. Whenever I share about the importance of listening with busy executives, they sardonically say, *'But who has the time for listening? We are so*

pressed for time and so pressured by fire-fighting that we can't even take a break for ourselves.' This is like a person chopping wood with a blunt axe and with blistered hands saying, '*Who has the time to sharpen the axe?*'

Just a bit of listening can resolve the problems of demotivated employees and confused colleagues.

As mentioned earlier, a common assumption is that listening is the same as accepting. If I assume that listening to another person and understanding her feelings means that I must do something about them or change my behaviour in any way, then I may not listen. In this case, listening is seen as a passive and a compliant act . . . a remnant of our childhood when we had to 'listen' to our parents. This is perhaps the most well-entrenched barrier to listening.

8. *Lack of listening skills.* One of the simplest barriers to overcome, and probably the most ignored, is the lack of *learnt listening skills.* The reason why listening skills are not consciously learnt is because the enormous benefits of good listening are not seen. Listening is not taught in school where we begin with reading and writing. Nor do colleges have 'listening' in their curricula.

A careful assessment of all the barriers to good listening shows that they all emanate from an identification with the mind. The underlying thought patterns and emotional state of the mind draw the listener's attention away from the speaker. Listening suffers when the mind is preoccupied with our own interpretations, expectations, likes and dislikes, fears, etc., or is outwardly distracted. *Conversely, good listening is based on a foundation of pure and total attention.* If I can witness what you are expressing (both verbally and nonverbally), and simultaneously also witness my own mind and its pre-occupations, I am present to the whole situation in an unbounded and aware way. This is like the open sky, free of the clouds and totally present to what is. Not distorting anything, not having its own axe to grind, not giving advice, but just being there, receptive and free. This is the foundation of good listening. Listening with this openness can enhance one's sense of well-being and deep connectedness with all human beings. At its deepest level, listening is identical to meditation.

Benefits of Listening

By now you would have got a feel of why listening is one of the most beneficial skills to learn. The pay-off in almost all areas of our lives—

both at work and at home—can be very high. Let us look at these concrete benefits.

1.   *Listening releases tension.* In exercises where people pair up with a partner to listen and be listened to well, they invariably report feelings of deep relaxation and relief. Listening enables people to get their problems, viewpoints, feelings and expectations off their chests. It helps clear the air of residual tension.

2.   *It encourages the other person to speak.* Receptive, active and total listening creates the space for others to freely express themselves. It makes it easy for the speaker to express himself. Reticent people are drawn out by good listening.

3.   *Listening can increase your capacity to influence.* Our ability to influence others depends upon how we have listened to them. People commonly assume that speaking more is the route to better influencing. They believe that *'talk is power'* and that when we have the floor we are in control. This is not always true. It often leads to increased tension, decreased trust and decreased effectiveness, especially when more than one person is vying for attention and control.

In practice, true power lies in listening to others. People like you for letting them talk and for listening attentively to them. They start feeling good about you because you gave them the floor. Besides, you clearly understand their needs and also how best to approach their needs. When it is your turn to speak, they will be more attentive to you and to your message.

4.   *Listening can help in persuading and selling.* Ask any good salesman the secret of good selling and he will tell you that he gets the customer to sell to himself! This means that he encourages the customer to first talk about his needs. And through excellent listening and by asking appropriate questions, he then presents his ideas in a manner that connects with the customer's needs. Exactly the same process can be used to sell an idea to your boss, or to another department. It is simply a way of discovering what constitutes a 'benefit' for the customer, and then showing them how your idea or product gives them this benefit.

Every lock has an appropriate key. Listening helps you to understand the inner shape of the 'lock of need'. You can then tailor the key of your benefits to suit the lock.

5.   *Listening helps problem-solving and decision-making.* When we listen, we expand our field of awareness. Many facts, feelings, ideas and insights, which we were not aware of, are uncovered by listening. This is

There is a Key to Everyone's Heart

invaluable for making more informed decisions, which are fully in touch with the total picture. Many new ideas for solving problems can be yours by asking people for suggestions and then listening attentively. Be ready to be pleasantly surprised by the number of good ideas you can pick up by asking people and just listening.

One of the features of good problem-solving is correct diagnosis, that is, discovering the root cause behind the symptom. Listening with an appropriate use of Rudyard Kipling's 'six honest men' (what, why, who, how, where, when) can enable one to get insight into the root cause of problems. When a person has a problem to discuss with you, listening to her not only gets you to the cause of the problem, but also helps the other person to release feelings. This clarifies the person's own thinking and gets her to tap into her own creative potential to find effective solutions.

> In the very act of listening, if one does listen with awareness, without any effort, in that very act there is a strange miracle that does happen, which is like light penetrating into darkness. Listening has importance only if, in the very act of that, you can go within yourself and uncover your own ways of thought, feeling and discover how one is a slave to a symbol, to a word, and actually, emotionally, directly experience that which is being talked about.
>
> J. KRISHNAMURTHI

6. Listening can help you to resolve disagreements and solve mutual problems. You can agree, or disagree, with another person only after you have fully understood their point of view. Listening, followed by paraphrasing and summarizing, can help in doing this.

It is only after two people have actually understood each other's viewpoints, feelings, expectations and objectives in a cordial setting, that they can creatively explore possible solutions to their mutual problem. That is why it is better to first understand another person before you can expect to be understood.

7. *Listening leads to better teamwork.* In a team, when people respect each other and show their concern through better listening, a sense of trust and openness develops. This is excellent for fostering a spirit of cooperation and togetherness, both at work and at home.

8. *Listening can help you learn.* In today's times one of the most important needs of a manager is to learn continuously. In a study we did of high potential managers in an organization, we found that *self-motivated learning* is a strong indicator of how far a person will go in his career. Listening is central to good learning. As we listen to people speak on various subjects, and observe life around us keenly, we expand our understanding. Our capacity for effective action grows.

9. *Listening can give you confidence.* Understanding another person is like opening one's eyes. It is like turning on the light where there is darkness. A lot of our fear comes from not understanding something. If you listen accurately to another person, you can be sure of making an appropriate response.

If you have listened carefully in a meeting, you will be confident about what needs to be done. If you listen carefully to the union leaders, you will know what course of action to take. Listening to your boss respond to your question, 'What do you expect from my department?' can give you a clearer picture of what your role ought to be. This gives you direction on how you need to carry it out. Listening to the wisdom of your body and to your heart can enhance your confidence in responding to the varied demands of life.

10. *Listening enhances your joyfulness.* Good listening can significantly improve the way you relate to people. You make more friends and learn to appreciate other people. Being more attentive to people, as also to good plays, films and music, can significantly expand your blissfulness. In fact, being totally attentive to *anything* invariably expands joy.

Action Ideas for Improving Your Listening

Good listening rests on a foundation of courtesy and care for the other person. Many of the ideas for action given below may seem like common sense. It is, however, amazing how often we forget these simple rules and unwittingly hurt the feelings of the speaker. We may not mean to do so, but our enthusiasm for our own viewpoint or our desire to hear our own voice make us forget basic courtesy. Remembering and practising these tips can make all the difference:

1. *Give your speakers total undivided attention when they talk.* Be courteous and allow them to complete what they are saying without any interruptions. Do not butt in with rebuttals and arguments.

2. *Fight off distractions and create an appropriate physical climate for listening.* This includes finding the right time and place for listening, as well as giving time to the speaker and making this known to her.

3. *Use your entire body to express that you are listening and to encourage the other person to talk.* Use your eyes, hands and posture to express genuine interest in what they are saying. Maintain eye contact in a relaxed manner (without staring) and nod your head affirmatively to show that you are with the speaker. Lean slightly forward with uncrossed arms and legs and sit alert to indicate that you are listening. Do not fidget or play with things on your table.

4. *Listen with empathy.* Just as songs have words and music, what people express has content and feeling. While the words convey the content of a message, the feelings are like music. They convey how a person is experiencing life in the here and now. The content is best handled by the mind, while the feelings need to be understood by the heart. This calls for listening with empathy

The word 'empathy' comes from the Greek root *em* which means 'in' and *pathos* which means 'feeling' or 'suffer-

> Before we can forgive one another, we have to understand one another.
>
> EMMA GOLDMAN

ing'. 'Empathy' means putting ourselves into the other's shoes to see her feelings as she sees them. It does not mean agreeing with the feelings but simply seeing them as the other does. Since feelings are mostly expressed non-verbally, we have to use our eyes and ears to pick them up. Add that extra element of compassion and you are fully in touch with another's feelings.

Acknowledging and reflecting back these feelings gives the other person an assurance that they have been understood. For example, telling a person that she appears a bit tense may actually help her to relax. She feels that her feelings have been empathically understood. Reflection means restating clearly what we are understanding. Acknowledgement is something we say or do to show others that we have received and understood their statements or actions.

5. *Withhold judgements.* Try not to be critical of what the other person is saying. Even if the other's viewpoint is different from your own, be patient. Enter into a spirit of dialogue (where the focus is on discovering *what* is right) rather than into a debate (where one is attending to *who* is right). Do not evaluate the speaker's delivery. The mind needs to be consciously kept non-directional and open. We need to free ourselves from our own inner prisons.

6. *Ask open-ended questions.* An open-ended question is one which does not have a 'yes' or a 'no' for an answer. These questions allow the speaker to freely express her feelings and thoughts. 'What?', 'Who?', 'When?' and 'How?' questions are the ones to use. Avoid 'Why?' It puts people on the defensive because it sounds like an accusation.

Some door-opening questions which can be used in listening are:

> 'Tell me more about it.'
> 'What do you think is happening?'
> 'How do you see the situation?'

> If I can listen to what he tells me, if I can understand how it seems to him, if I can sense the emotional flavour which it has for him, then, I will be releasing potent forces of change within him.
>
> CARL ROGERS

Such questions tell the person that you are interested and want to understand things in their way. They can help to clarify potential ambiguities, expand horizons of understanding and also show the speaker that you are actively listening. Use silence appropriately to encourage the speaker to open up.

7. *Watch out for the speaker's main ideas.* Specific facts and details are only important as they relate to a certain context. They can cause misunderstanding if taken out of context. A good listener, therefore, relates to what is being said to the main arguments of the speaker, and constantly aims at getting the big picture. He makes use of the excess capacity of the mind to periodically review what has been said and to get an overview of what the speaker is really saying. It helps, sometimes, to jot the key points down in the form of a mind-map which creates an integrated picture of what the speaker is saying. This will help you to grasp the essence of what the speaker has said and to jog your memory later on. However, please keep your notes brief. Listening ability is affected when you are writing. The mind cannot do two things at a time.

8. *Paraphrase and summarize.* It is difficult to listen in situations where

emotions are running high. Each person may have actually stopped listening because they are ready to attack the other. Two basic skills that can help in such situations are *paraphrasing* and *summarizing*.

Paraphrasing involves reiterating the essential meaning of the statement in your own words. *Summarizing* involves reducing several statements into one concise restatement of the other person's point of view. When another person does not listen to you, you can paraphrase their point of view, reflect back their feelings and ask them to paraphrase and summarize yours.

For example, after listening to an emotionally charged mouthful, a person practising good listening might sound something like this: *'You are feeling . . . about . . .* (reflection). *The gist of what you have said is . . .* (paraphrasing). *I understand your point of which view is . . .* (paraphrase).' You would probably find a pacified person after this exercise in good listening.

The deepest form of listening is meditation. When I can listen to my opinions and watch them unpeeling like the layers of an onion, witness my feelings and the corresponding sensations in my body, watch my mind and its hankering for this and that, see the movements of my own ego, I transcend all these. This listening to the movements of my body–mind, and being a oneness that integrates the listener, the listened to, and the process of listening into one, is meditation.

Expressing Oneself and Assertiveness

Life is at its best when we are relating to others in a harmonious manner. We experience a sense of ease and freedom. However, when we have to deal with people who are overly pushy or who keep interrupting us or criticizing us rudely, we often feel a sense of anger and irritation arising inside us.

How does one deal with such people? *While it is important to listen to others and understand them well, it is equally important to express yourself and make yourself understood.*

Assertiveness is about standing up for our own rights in a way that is honest and caring of the other person, yet direct. It is expressing our thoughts, beliefs, viewpoints, expectations and feelings in a way that is respectful of ourselves and others. It is a way of balancing our own needs with those of other people.

Imagine a situation where you are standing in a queue in the office canteen and a person jumps the queue. Assertive behaviour would mean politely acknowledging that the person appears keen to have his food, or seems to be in a hurry. However, there's a queue and everybody else is also busy, and so could he please go right back to the end of the queue and wait there for his turn.

This is not always how such situations are handled. When it comes to standing up for their rights, people are either submissive or aggressive.

Submissive, timid or non-assertive behaviour This is behaviour in which we fail to stand up for what we believe in or are feeling. It is also behaviour that is apologetic, over-cautious and self-demeaning. In a nutshell, it is being violent and disrespectful to oneself. In the example of the canteen queue, this kind of behaviour would be to outwardly quietly accept the situation and inwardly curse the culture of the organization!

Aggressive behaviour, on the other hand, is standing up for what we want in a way that is abusive to other people. It involves blaming others, showing contempt, arrogance, hostility and attacking or putting down other people. It is based on the assumption that standing up for one's own rights necessarily involves being disrespectful to other people. It also assumes that our views are more important than those of others. It is being violent and disrespectful to others. In our example, pulling the person out of the canteen queue and giving him a few slaps would fit into his category.

Many managers believe (erroneously) that the only way they can exercise influence is by being aggressive. It is seen as an antidote to the other end of the spectrum, which is non-assertive behaviour.

A simple way of viewing these three kinds of behaviour is shown below.

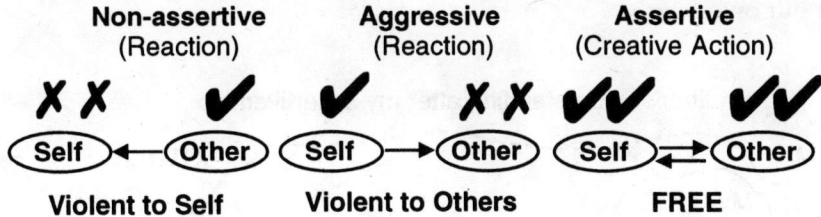

It is up to us which kind of behaviour we choose to follow.

Let's take the example of Mohan. He has to attend the birthday party of his son at 6 pm this evening. He is feeling quite excited, and is eagerly looking forward to the celebration. At 4.45 pm, just as Mohan is getting ready to go home, his manager announces that an urgent meeting is to be held from 5.30 to 7 pm and that all members of the team must attend. Mohan now has three choices before him:

1. To go along with the meeting without saying anything.
2. To get upset and angry and tell his boss about how unreasonable and uncaring he is. Then to go home in a furious rage blaming the organization and its culture for this sorry state of affairs.
3. To calmly, firmly and honestly express his understanding of the importance of the meeting and also mention his prior commitment and consequent inability to attend the meeting. He could offer some alternatives to make up for his not attending the meeting. Both the manager and he emerge feeling happy and contented with the solution.

You can now identify for yourself which choice before Mohan corresponds to which type of behaviour.

The consequences of choosing assertive behaviour are always positive. Even though we may not always get what we want, we at least have the satisfaction of freeing ourself inwardly. This enhances our own self-confidence and inner peace. People who have practiced assertive behaviour in our training programmes have reported feelings of relief, peace, freedom and growing self-confidence.

After I have chosen to be assertive, I get the other person to see things she never did earlier. *In effect, I have actively expanded the others' boundaries of awareness by being assertive.*

The other advantages of assertive behaviour are:

1. *It increases personal responsibility* and helps us to operate in the accountable mode. This is distinctively different from reacting and blaming others or ourselves (aggressive and non-assertive behaviour). This also gives us a better sense of being in charge of our lives. We choose what we value rather than being controlled by people, places, and events, or our own fears.

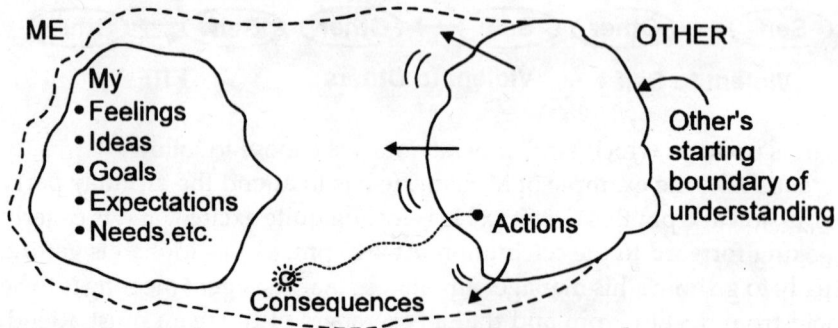

Assertiveness Expands Others' Understanding

2. As we honestly express feelings and state clearly what we want, our *relating to others improves*. We help people to understand us as we truly are and to see things from our perspective. This not only clears the air, but also improves trust in relationships. It also releases our stress.

3. *Energy and time are saved* as things become clear. Both non-assertive and aggressive types of behaviour have a serious negative impact on our available energy. This works somethings like:

$$\text{Available energy} = \frac{\text{Energy released}}{\text{from within}} - \frac{\text{Energy lost in supporting}}{\text{negative behaviour}}$$

Both the terms on the right-hand side are adversely affected when we are aggressive or non-assertive. The energy released from within is reduced. This is just like a spring clogged up with debris blocking the flow of pure water from below. At the same time, the amount of energy required to support this negative behaviour increases. So, the available energy reduces drastically.

I have yet to see a joyful person who chooses aggressive and non-assertive behaviour all the time! They mostly choose assertive behaviour. Since conflicts and decisions are handled quickly without wasting energy on 'not-upsetting people', or on 'power trips', the extra energy saved flows out in 'joyful relating'.

4. The likelihood of everyone getting what they want increases as people become more assertive. Peoples' ideas and opinions are aired, things are seen more clearly, and chances of every ones' expectations being met are improved. Being assertive, however, does not always ensure that one will get what one wants. Not being assertive, on the other hand, will ensure that the person does not get what he wants.

5. Assertiveness develops a healthy confidence in ourselves and in others. We see ourselves and other people as they are, in a balanced and respectful way. It clears up understanding, thereby making way for clarity and love. Understanding is the foundation of love.

6. Assertivenss also enables us to discharge feelings when they occur rather than 'gunny bagging' them until they all explode inappropriately at some other time. If I store up my anger, it may express itself onto someone who does not deserve it. Moreover, bottling up feelings can make us physically sick. I have seen many patients of heart disease and asthma who chose non-assertive behaviour for many years. On the other hand, people who freely express themselves have better physical and emotional health.

Steps in Assertive Communication

After this background on assertive behaviour, and its many advantages, you would be keen to put it into practice. There are two things to remember about practising assertive behaviour. One is the 'how' part, or the way we say things including the way our body expresses its feelings. The other part is the 'what' part, or the content of what we actually say while being assertive.

Let us start with the *'how' part*. Your body language and non-verbal behaviour needs to come naturally from an inner space of confidence and courage to enable you to come across as being assertive.

However, following some of the points given below can make a difference to how you feel:

1. *Maintain balanced eye contact.* Keep your eye contact relaxed and easy. Looking at a person directly in the eye, without trying to stare at or dominate him, creates a feeling of trust and credibility. It also gives the receiver the impression that you are firm about your point.

2. *Keep your body posture upright and relaxed.* An upright posture with no slouch reflects ease and poise. It is not intimidating. The head is held straight and the person is faced squarely. The hands are open and free to express feelings. Facial expressions are balanced and aligned with the feelings being expressed. This means that you smile or laugh only when you are actually happy.

3. *Keep the tone of your voice firm and clear.* It should have a sincere and authentic ring to it. It should be neither too loud (as in aggressive behaviour) nor too soft (as in non-assertive behaviour). The tone should be variable, emphasizing key feelings and important words. Generally speaking, assertive behaviour is a reflection of being comfortable and present in the here and now. This is born of deep caring for oneself and the other.

Now for the *'what' part*. Considering that assertive behaviour is born out of focusing on the 'I' factors (accountable mode) rather than on the 'they' factors, many of the points given below are based on choosing 'I' messages rather than blaming or 'they' messages. Assertive behaviour is also direct and non-apologetic. It is taking responsibility for our feelings.

1. *Start by acknowledging the other persons' viewpoint, and state your understanding of how the other person feels (reflecting feelings).* Remember that assertive behaviour is not only about stating what **you want**, but also of **understanding the other**. It helps to start with

understanding the other person's viewpoint before you express yours. This puts the other person in a more open frame of mind and thus, more ready to receive your honest and direct feedback.

2. *Describe specifically, in a straightforward, direct and descriptive way, your own viewpoint, needs, wants or opinions.* Be as descriptive as possible. Use data and facts. Facts are friendly, and hard to dispute. Use '*I*' statements such as 'The way I see things is : . . .' or 'What I would like is . . . .' Avoid judgements, 'they' blaming, verbal attacks, shoulds and musts, vagueness and generalizations. These poison a relationship and do not reflect assertive behaviour. Examples of such 'toxic' statements are:

> *'You never come home on time.'*
> *'You always fail to get up early and miss your exercise.'*
> *'Your attitude is not up to the mark!'*

3. *Describe your feelings using 'I' messages.* For example, 'I choose to get bored when you're not around' or 'I get scared when you drive too fast'. Describing our feelings is a simple process of making the other person aware of what is going on inside our mind. They are not attacks on the other person and we retain responsibility for how we feel. 'I' messages can give another person a concrete description of the specific behaviours that bother us and also how we feel about them.

4. *Show the other person the consequences of their behaviour.* Use specific descriptions giving examples such as: 'When your department does not send us the sales data by the second of the month, our reports are delayed. I feel very concerned about slipping out on our commitment to the Head Office.'

5. *State specifically what you want.* This may include what you want the person to start doing, or stop doing. 'I would like you to give me this report by 5 pm tomorrow evening.'

Let's look at an example on how these steps might work in practice.

Mohan's manager has the habit of not looking at him when he is speaking. He also interrupts his talk before Mohan has finished his sentence. Mohan finds this behaviour irritating. He also feels that many important things that he would have liked to share with his manager are not getting shared. He needs to make his manager more aware of his viewpoints and feelings on many issues. Here is how he might be able to do so using the steps described above.

Choosing an appropriate time, he goes to the Manager's cabin and tells him: 'I appreciate the number of things that you have to attend to. These are probably keeping you quite preoccupied and you must be feeling quite harassed by all the pressures. *(Step 1: Acknowledging the others' viewpoint, reflecting feelings.)*

'However, when I am with you, I observe that our eye contact is missing 90 per cent of the time. Also, I am interrupted before I finish what I have to say 100 per cent of the time. For example, when I was sharing about our need for a water cooler on the shop floor, I could not complete what I was saying. *(Step 2: Describe your viewpoint with facts, examples.)*

'I choose to feel pretty upset by this because I am telling myself that you are probably not interested in what I have to say. *(Step 3: Describe your feelings while retaining responsibility for them.)*

'The consequence of this is that important information which would help you and our department does not reach you. I also am not getting across my feelings to you. *(Step 4: Show the other person the consequences of their behaviour.)*

'Therefore, what I would request you to do is: maintain eye contact with me when I am speaking, and also listen to me completely without interruptions so that I can share all that I have to tell you.' *(Step 5: Stating specifically what you want.)*

While the steps given above are in a certain sequence, you can use them in any order as appropriate.

It may appear at this point that assertive behaviour is the 'right choice' in every single situation. This is not so. There are occasions when you may choose aggressive or even submissive behaviour.

If you are mugged on the streets of New York, it may be wiser to quietly give up your wallet rather than face a physical attack. Or, if someone is trying to take your child away from you while you are on a walk, you would probably need to choose aggressive behaviour. The important thing is that you are 'consciously choosing' the approach that is the most appropriate one in that situation.

Assertive behaviour is all about being free to choose one's response. It even includes the choice of being aggressive or non-assertive, if required. It is about operating from truth and integrity: a condition in which what I think, feel, say and do are all one. It is about showing other persons things they are not seeing. It is about turning on the light of awareness in a respectful and caring way. It is an expression of operating from love in which there is a sense of oneness and shared understanding. It is a courageous standing up for what we truly value, and also respectfully acknowledging what others value.

Interpersonal Communication

Both sensitivity to others and expressing yourself need to be balanced in our relationships. An overuse of either one leads to partial and imperfect understanding. The table below shows four different situations of using both these skills.

Box A (low on listening and low on assertiveness) represents the behaviour pattern of a person who is neither listening nor expressing too much. He chooses to remain in the dark and keep others in the dark about what he is experiencing. For all practical purposes, his existence in a team would hardly make a difference. He would choose to be like a tortoise sitting inside a shell.

Box B (high on listening and low on assertiveness) represents the choice of a person who is an excellent listener but does not say much. When I ask participants if they would like a boss who behaves like this, many people say they would be frightened of such a manager! The reason for this is that they would not know what he is thinking or where they stand in relation to him. Such people in a team would not contribute very much. They would be silent spectators not sharing any ideas or information that might help the group's work.

Box C (high assertiveness and low listening) is another example of unbalanced behaviour. Like Box B, this also will lead to stressful situa-

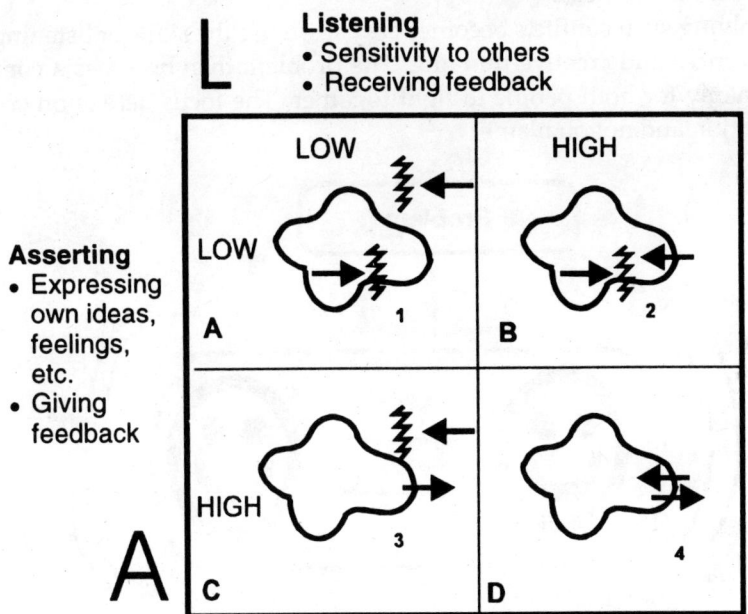

tions. It is characteristic of people who speak too much and are not willing to listen to others. These are people who do not receive enough feedback on their actions and the consequences of these actions. They have 'blind spots' about things that others can see and they cannot. Their behaviour in teams is unyielding and they create a loss of goodwill by refusing to listen.

Box D (high on assertiveness and high on listening) is the behaviour of people choosing to use both skills in a balanced manner. Being open to others' viewpoints and also honestly sharing one's own creates the conditions for creating harmony in relationships. It releases stress in people by creating oneness and understanding. This is like turning on the 'light of awareness' on both sides. The opposite of this would be fear, misunderstanding and darkness. Behaviour represented in this box helps us to see things in totality and work towards resolving differences amicably, whenever conflicts arise.

Solving Problems and Resolving Conflicts

Whenever two people want to achieve their own outcomes and cannot, because of another person, there is a conflict. Suppose you would like to change the way something is done in the office and your colleague does not want to change it, you have a conflict of approaches. You could even have a conflict of ideas.

Resolving such conflicts becomes easy if we use the skills of listening, assertiveness and creative thinking. The problem then becomes a common enemy for both people to fight together. The focus here is on creative action and not on blame.

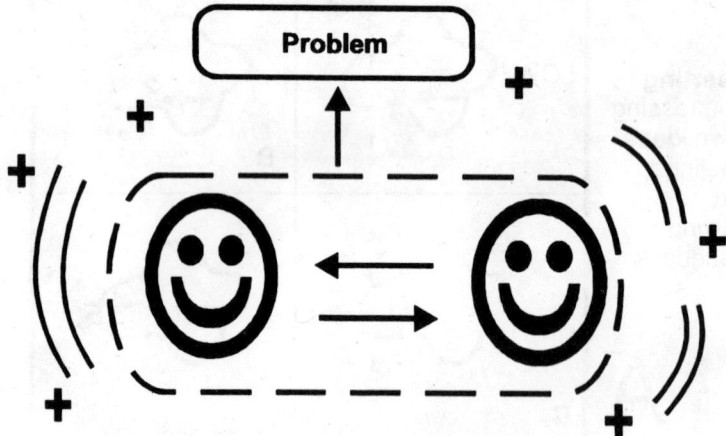

If they do not use these skills, then the issue remains as it is and people end up spending energy attacking each other.

Thats why the adage, '*Attack problems and not people,*' is so popular.

A few steps to resolve conflicts are :

> **Before we can make friends with anyone else, we must make friends with ourselves.**
>
> ELEANOR ROOSEVELT

1. *Create a good atmosphere for discussion.* It helps to have a conducive physical and emotional framework before you begin resolving the conflict.

2. *Understand the other person's viewpoint completely.* Use good listening to bring out the other's viewpoint and feelings.

3. *Assertively express your viewpoints and feelings.* Remember to specifically state what you want. The more clearly you can describe what you want and also the more accurately you capture what the other wants, the better position you are in to find a mutually acceptable solution. It is better to walk on a moonlit night than to grope around in the dark. The clearer the terrain, the better our choices and actions.

4. *Generate many alternatives using creative thinking.* Spending time on generating ideas can help us to find a solution beneficial to both. This is a step often overlooked by people. They assume (erroneously) that there are only two ways to solve a conflict . . . either my way or their way.

5. *Mutually select the best alternative which has a high likelihood of being accepted by both parties.* Suitable criteria for evaluating alternatives can be fixed in advance. Life is infinitely creative and possibilities to solve conflicts always exist. They are available to us only if we search for them.

6. *Focus on the common goals and the 'big picture' in every conflict.* When we connect with the common well-springs of human values in our relationships, petty differences are relegated to the background.

7. *Adopt a positive underlying attitude to solve conflicts.* The attitude on both sides needs to be:

- 'We can work it out together.'
- 'I will focus on action and not on blame.'
- 'There are always possibilities which will be open to us if we keep our minds open.'
- 'I will attack problems and not people.'
- 'Love conquers all.'

I'm often asked the question, 'What can I do if the other party is rigid and hostile?' The answer is, trust your own bliss and keep doing what you think is the right thing to do in the circumstances. A block of ice eventually melts under the warm glow of a coal fire. Your own integrity, honesty and genuine desire to resolve the conflict in a mutually beneficial way (and not to 'win' it) will have its own rewards. It may take time however. This approach is not easy. It draws upon all the reserves of patience and maturity that you have.

Ideas for Playful Action

1. Think of a few people who you think are excellent communicators. What is it about them that makes them good at communication? List down these traits.

2. Having read this chapter, identify your strengths in communication. Also identify some areas where you can improve. Write down what you can do to improve, and set a deadline for achieving this.

   Strengths   Areas of Improvement

3. Think of all your relationships. Which ones are in need of healing. What are the few steps you can take to do this? Where can listening help and where can assertiveness be handy?

4. Look at the diagram on page 137. Which quadrant do you normally choose and with whom? What changes would you like to make in this behaviour?

≋ 6 ≋

Acting

Skills for Managing Time and Life

Time is God. Time is divine. Time is a lightening bolt.
Time is the flow of consciousness.
When you have this sublime awareness of time,
every breath you draw brings you the vision of God.
SWAMI CHIDVILASANANDA

Communication enables us to understand each other and see things differently. It changes our view of things and alters the vision or images we hold in our mind. This vision needs action to convert it into reality.

Taking *inspired action* however is not as easy as it sounds. Forces that drag us back abound. Words come cheap, notions and ideas are all fine, good intentions are all right, but they are all useless without action. As one wit remarked, *'A little bit of something is better than plenty of nothing.'* The challenge is to use our energy to cut through and go beyond all our fears, insecurities, uncertainities and doubts. We need to confront and transcend our lethargy and apathy, and *act* rather than make excuses.

Taking inspired action is not about ridding ourselves of self-doubt, insecurity and that inner tape that keeps telling us things, such as, *'You will fail; you can't do this. You will hurt yourself.'* It is doing things despite all these.

Making things happen is perhaps the most important skill of all out of the ones we have covered so far. Anything thought of and considered useful must finally be converted into inspired action. As the Chinese master Lao-Tsu says, *'Even a journey of a thousand miles begins with a single step.'* Our zone of action is this present moment. The past is a set

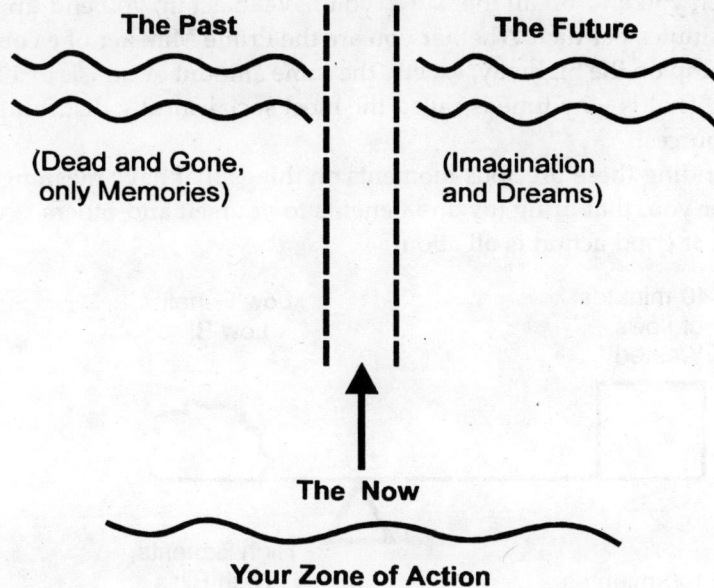

The Past

(Dead and Gone, only Memories)

The Future

(Imagination and Dreams)

The Now

Your Zone of Action

of memories. The future is only a dream. It is action today, which creates the future. We are planting thought, word and action seeds all the time. These will bear fruit in the future.

Making things happen is all about using our present moment well to create the events that we want. It is about managing time in the here and now. Managing time is the same as managing our life. What we do with our time will determine what we do with our life. Time, in turn, is nothing other than a series of 'NOWS'. The only time you have control over or which you really have to do anything is *now*.

> The present moment is a powerful Goddess.
>
> GOETHE

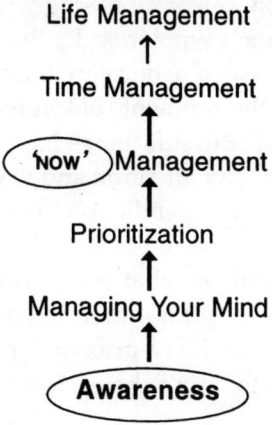

Life Management
↑
Time Management
↑
'Now' Management
↑
Prioritization
↑
Managing Your Mind
↑
Awareness

When you add up all the 'NOWS' you have to act in, you end up with 1440 minutes per day. Whether you are the Prime Minister of a country or a tramp on the highway, exactly the same amount of time is available to you. That is why time is called the most socialistically distributed of all resources!

Spending these precious moments on things that have meaning and soul for you, that bring joy and benefits to yourself and others is what the art of good action is all about.

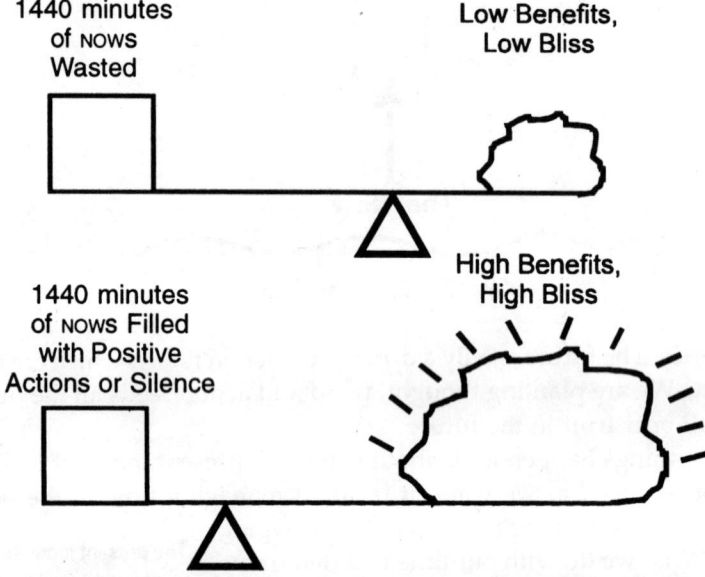

1440 minutes of NOWS Wasted

Low Benefits, Low Bliss

1440 minutes of NOWS Filled with Positive Actions or Silence

High Benefits, High Bliss

Remind yourself of a recent day you spent well. Remember the joy of inspired action, the warm and easy interactions with people, the moments of creative reflection, celebration, singing, the walks and exercise with the children, the lunch with friends, the kind acts of giving. A picture of time used well. Good actions are blissful in themselves. They are free and peaceful in the moment. Blissfulness can guide you and give you the energy to make useful things happen every moment. This will mean that you have to pay attention and watch what you are doing and why. What you do now depends upon what you are putting your attention on.

This, in turn, is governed by what your priorities are. If a manager thinks that developing his people is important, he will consciously spend time on it. Similarly, if I think it is a priority for me to keep my body fit because I value good health, I will choose to spend some time to take a walk every day. My priorities will govern what I finally decide to direct my will and choice towards.

So, *identifying and setting priorities* is an important skill in time management. It calls for being aware of our deepest guiding principles, and also of the way in which we harmonize our efforts with the needs of our environment.

> Things which matter most must never be at the mercy of things which matter least.
>
> GOETHE

Identifying priorities by itself is not enough. We need to set *objectives* for achieving these. A group of managers I knew said they could not achieve their objectives. When I asked them if they had written them down, they said, *'Yes'*. I next asked them where they kept these written objectives. The answer was, *'In our desk. We see them only before our six-monthly review!'* Out of sight = out of mind = out of action. With their priorities locked up in the desk, their attention was *'grabbed'* by the 'fire of the moment' or just anything that came along. Consciously watching our moment and reminding ourselves of our objectives will enable us to spend our time and energy on our priorities.

A Different Kind of Watch

W ords

A ctions

T houghts

C haracter

H abits

Being aware of what tries to *'grab'* our attention in the moment besides our priorities (to which we commit ourselves by choice) calls for tremendous awareness and insight—a quality that is at the core of good time management. We have to be watchful of each action of ours.

A person who utilizes her time well is totally and fully in control of her life. She knows what she wants and is committed to achieving it. She accordingly plans her work and expenditure of time. She is the master of her destiny and makes things happen. Good use of time is one of her most important tools.

Yet, how many of us really behave like this? Most of the time we are racing towards deadlines, not being able to show results, having too much paperwork to deal with, irate bosses and unhappy subordinates, not to mention stomach ulcers related to stress! There is too little time and too much to do.

It appears as though we are no longer in charge. Life seems to be pushing us along relentlessly. It is no wonder then that most managers suffer from symptoms of stress. No one would like to waste time deliberately. Time Management is not something that one just acquires. It is a skill, a technique and an attitude that one can learn. It develops ways of making inspired action happen and of living and working from the Heart.

> Lives of great men all remind us
> We can make our lives so sublime
> And departingly leave behind us
> Footprints on the sands of time.
> H.W. LONGFELLOW

Getting Our Objectives in Place

Just as an architect creates the plans for a house before it is actually constructed, we too can create a picture of our future. A clear picture of what we would like to see happening is a starting point for its manifestation in the realm of reality. When we visualize something clearly and keep putting our attention to it, our feelings and actions are drawn in that direction. Our goals pull our thoughts, feelings and actions towards them.

> When the soul wishes
> to experience something,
> She throws an image
> Of the experience out
> Before her and enters
> Into her own image.
> MEISTER ECKHART

Our energy then begins to follow our intentions. The more specific and clear the picture of an outcome is in our minds, and the more it is aligned with our deeper values and strengths, the greater is the probability of it happening. Setting objectives is an important device for making this happen.

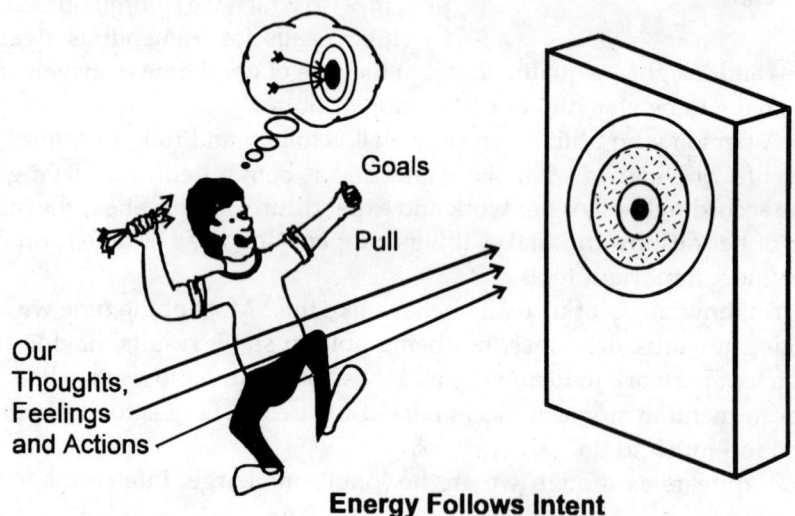

Energy Follows Intent

What is an Objective ?

An objective is a statement of a desired result to be achieved within a specific period of time. An objective tells us in concrete, measurable, terms what we want to achieve. It helps us to track whether or not we are moving any closer towards our goal.

The key word to remember while setting objectives is SMART!

S	*Specific.* They indicate *what* must be done to achieve the desired result. People must be able to *see* your achievement.
M	*Measurable.* How will you know that the objective has been achieved? Set up a standard of performance that is quantifiable.
A	*Attainable.* Can you realistically achieve it?
R	*Relevant.* The objective should be related to your role and priorities.
T	*Time-bound.* By what time does it have to be achieved?

There is another dimension to the SMART acronym. While the one mentioned above is related to the outer aspects of setting objectives, your objectives must also be aligned with the best for you and others. So, here's another test to check for the inner SMARTness of your objectives.

S	*Spiritual.* Are these objectives aligned with the calling of your deepest wisdom, your innermost self?
M	*Mindful.* Are these objectives born out of the mindfulness of all factors, for example, your strengths, need for balance, etc.
A	*Aware* of this moment, of my values.
R	*Responsive* to the needs of other people, and both internal and external customers.
T	*Timeless and trusting.* Do they remember that some of the most valuable things in life are timeless? Do they trust Existence?

These two dimensions of SMART need to be in harmony with each other. You cannot afford an inner conflict here!

All objectives that you set must be mutually consistent (to avoid conflicts), and written down (for easy reminders and review).

Correctly stated objectives help us to do the following:

- Plan our activities effectively. We can map out the steps we need to take to make them happen.

- Measure performance against the plan. We can track progress by comparing performance with the objectives.
- Inform others about what we are tying to achieve, by sharing specific ideas.
- Enhance our communication, since we are giving concrete information to the receiver.

Where Do Objectives Come From?

SMART objectives emerge from looking at situations objectively. When we look within, at our values, our deepest desires and inner promptings, as also look around us at the needs and expectations of other people, we see the beginnings of a new direction. Objectives are like seeds. They hold within them the power of creation, and the capacity to grow into tangible outcomes. They are like the forerunners of the future—the shape of things to come. Writing down SMART objectives can be a very creative act. It is a way of harmonizing and balancing the various factors and crystallizing them into a clear statement of intent.

While setting objectives in an organization, a manager has to consider the objectives of the organization as a whole, the objectives of his department or boss, as also those of his own as well as his colleagues and subordinates. Some of these could also be his internal customers or people who receive the output of his department's work.

Here are a few areas you may have to look at to decide your objectives:

1. *Objectives that come from the top*
   - The objectives of the organization, and what that means for my role.
   - Things the boss wants me to do arising out of the corporate plan.

2. *Statutory objectives, or things connected with legal requirements*
   - Objectives arising out of external law or internal company policies.
   - Legal requirements, routine checks (for example, closing of accounts, safety audits).

3. *Improvements to ongoing work*
   - Objectives arising out of a desire to achieve a higher standard of existing work, such as improving quality, or the response time to customers' complaints. Some questions can help here: Can I do more? Can I do better? Can I do differently?

4. *Things that the manager alone can see*
   - New ideas, developments, research—things that can make a big difference.
   - New possibilities which can be developed on my own initiative.

5. *Manager's own development*
   - What are the deeper values my life rests on? How can I come closer to realizing my own vision for my life?
   - What do I need to learn/do to improve my performance?
   - Do I need to develop any new skills, say, to coach my subordinates better?
   - Do I need to be more friendly and informal?

6. *Staff development*
   - How do I develop my staff better?
   - What are their development needs?
   - What is the knowledge, skill and attitude that they need to develop?

Let us look at a few examples of *good objectives:*
- I will reduce my weight from 65 kg to 60 kg by 31 December 1999.
- I will master the use of all features of the software package MS-Office by 15 August 1999.
- The quality of product X will be improved from the present 90 per cent acceptable to 100 per cent acceptable by 30 November 1999.

These objectives are SMART. This is because each one specifies what has to be achieved, that is, the desired result (S), and they are all measurable and can actually be tracked using a graph or a checklist (M). They are attainable (A) *and* relevant to the person's role (R), and have a time-bound date of completion (T). I'm assuming that the inner dimensions of SMART have also been considered in writing them.

Good objectives are a device to initiate, monitor and track progress towards our desired goals. They also connect what we are doing now (at this moment) with the outcomes that we are seeking to create in the future. Achieving our objectives is primarily a process of reminding ourselves of what we want to achieve and then taking the necessary action to make it happen. Mechanisms to remind us of our objectives are therefore very important.

Reminding Ourselves

Some methods I have seen people use to remind themselves to ensure that they achieve their goals are as follows:

- They put their objectives up in *writing*, preferably where they can see them often, for example, on a felt board in front of their desk, or in their drawer, or up on a whiteboard on the facing wall, or even under the glass top on their table.
- Some draw a *colourful picture* capturing the essence of their goal. They make it visually creative and specific. We found dramatic proof of the efficacy of this method when we created a scrap-book of pictures and cuttings of what we thought our new house should look like. The actual house turned out to be a lot like what we had imagined together as a family.
- Some people make a *mind-map* of their objectives and show its connections to other aspects of their life.
- I've seen people make *small cards* with their objectives. They carry them in their wallets and see them often.
- One common method is to put the objectives in a *diary* and refer to them regularly.

Using the 'Now' Well

The working unit of our life is really the 'now'. It is really all we have and will ever have. To be blissful in the 'now', celebrating and enjoying it, and totally doing whatever has to be done automatically creates the seeds for future excellence. A moment lived creatively and totally with full energy devoted to whatever is at hand creates its own positive ripples.

When we are total in our work and are fully and completely engrossed in it, we tap into a source of creativity and power which helps us to do the work joyfully. An easy way to remember this is through the meanings of *en* and *ergy* in Greek. *En* is '*in*' and *ergy* is '*working*'. So when you are fully immersed in your work i.e. totally present to what you are doing, and your work is in you, i.e. born out of your own mission, then you experience an abundance of energy! Working in this way is close to what Polish-born psychologist, Mihaly Csikzentmihalyi, calls the 'flow' state. His research shows that the type of activities which people all over the world consistently report as the most satisfying psychologically and which make them feel good involve:

- A clear objective
- A need for concentration so intense that no attention is left over
- A lack of interruptions and distractions
- Clear and immediate feedback
- A sense of challenge

The 'flow' state happens when we are intensely focused on our work. Since action can only happen in the now, being *in* our work also implies being in the present. That's when real energy begins to flow, and we are enthusiastic about our work.

The word 'Enthusiasm' comes from *En*, which is 'in' and ' *theos* ' which is 'God'.

When we are totally 'here–now', the only place where *ergy* or work can happen, you are joyful and enthusiastic! Totally in it, totally present.

Working with bliss and inner peace as a foundation will ensure that what we do will yield good results. Seeds of thoughts, words and actions sown with joy, freedom and peace will always yield good fruit. The secret of making things happen is to focus on a good process aligned with our objectives, and to trust existence to take care of the rest. While it is important to have objectives, they must always remain our slaves. While it is good to give them a good shot, we must never become obsessed with them. *The key is staying free.*

Our expenditure of time at the point of action needs to be connected with our own inner freedom. Whatever we do must link up with what we consider important.

While this is clear to many of us, we often allow other things which are not so important to encroach into our here and now. For example, useless gossip, unproductive meetings, watching trash programmes on TV, and squandering time on laziness eats away our time. All these happen because we have lost touch with our inner baro-meter of peace and silence. We often suffer people non-assertively, or painfully sit through a boring meeting because we have forgotten that we have the creative power of free choice. What is urgent or urging us for attention in the here

> It seems essential in relationships and all tasks that we concentrate only on what is most significant and important.
>
> Soren Kierkegaard

and now is not always important. Spending time on carefully reading junk mail on our desk is to get carried away by the urgency of the matter and to forget that it is not important. Similarly, the truly blissful and liberating things in our life may not always present themselves in this moment. Sitting with our team mates to give and receive feedback may be very important, but it rarely urges you to make it happen. *The art of good time management lies in consciously saying 'Yes' to the positive energies of life and reminding ('re-minding') ourselves of those things which bring us the greatest inner satisfaction and growth.*

Things I genuinely need to do are like a vein of gold in the ground—high-value things, which will bring me peace, freedom, health and prosperity. Things I do not need to do are like the surrounding rubble.

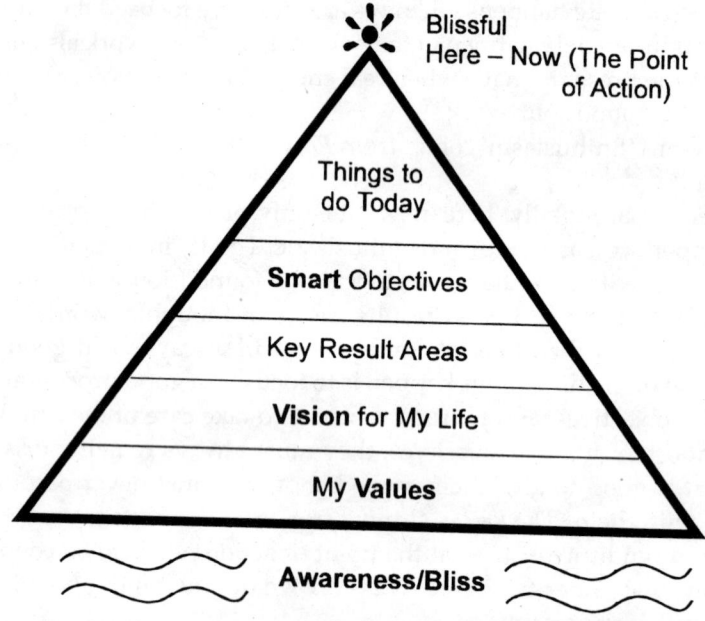

How can I stay focused on the gold vein? Once we discover what is truly important in our lives, our decisions begin to reflect the whispers of our soul rather than the agitated promptings of our personalities and egos.

One of the things that robs us of the now is submitting to the pressure of urgency and losing sight of the important. We tend to forget the important things in our life because they do not often create a pressure for completion. The matrix below is another way of looking at this issue:

Urgent vs Important Matrix		
	URGENT	NOT URGENT
IMPORTANT	• Crisis • Fire-fighting • Last-minute deadlines *Quadrant I*	• Planning • Innovation • Creative work • Self-renewal • Research *Quadrant II*
NOT IMPORTANT	• Some phone calls • Some interruption • Some meetings • Some papers, mail, reports *Quadrant III*	• Gossip • Chit-chat • Long tea breaks • Useless diversionary activity *Quadrant IV*

There are basically two factors that define an activity as far as time management is concerned:

The song that I came to sing remains unsung. I have spent my days in stringing and unstringing my instrument.

RABINDRANATH TAGORE

1. *How urgent is it?* To what extent is it urging us to act now, pressing you to give it attention immediately.

2. *How important is it?* To what extent does it contribute to your deepest values and objectives?

Quadrant II is where we should be focusing most of our time and energy because it is these very activities that will carry the organization ahead. This includes the time spent on planning of projects, staff development, research, documentation, improvement of quality, etc. Typically, most of us do not spend enough time on these activities.

If we focus our time and energy on *Quadrant II* activities—namely planning, project management, setting up of systems and procedures, internal meetings, etc.—then we reduce the time on *Quadrant I* activities which are mainly fire-fighting activities. Fire-fighting activities arise because of poor planning and inadequate time management.

If we practice good principles of time management, we will reduce the time spent on *Quadrant III* and *Quadrant IV* activities. In fact, *Quadrant IV* activities should be completely eliminated.

Two vicious cycles arise when we do not spend enough time on *Quadrant II* activities:

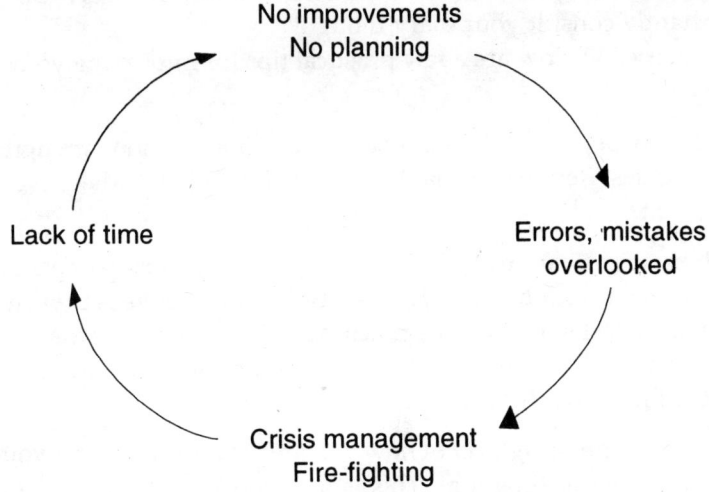

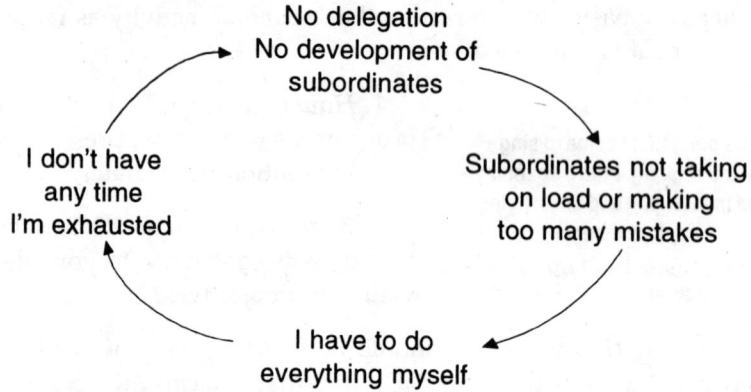

As we consciously decide to spend our time on *Quadrant II* activities, a sense of discipline and control arises and there is a decline in the number of crises faced by managers. A useful device to enable us to stay focused on our important activities is a good *diary system*.

The purpose of a diary is not only to remain focused on the important and priority aspects of our life, but also to plan and track the implementation of actions taking us closer to these objectives. It gives us a sense of better control and it also becomes a device for recording our ideas and thoughts about our goals. This helps unclutter the mind and keep it free from undue pressure and stress. I find it very relaxing to write things I need to remember in my diary to get them off my mind. One has to be careful to constantly consult your diary though!

> **Vision isn't enough unless combined with venture. It's not enough to stare up the stairs unless we also step up the stairs.**
>
> VANCE HAVNER

Summarised below are a few practical tips for improving your use of the 'now' well:

1. Set your objectives in alignment with your mission, strengths and deeper values. Remember that this life is all you have. Make every moment count.

2. Make specific action plans showing the action steps you need to take to achieve your objectives. When each big objective is broken down into smaller tasks, it becomes much easier to move towards. *'Inch by inch, it is a cinch!'* With small mouthfuls of rice, you can eat up a whole granary. Prioritise all tasks.

3. Become more insightful of how you are actually spending your time by maintaining a 'time-log'. This is a record of your activities in the format shown below:

Date	Activity	Time		Time Spent	Quadrant
		From	*To*	(min)	
5.6.98	Dressing up	7	7.30	30	I
	Breakfast	7.30	8.15	45	II
	Travelling	8.15	9.15	60	I
	Project report	9.15	10.45	60	I
	Meeting with project staff	11.00	12.30	90	II

Total time spent:

Quadrant I = _____
Quadrant II = _____
Quadrant III = _____
Quadrant IV = _____

When I first prepared a time-log, I received quite a shock. I realized (through data that I could not escape from) that a substantial amount of my time was wasted on long phone calls and just lying in bed doing nothing! The time-log is a beautiful device to expand your insight about how you are using your time.

4. Eliminate time-robbers. The time-log will help you find them. Start with your biggest time-wasters. Generate creative ideas to lick the problem. All problems also come with solutions. We have to look for them.

5. Schedule and plan your days and weeks just as a good artist would make beautiful paintings. Bring in harmony and balance. Avoid over-commitment and be realistic while planning schedules. Allow flexible time for crises and interruptions, and schedule at least one hour each day for self-development and exercise. Do not forget to schedule some time for meditation. Treat each week as a work of art and yourself as its creator. It is amazing how life actually begins to follow the pattern that you create for it. As you think, so you become. Make your whole life a beautiful work of art.

6. Take care of your energy balance. Remember the equation discussed in Chapter 5.

$$\text{Available energy} = \begin{array}{c}\text{Energy released}\\\text{from within}\end{array} - \begin{array}{c}\text{Energy lost in supporting}\\\text{negative behaviour}\end{array}$$

Keep the energy levels high by regular exercise and meditation, focusing on meaningful goals and a constructive attitude of positivity and gratitude. Eat well and rest well. Reduce the energy wasted by dissolving the ego and being as far as possible in the here and now. Avoid actions that dissipate energy. When the energy available is high, tasks are done much faster and more creatively.

7. *Use a good diary* to record and track your objectives, prioritise your schedules, put down your ideas and a variety of other uses, which you can creatively think of. Do not let the diary become your master. Remember that goals, diaries and schedules are your creations and slaves, and not the other way around! Remain masterful, relaxed and free.

8. *Maintain a neat and organised desk and filing system.* Use the TRAF method to sort out the paper messes on the desk. The TRAF method is a simple device which says that every paper on your desk needs to be processed using one of the four actions given below.

T	*Trash* Throw the paper away into the wastepaper basket, often described as a man's second best friend (after the dog!).
R	*Refer* it to somebody else for action along with brief comments.
A	*Action* Prioritise all the papers based on their importance and hold them for action. Keep them in neat folders for easy access.
F	*File* the papers in a good filing system.

A neat and well-organised workplace can be your best friend. Good house-keeping can be of enormous help in making inspired action happen.

9. If you work with other team members, make sure that you do this. *Use everybody's strengths to the fullest.* Rather than think of this as delegation, if we see it as enabling people to give their very best, you will not only release their energy, but also save some of your own. Always look out for opportunities to let others use their strengths and talents. This liberates your time and it helps others to grow.

10. *Learn to understand and dissolve the habit of procrastination.* Procrastination, or putting off till tomorrow what we can do today, is a great barrier in the natural flow of creative action. Develop the habit of completion and action now by tapping into your core of pure awareness.

Developing the Habit of Completion

The Roman philosopher, Marcus Aurelius, once said, *'Do not act as though you had a thousand years to live.'* Many of us often do this. We put off things perpetually, and in the process miss the ever-flowing joy of dynamic action.

Whenever we are stuck with any unproductive habit, there is always an underlying mental pattern that supports it. This is like a deceiving, luring mechanism that gives us a false sense of comfort or a pseudo-benefit. This is really a certain desire which is getting fulfilled and is always connected with not being present in the 'here-and-now'. Remember the 'rest house' we discussed in Chapter 4.

This rest house keeps us away from inspired action in the 'here-and-now' which would take us forward in life's journey towards real success!

An example of rest-house behaviour is excessively 'resting' in bed instead of being up working or exercising. The underlying benefit is comfort and physical ease based on the false notion that I am the body. This pseudo-benefit, or false lure, keeps us away from exercise and total work which would have given the body greater ease and better health in the long run.

Coming out of the rest house requires 'non-judgemental awareness'.

Non-judgemental Awareness is the Key

Habits are like old comfortable shoes. Changing an unproductive habit requires awareness, action and a review of the consequences of our actions. Judging, fighting and condemning yourself does not change a habit. It only creates an inner conflict—an inner *Mahabharata* raging between two parts of your own mind. This brings in tension which only makes things worse.

> Delays are always dangerous, useless, barren. Today is the only day to attempt any great and worthy purpose. Opportunity comes to all of us; the diligent catch hold of it; the foolish let is pass.
>
> SWAMI CHINMAYANANDA

The more productive and creative approach to changing habits is to *witness your habit* with non-judging awareness. Observe what you are doing. Observe the inner movements of your mind which support your actions and understand the consequences of what you are doing. As this alertness grows, your unproductive habit will change just as a source of light spontaneously dispels darkness.

Getting Rid of Procrastination

Procrastination has a lot to do with the mind. The roots of the problem as well as the solutions all find their locations in the way we think. For example, look at a common vicious circle which many people who 'choose' to procrastinate find themselves in:

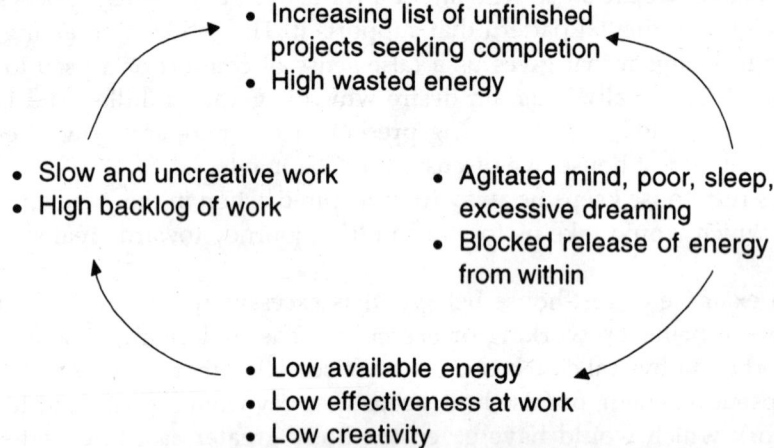

The unfinished work or accumulated backlog begins to look far more formidable than it actually is. It assumes gigantic proportions in thought. This, in turn, blocks further release of energy and aggravates the problem. In reality, the work to be finished is downright simple when we get down to it. The funniest thing of it all is that we actually 'enjoy' doing the work once we move forward on the journey of inspired action. The heart of the matter is to remember the following connection:

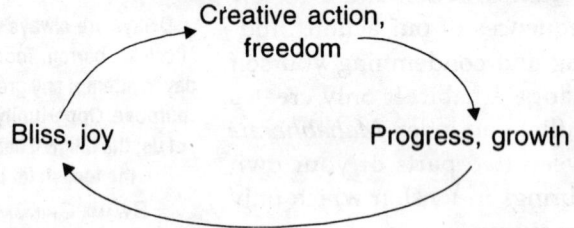

As this engine of energy unfolds its light in our lives through our own understanding and actions, making things happen becomes as easy as breathing in fresh air.

A Practical Exercise for Changing Habits

1. Write down the habits you want to change. The inner stance should be of a loving witness and not a condemning fighter or judge.

2. Write down your goal in a finished form. Make your results measurable. Describe the goal positively, for example, 100 per cent completion rather than 0 per cent procrastination.
3. List down all the problems created by the habit for you.
4. Now list down all the benefits of changing the habit.
5. Visualize yourself actually carrying out the new behaviour. Picture yourself behaving in the exaggerated opposite way of your unproductive habit. For example, if you want to improve your assertiveness, visualise yourself behaving in an extremely positive, open and energetic way.
6. Allow no slippages. Each time you find yourself slipping, *stop*. Take a few deep breaths. Draw strength from your silent and free innermost core, and change to the new pattern.

> **For all sad words of tongue or pen, the saddest are these: 'It might have been done!'**

7. Enlist the support of others. Involve close relatives or friends in the change process to encourage consistency, persistence and firmness.
8. Use visual reminders in the form of affirmations, sentences on cards fixed at prominent places which state your new behaviour.
9. Be positive. Reward yourself. Meditate.

Practical Tips to Overcome Procrastination

- Imagine you had only six months to live. Look hard at life and act now.
- Substitute anxiety about the future with ACTION NOW.
- Do it in small bits. Live fifteen minutes at a time.
- Begin now . . . you'll enjoy it!
- Choose timings and set-ups that match your natural energy rhythms.
- Give your own identity and goals a chance. Ask what is really important to you. Keep time for your own needs.
- Overcome fear of failure or of being judged by action. One act of courage can eliminate fear.
- Doing is far more important. Settle for less than perfect. Don't attempt the impossible.
- Look at your 'now' with awareness. Look at your fear and ACT.
- Remember the Hassidic prayer: *'If I am not for myself, who will be for me? If I am for myself alone, what use am I? And if not now, when?'*
- Say, *'I am doing it now (about a task)'*, and then act on the task each time after you have said it. This builds a powerful habit.
- Take an incremental approach to completion.

- Use a 'leading edge' or key task to trigger the whole action.
- Make a public commitment.
- Reward yourself when the task is completed.
- Compete with yourself. Get into the completion habit.
- Finish one task at a time. Then move on to another. Prioritize and attack 'A' category items.
- Focus your attention on the job until you finish it.
- Complete what you start.
- If you want the world to change, don't complain about it. Do something.
- Use the GOYA (Get Off Your Anatomy) approach!

> VISION without ACTION is merely a dream. ACTION without VISION just passes the Time. But VISION with ACTION can change the World.
>
> JOEL ARTHUR BARKER

The art of inspired action can be a formidable force to meet any challenge. Developing this habit, along with clarity of direction can enable you to achieve almost anything you want in life. It also helps to unfold joy and spirit in ourselves and our organizations.

Ideas for Playful Action

1. Where and how are you spending your time? How much time are you giving to others? To yourself? Maintain a time-log for a week to give yourself valuable insight into your actual time usage.

2. List down a few smart objectives for yourself covering the important aspects of your life. Break it down into steps with 'alive-lines' (against the obsolete dead-line!). Schedule these in your diary and JEDI (Just Enthusiastically Do It).

3. Plan and schedule for one week and systematically follow the schedule with discipline.

4. Make a list of a few things you have been putting off and which you enjoy doing. Read through the list on overcoming procrastination and select a few inspiring triggers to make it happen. Make a public statement of your wanting to do it, and work towards it.

5. Draw a circle and divide it into six equal sectors. It will look like a wheel with spokes. Now label each of these six sectors with result areas important to you, for example, Work, Family Well-being, Friends, Health, Finances, Contribution to Community, Self-development, and so on.

Now place a dot in each sector showing how satisfied and joyful you are in that area (the outer rim would be 'ecstatic', and closer to the centre 'not so happy'). Connect the dots together. How balanced and 'whole' does it look?

6. What small incremental changes would have a big payoff in your life? List them down. Select a few and make these changes. Watch the release in positive energy as you say '*yes*' to yourself.

7. Imagine you are a hundred years old. Describe yourself at this age. Picture yourself healthy, successful and at peace. Get into the skin of yourself at hundred. Now, from this perspective, write a loving letter to yourself now. What advice would you give yourself? What would you tell yourself to do now? What visions would you encourage yourself to materialize?

8. Think of one situation in your life that you feel you need to change but haven't yet. What is the 'pseudo-benefit' for you in staying stuck in this 'rest house'?

7

Learning
The Evolutionary Edge

*In times of change, learners inherit the earth while
the learned find themselves beautifully equipped
to deal with a world that no longer exists.*
ERIC HOFFER

How would you characterize the business and social environment that we are working in today? It may be difficult to provide an all-encompassing description. However, one thing is very clear: we are in the midst of turbulent, chaotic and often unpredictable changes. It is a time in which the only constant is change. Not only is there continuous change, but the speed of change has significantly increased in the past decade. If we think of managing ourselves and our organizations in these times as rowing a boat, what kind of a situation could we describe it as? Is it rowing on a placid lake, where everything is calm and peaceful, or is it like rowing in a turbulent white water rapid? On the one hand, newspapers and business magazines talk of new technologies, innovations and new ways of working and doing business. On the other hand, you also see many examples of rising tension, growing stress and deep despair and confusion about the future of things.

A friend who recently returned from Singapore talked of the very high levels of stress that he encountered there. In 1996, a record 11,000 workers were retrenched in Singapore. This was the highest since that country came out of the 1985–86 recession. American banks eliminated 39 per cent of their workforce with automatic tellers between 1983 and

1993. In 1982 there were 32,000 robots in the USA. Today there are 20 million. Talking about robots, the well-known management academic and writer, Warren Bennis, was once said to have remarked that the factory of the future will have just two people in it. A man and a dog. The dog's work will be to keep the man away from the machines.

Let us take another example about the kind of change we are undergoing right now. If the technology of cars were to grow at the same rate in terms of technology and performance as computers have grown, then you could buy a Mercedes car for two dollars! It would travel at the speed of sound and would go 600 miles on one teaspoon of petrol. This is the amazing level of change that we are encountering at present. I often ask participants in my programmes to assess how the world is going. The general feeling points to an increase in tension and competitiveness leading to a tremendous hurry to catch up with the others and not be 'left behind'.

A few years ago I met a Pakistani gentleman whose ancestors were from my home town. We were sitting together under a tree chatting about life. He told me with a tinge of sadness in his voice, *'Once business was for life. Today it appears that all of life is for business.'*

Business seems to have become the overriding force driving everything else. The work environment in many organizations that I have come across parches the human spirit. Some of the most financially successful organizations are also the ones where people have reported that the whole organization has little or no Heart. The new *mantras* for success seem to be 'Downsizing' and 'Re-engineering', which often lead to more work being heaped onto the shoulders of fewer workers. This leaves little time for the heart and spirit, or for some of the things that make life meaningful. People seem to have forgotten what Dennis Burkitt, who writes on healing, once said, *'Not everything that counts can be counted.'* Millions of people all over the world have begun to voice their discomfort with de-spirited workplaces. There is a crying need for work to have more soul and more heart. Almost all aspects of life need and want positive change. It is a time of crisis for earth. The pictogram in the Chinese language for 'crisis' is shown alongside.

Danger

Opportunity

Crisis = Danger + Opportunity

This pictogram is the combination of the symbols for 'danger' and 'opportunity'. Today's times are dangerous because they are challenging some of our old beliefs, paradigms and ways of working. On the other hand, life today is throwing up opportunities for creating new ways of working, new ways of doing business and new ways of living—in short, more wholesome and balanced approaches to life. While we are in a crisis and there is little time to lose, we also have the opportunity to reinvent our own individual and organizational lives.

Coming back to the rowing boat example, imagine yourself rowing a boat upstream. Let's say that your rate of rowing is R. If R is greater than the rate of current of the river, you will move upstream. If your rate of rowing is equal to the rate of current of the river, you will stay stationary at one point. If your rate of rowing is less than the rate of current, then you will slip back and be carried downstream by the river.

Now imagine that the rate of learning, L, replaces the rate of rowing and the rate of current becomes the rate of change, C. For organizations or individuals, if the rate of learning is greater than the rate of change around them, then they can respond intelligently to the challenges being thrown at them. In other words, for effective learning, $L > C$.

> **Learning is but an adjunct to oneself, and where we are our learning likewise is.**
>
> SHAKESPEARE

Just as the effects and impacts of change have been varied, the responses and reactions of companies have also been very different. Some companies have taken conscious steps to respond to the changes and to make learning a way of life. Other companies, in contrast, have languished to the point that they have become victims of hostile takeovers or have just gone out of business.

Learning will always be needed. The reason for this is that life will continue to change all the time. So, responding in new ways will be required at each step. This will call for constant flexibility and innovation, so that individuals, teams and organizations can keep growing. Whatever is rigid and blocked will atrophy and die. Life lived from the Heart is a life of joyful living.

Whether it is total quality management, the development of people in organizations, or the improvement of customer service, each one of these is basically a process of learning. New theories or new ways of seeing will lead to new methods and tools. These in turn, will lead to newer insights and more integration within organizations. As we saw earlier, what is needed urgently today in many organizations is:

- *Insight* to understand what is happening within and outside the organization, to understand the pattern of events and processes that are currently happening

- *Integration*, working together, learning together, enjoying work together
- *Inspired action* to make things happen.

Arising out of these is the fourth '*I*' required in today's turbulent times: *Innovation*, or the capacity to make new things happen.

All these ideas hinge around *learning*. Learning is the central process that will be required to unfold spirit in people and organizations.

A question that we can ask at this point is, 'Can learning be done alone or does it have to be done along with other people?' When we harness the immense potential of our collective experiences, we can learn from each other. This is through conversations, dialogue, networking and a whole range of other processes which can be brought into play. With the power of the Internet coming into our reach, learning has become an activity that transcends the boundaries of organizations and nations. It has become a global process. Can this learning together be unfolded to enhance well-being, Heart and excellence at the workplace? The answer is: 'Yes.' Before we see how this can be achieved, let us learn a bit more about learning.

Learning—What is It?

Learning is all about changing behaviour in a manner that improves our ability to respond to situations in a given moment. *It is about the capacity to take effective actions and to respond intelligently to life in the here and now.*

Ultimately, learning must result in action. I may read many books but if I do not *act* on the knowledge, then I cannot claim to have learnt. Even an iota of doing something in an improved way is better than speaking about it for a long time. Merely reading about water will not quench my thirst. Similarly, If I write an article on 'water', do a Ph D on the molecular properties of water, I will still remain thirsty until I *drink* some water myself.

No amount of information can substitute for the direct experience of knowing for ourselves. When we open our eyes and we see things for ourselves, we have truly experienced something. In a world where we are constantly bombarded by external suggestions, the need to think for oneself becomes an important basic virtue. Remaining prisoners of what others tell us

> To read without reflecting, is like eating without digesting.
> EDMUND BURKE

or of our own worn-out past will not help further learning.

Direct knowing has a silent purity about it. People who know do not seek to impress or show off their knowledge. Neither are they caught up with the *'malady of a myriad whirling thoughts or the endless pursuit of mental wealth'*. They have digested their experiences, reflected upon their meaning, and quietly nurtured the expansion of their spirit. They eschew banks of memory and rely more on a direct knowing of reality in the moment. This is a state of humility . . . of supreme openness to life and learning. Their inner stance is: *'I don't know; I am, things are.'* Contrast this with a knowledgeable person who carries the weight of his wisdom on his mind. With the ego enhanced by concepts, ideologies and various conditionings, he is subject to confusion where there should be fusion. His Heart is covered in layers of the mind.

I have come across managers and consultants who are so full of their own knowledge that there is little space in their minds for others' ideas. Predictably, they are poor at listening. On the other hand, some of the

Y	Your
O	Own
G	Guru
A	Always

most profound and deep thinkers are almost child-like in their simplicity and full of playful humour. They radiate peace and presence. I am sure you must have encountered such people.

Moving towards such an inner openness has more to do with **unlearning** rather than learning. It is about relying on one's own inner resources and connecting with your own guru which, is the Heart, our inner guide—the reference for all meaning.

This process generates new insights. We see things afresh and are inspired by what we see. Our feelings are churned up and they crystallize into new actions which bring us new experiences.

The Learning Loop

Learning is a cyclic process as seen in the figure on the following page.

When I see things in a new light and get new insights, I experience a surge in energy. This propels me in the direction of new action and new initiatives. These lead to new outcomes and achievements which set the foundation for new views and vistas in life.

Let's take an example from an organization in which customer service is of paramount importance. As feedback from customers in the marketplace is collected and examined, people in the organization begin to see things differently. Their questioning and reflection lead to new theories. It unfolds new energy to make action plans for corrective action. After the new actions are implemented, the result is a change in the

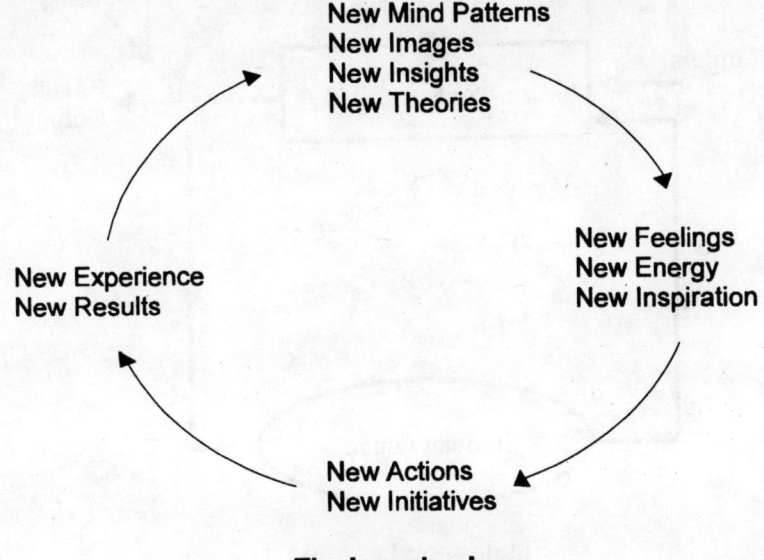

New Mind Patterns
New Images
New Insights
New Theories

New Feelings
New Energy
New Inspiration

New Experience
New Results

New Actions
New Initiatives

The Learning Loop

level of customer satisfaction as reflected in a new survey conducted after some time. The loop of learning is thus complete. It goes on continually as the organization strives to add more value to its customers.

The learning loop can occur at many different levels and can take on many different forms. To me, the cycles of:

- Performance review discussions and performance planning between boss and subordinates, or
- Problem-solving for quality improvement by a cross-functional team, or
- A strategic review and plan by a top management team for the whole organization based on environmental scanning, competitive analysis and customer feedback,

are all examples of the learning cycle in action at different levels of the organization. It would not be an exaggeration to say *that all of life is a dance of interconnected learning processes, which move people in the direction of oneness and love.*

The Three Levels of Learning

There are basically three levels of learning in life that we need to be conscious of:

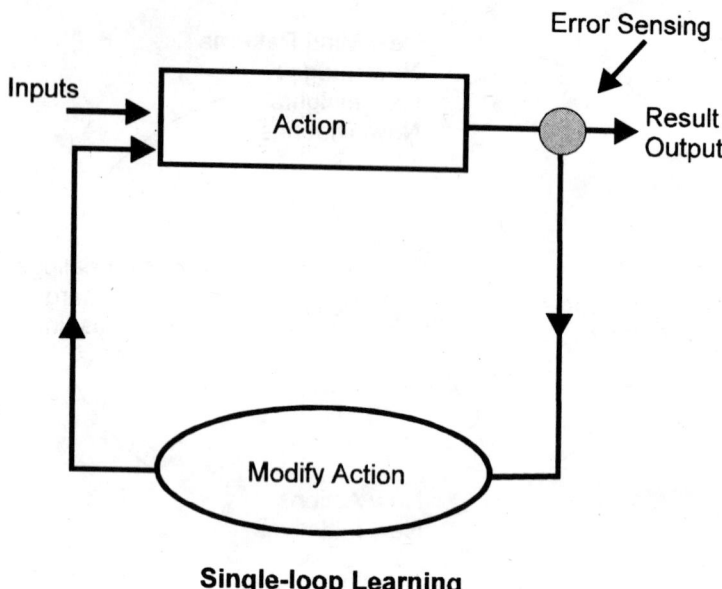

Single-loop Learning

Level 1 learning is about changing our actions. If I was doing something which I now do better, I am modifying my actions to achieve better results. For example, if I modify the way I sort and store the papers and other items on my messy desk, I am more likely to find something faster when I need it. A sensing of how well I am doing and comparing that with a standard (error-sensing) can help me to further modify my actions until results get better. A simple loop of learning is thus completed. That is why, this level of learning is also called *single-loop learning*.

The second level of learning, *level 2* or *double-loop learning,* involves a change in the way we think. It involves a modification at a deeper level, where the underlying ways of thinking are changed. The first loop is nested within the second loop. Patterns of thinking alter my actions which affect the process of achieving results. For example, going back to our messy desk, I might question the whole need to use so much paper, pencils, erasers and physical files. My whole thinking and approach would be dramatically re-framed if I started thinking of using a computerized Local Area Network (LAN) and the Internet. Many of the papers, pens, erasers and files would disappear from my desk. This would be the outcome of creative or new thinking (discussed in Chapter 6).

We can still go one more level deeper. *Level 3* or *triple-loop learning* represents change and transformation in our basic view of ourselves, and our world. It is about changing values, identity, mission and notions

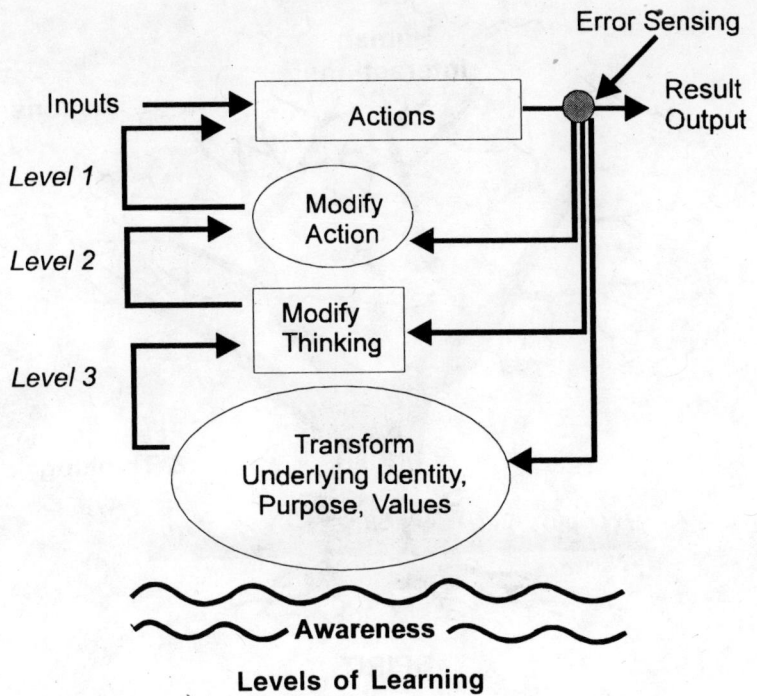

Levels of Learning

about why I am here on earth. Change at level 3 is about deep fundamental changes in our paradigms of thinking.

In our earlier example, imagine I re-examine my life and discover that I would deeply love to use my talents, resources and contacts to set up an organic farm away from a city. The whole issue of tidying the desk and using computers may then no longer be relevant!

Level 1 learning is about simple change in actions. Level 2 is about changing process, the most commonly referred to level when we talk of 'learning'. Level 3 learning is about 'learning how to learn', or changing change or *'evolution'.* It represents the slowest, deepest, but most lasting level of change. When learning at such a deep level occurs in people, organizations and societies, major changes in consciousness take place. Whenever a flow of conscious transforming energy moves up from the depths of our being, great transformations can occur with dramatic speed.

Another simple analogy to look at these three levels is to look at the tree shown above. The actions represent the leaves, the feelings and attitudes the branches, and the spirit the roots. If we really have to rectify a situation in which the tree has yellow leaves, it would not help

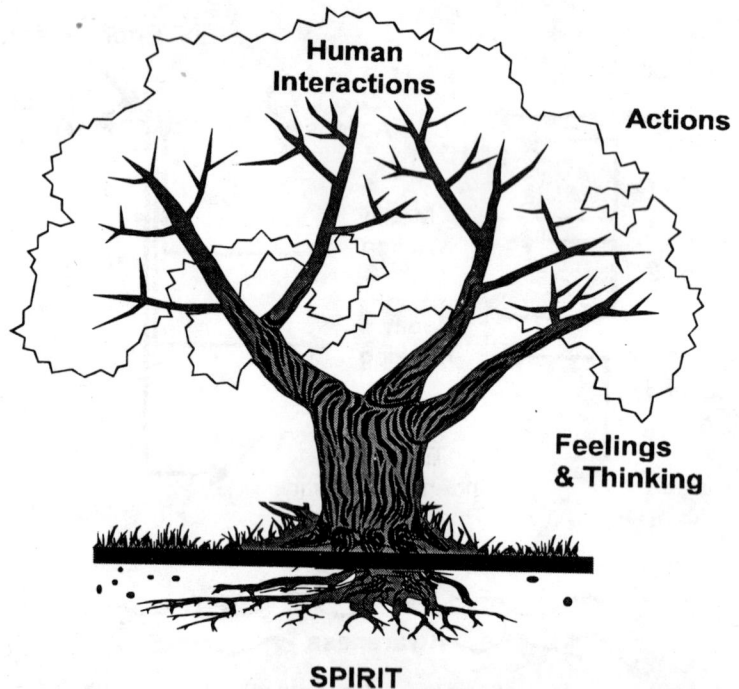

to paint the leaves green. We would have to work at deeper levels. We would need to water the roots to nourish the whole tree back into health.

In the same way, in organizations and in teams, it is often not enough to just tinker around with actions and processes. We need to surface and re-examine the basic assumptions and paradigms that we are working with. We may need to question them, to recreate them, to cast them aside or create new ones. This new way of looking can change our way of working. *As we come closer to the level of spirit and the deeper we go inwards, the more we experience a sense of freedom and peace*. At its innermost core, the spirit is free of all theories, all definitions, all contents. It is pure creative intelligence and pure potential which has within it the capacity to create the most appropriate response to any situation. However, the free flow of creative spirit does not always happen. Learning in all its fullness is therefore often blocked.

Barriers to Learning

Some of the factors that inhibit learning in people and organizations, as I have experienced them, are as follows:

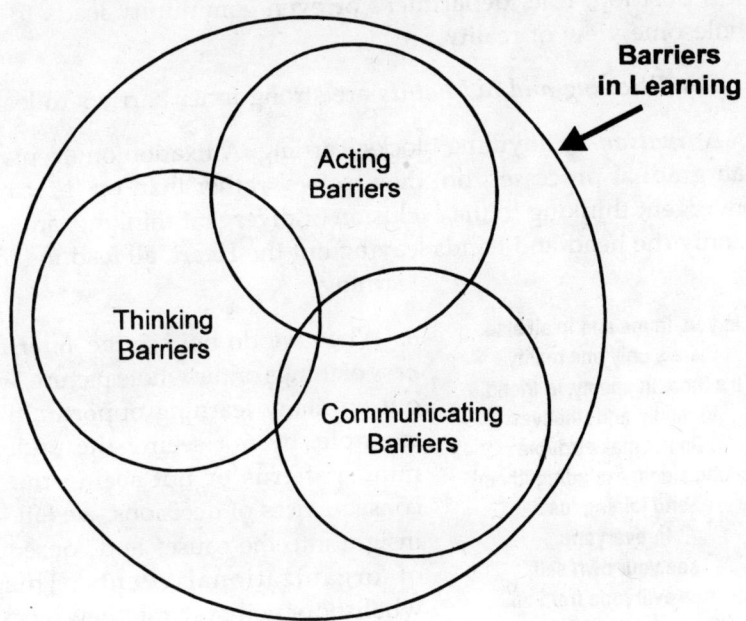

All barriers in communicating, thinking and acting are sub-sets of the barriers in learning.

Let us take a look at some forms that these barriers take:

1. *Fixation with short-term results and constantly being driven by what is urgent.* As we have seen earlier, reacting to the urgent displaces a proactive focus on the important in many managerial lives. Learning from subordinates, peers or other professionals is usually put on the back-burner.

2. *The assumption that one's undigested experiences automatically lead to insight and learning.* This is not true. Conscious reflection is needed to get the juice of learning out of an experience.

3. *A long history of success,* which leads to complacency. The 'failure of success' can become a dangerous block to learning. Many organizations have gone the route of the dinosaur because of this block.

4. *Fear* and an atmosphere of mistrust, accusations, judgement, and fault-finding creates defensiveness. This blocks openness to feedback, which is a powerful source of learning.

5. *Distortions and deletions* connected with getting over-identified with

one's position, role, department or even community leads to a non-wholesome view of reality.

6. *Conditioning and old habits* are strong inner barriers to learning.

7. A *fixation* on anything blocks learning. A fixation on events rather than gradual processes, on 'they-factors' rather than on 'I-factors', on convergent thinking to the exclusion of divergent thinking, and a focus on only the head and hands leaving out the Heart, all lead to blocks in learning.

> In you, in me and in all else,
> there's only one reality.
> It's there in enemy, in friend,
> in family and relatives.
> Do not make trouble
> taking sides, excluding 'them'
> and joining 'us'.
> In everyone,
> see your own self,
> free everyone from all
> *discriminating prejudice.*
>
> SRI ADI SHANKARA

8. When we do not see the *interrelatedness* of things or the whole picture, we miss out on many learning opportunities. For example, by not seeing the underlying mind patterns or not seeing the larger consequences of decisions, we fail to gain insight into the causes and consequences of organizational events. This non-wholistic or non-systemic view blocks total learning. A typical block is to segregate 'them' and 'us'. One imagines that the enemy is 'out there'. Systems thinking implies that there is no 'out there'. All is one interrelated whole. Consequences are nothing but the cause unfolded in time.

What Helps Learning?

At the silent, peaceful, level of awareness, one is truly at the goal of all learning. Being your own real self is the whole end of learning! Let us now see what else can help the process of learning:

1. *Learning is really about unlearning.* It means an openness to new possibilities, alertness and flexibility and the capacity to let go off one's old conditioning, dead ideas and theories. This clears the space for new insights.

2. To that extent it is really *an ability to take risk,* to venture out of the comfort zone of my own beliefs and ideas, to jump out of my mental stagnation and leap out into the adventure of new views, new vistas, and therefore new feelings in energy, new actions and new outcomes.

3. *It is about a certain vulnerability, a certain honest, openness to life.*

It is about saying 'yes' to life and moving with the flow of life. Taking everything to be my own guru, my own teacher.

4. Some of the best learning happens when there is no *agenda* or *no fixed notion* of what I have to learn. If I just flow along with life and remain alert to whatever happens, whatever comes my way, I will learn the art of intelligent response which is what learning is all about.

5. *It is about taking every event, person, place, and situation as an opportunity to learn and grow.* One of my favourite affirmations which has been shared by one of my mentors, Swami Bhoomananda Tirtha, is:

Everything in life will nurture me. All that happens will strengthen me. Everything in life is my Teacher.

Accepting all people, places and events in my life as adjuncts to the process of evolution is an empowering way to face the challenges that life will invariably present us with.

When I half-jokingly tell my manager participants to be grateful for a 'difficult' boss, they all burst out laughing. On closer examination, we see that an aggressive boss, for example, can give me excellent practice on my skills of assertiveness. He can also help me to stretch to higher levels of performance and tap into reserves of talent, patience and perseverance that I did not know I had. All this can help me grow and develop, and hence is a learning experience. This attitude of acceptance was called *Prasadam Bhavna* by our ancient seers. *Prasadam* means that which nourishes.

That everything can be my teacher is illustrated by a story about the famous Sufi master, Hasan. On his deathbed, he was asked who his greatest teacher had been in life. He replied, 'A thief, a dog and a child.' When probed, he further said that the thief had taught him about being happy and always hopeful. The thief would never get to rob anyone's home. But he was always willing to go out tomorrow for a fresh start. His motto was, *'God willing, tomorrow it's going to happen.'*

'My second master,' said the Sufi mystic, 'was a dog. When the dog was thirsty, he would go to the river. There he would see another dog, his own image, and would become afraid and run away. His thirst, however, was so much that in spite of his fear he jumped into the river and the image disappeared. From him, I learnt that one has to jump in spite of one's fears.'

Hasan's third teacher, was a young child carrying a candle. Jokingly, the mystic asked him, *'Can you show me the source of the light from where you lit the candle?'* The child laughed and blew out the candle saying, *'The light has gone, where did it go?'* The Sufi master's ego was shattered and from that moment he dropped all his knowledge.

Today's world, with its social, cultural, economic and technological upheavals is a rich field for learning. Advances in the media, with additions like the Internet, have further added many opportunities for learning. All that we need is an unblocked openness to life as a sacred learning process. We need to see all things as compassionate teachers.

Enhancing Your Own Learning

Here are some things that successful leaders do to stay on top. We can learn from their example:

> We should think of learning as the expression of one's capacity to create, to produce results.
>
> PETER SENGE

- They stay in touch with what people are doing outside their functional area. For example, some outstanding human resource professionals I have met are well versed with finance, law and business strategy. Their counsel counts because they understand the whole picture and so have greater credibility.
- They network with people who are cutting-edge thinkers—both inside and outside their organization.
- They choose mentors who can give them insights into different skills and perspectives. They choose them from different cultures, fields, and areas of expertise. Easy accessibility and excellence in their fields influence their choice.
- They consciously plan their learning by setting SMART learning objectives and making a development plan for themselves.

> Change while you've still got time to do it voluntarily.
>
> JOSEPH GORMAN

Today's environment of constant change requires conscious choices at each stage. It requires us to constantly upgrade our capacity to share and contribute. The well-known management consultant, Tom Peters, advocates that you write your bio-data every six months and compare it with your previous bio-data. If there is positive change showing new things done and learnt, you are on the right track.

Here are some more ideas to enhance your own learning:

- Move away from the paradigm that sees learning as something that only happens in a classroom. Think of all the other possible opportunities that you can give or create for yourself for your own learning. Here's a list for you to reflect on:

o Conduct classes for young professionals (their questions will force you to read and prepare!).
o Attend short courses sponsored by your company or yourself.
o Study competitive analysis reports of your industry.
o Read the *Economic Times* daily and other business publications regularly.
o Take responsibility for your own career development and constantly upgrade your employability.
o Attend seminars, conferences, exhibitions, trade fairs, and supplier-sponsored programmes.
o Attend, and conduct, in-house training programmes.
o Go on trips abroad to attend training programmes, meet collaborators, etc.
o Visit other companies/organizations in India to see how they work and learn from them.
o Take membership of professional agencies/organizations/associations/networks.
o Take on new or challenging tasks; enlarge the scope of your job.
o Go in for job rotation.
o Make a plan for self-study/reading. Sign up for a distance learning programme.
o Undertake supervised self-instruction programmes using self-learning manuals, videos, etc.
o Fill in for your boss/other staff members at meetings.
o Serve on task forces/improvement projects and project teams.
o Get feedback from boss/peers/subordinates.
o Visit other departments, individuals in the organization.
o Attend study circles/study groups/problem-solving groups.
o Take memberships of teaching–learning communities.
o Tackle individually challenging problems/projects/assignments.
o Specify clear-cut results expected/accountability.
o Communicate high expectations.
o Write and present a professional paper.
o Meditate and do self-awareness exercises.
o Sign up for a university course (long-term) sponsored by your company.
o Have close interaction/apprenticeship with persons knowledgeable in some area.
o Observe and discuss with others expressing a particular skill. Model your behaviour after them.
o Use library and information services, bulletins, reprints etc.

○ Use national data banks/international data banks, e.g. UNIDO.
○ Go on a sabbatical leave.
○ Regularly browse the Internet for useful sites.

That's quite a long list to choose from. Pick a few which resonate with your Heart, and plan your action now. Jot these chosen ideas down in your learning journal. If you haven't yet started one, think of doing so right away.

While all these actions can facilitate your individual learning, this is not the same as your organization learning. We will see why.

Learning Organizations

The learning organization is an organization that facilitates the learning of all people in it and thereby continually transforms itself. It is the process of doing something better than before. It involves the process of identifying, acquiring, discriminating, retaining, sharing, updating and creating useful new knowledge, which expands our capacity to produce useful results.

> An organization that has adopted a learning strategy, in addition to a planning strategy, has a better chance than others, not only to succeed, but also to grow at a rapid rate.
>
> ARIE DE GEUS

Organizations learn only through individuals who learn. Without individual learning, no organizational learning can take place. Individual learning, however, does not always lead to organizational learning. If a member of an organization acquires new knowledge about how to use a powerful computer package to plan and track projects, this may not necessarily benefit the organization. However, if he shares this knowledge with others, and one or more project teams in the organization actually use this software for enhancing the quality, timeliness and customer satisfaction of their projects, we can say that organizational learning has taken place.

Organizational learning leads to enhanced effectiveness of individual, team and organizational behaviour. Spreading outwards from organizations, as they learn, customers, suppliers and the members of the organization themselves all benefit. Society too benefits from this process. The impacts radiate out to the farthest corners of planet earth. *What is needed today, more than anything else, is a powerful movement for learning in all spheres and all areas.* It has been said that all the knowledge we need to solve our problems today is available. What is

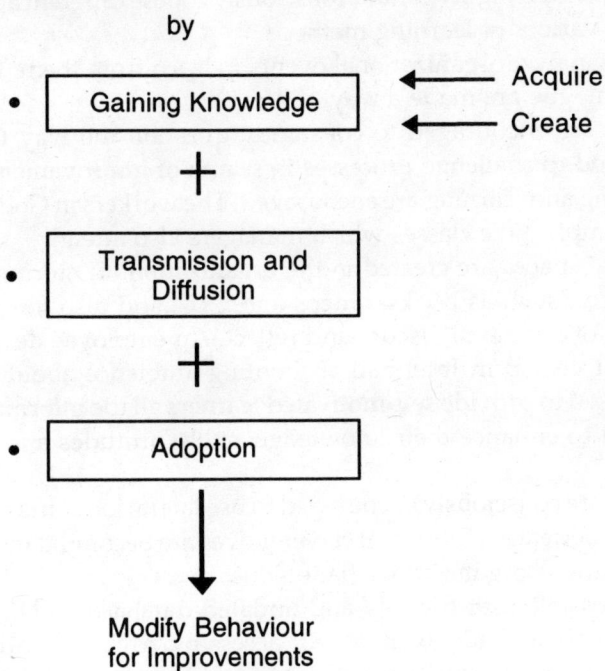

Learning:

An Expansion in Our Capacity to take Effective Action

by

• Gaining Knowledge ← Acquire
← Create

+

• Transmission and Diffusion

+

• Adoption

↓

Modify Behaviour
for Improvements

Learning Organizations

lacking, however, is a conscious, inspired and effective process of collective learning.

Enhancing Learning in Organizations

This is what many leaders are doing to enhance learning in their organizations. You can take cues for your own organization:

- Learning is made an important part of the company's value system and the word 'learning' is frequently used as part of everyday language.
- Managers take ownership of their own development and also of the people they are responsible for. They see this as a key element in their job. Documents such as the appraisal form are used to mutually discuss learning plans.

- Giving and receiving feedbacks are a way of life in the organization, and people are trained in the process.
- People sit down to diagnose problems. They examine their assumptions and learning styles, and consciously choose different approaches from a variety of learning methods.
- People analyze organizational events to learn from them. Reflection and dialogue are made a way of life.
- People are encouraged to constantly question the way things are done and to challenge processes in search of improvements.
- Teaching and learning are encouraged. The workers in Godrej Soaps, for example, take classes which managers also attend.
- Physical spaces are created in the organization for storing learning resources, such as books, videos and CDs, and also for providing places for people to discuss and reflect. An employee development centre I visited in Intel had an inviting ambience about it. It was organized to provide self-motivated learners all the information they needed to enhance their knowledge, skills, attitudes and job prospects.
- People are consciously encouraged to use lateral job shifts to enhance their experience. Horizontal career moves are becoming increasingly important as organizations flatten out.
- An accessible user-friendly and updated database on key business parameters is made available for access by anybody. Intranets are used to share information and messages. Electronic bulletin boards on topics of common interest are maintained within organizations. We have successfully used this method to connect together learners who took our 'Empowered Trainer Programme' in several organizations.
- Benchmarking as a device for comparing one's organization with others is used to improve processes.
- The top management actively sets an example by learning themselves and being involved in the learning of others. They foster a culture which focuses on action, rather than on blame. Mistakes and failures are seen as opportunities to learn.
- The reward system is used to reinforce the motivation to learn.
- The channels of communication are kept open. Spontaneous and informal networks are allowed to exist. These are seen as legitimate, and even necessary, ways of learning in an organization. Integrity, authenticity, open and freely shared information are the hallmarks of communication in the learning organization.
- People are involved in key decisions and improvements. They are empowered to apply learning on the job.

- Attention is paid not only to generating new insights and capabilities, but also to transferring these to all people in the organization.
- The boundaries of the organization are kept porous. New ideas and insights are welcomed through new recruits, consultants, and information down loaded from the internet. Dialogue and conversations with other professionals in forums, such as exhibitions, trade fairs, conferences and industry publications are actively encouraged.
- Learning requires stepping back from day-to-day operations. *Leaders of learning organizations make time for detached reflection.* They encourage others to make time for this.
- New patterns of thinking are nurtured in the organization. The unexpected is treated as an opportunity to learn and not as a mistake.
- All assumptions are brought to the surface and questioned. Alternate assumptions are developed. Letting go of old conditioning, useless paradigms and pet-beliefs, i.e. unlearning, is made a part of the learning process.
- When everything is going fine and they are 'succeeding', people in learning organizations stop, and say, *'What we're doing is all wrong!'* They look again.
- Learning organizations work as wholes. They are more like organisms where people act responsibly because they understand the big picture. This begins with 'wholistic thinking'—a way of seeing the totality and relationships rather than only things. The whole picture is actively shared by all.
- An organization's vision grows as a byproduct of individual visions, a byproduct of ongoing conversations. Dialogue is the key to evolving this larger vision. Dialogue and conversations are encouraged. 'Spaces' for these are provided.
- To take individual learning to the maximum, jobs are designed around people. This enables them to reach the next stage of development.

To ensure that people work at their peak learning potential, they are encouraged to work from their motivated skills. This matching of work with their creative and unique best, also provides the most fertile ground for natural learning. *Harmonizing the needs of the individual with the needs of the organization is needed for organizational learning.* Personal growth and self-mastery are valued.

Here are a few more pointers towards enhancing organizational learning:

- If a company has to survive, the people inside it will have to tell one another the truth.
- No single point of view dominates decision-making. *Information is free to act*. People feel free to speak their minds about what they have learnt. People communicate fully and honestly.
- Peoples' commitment and capacity to learn is tapped at all levels in an organization. Employee Involvement is at the heart of organizational learning and the empowerment of people.
- People are continually learning how to learn together.
- Organizational learning works best when learning collaboratives and communities are supported and encouraged throughout the organization. It works by people empowering other people. People in the learning team become 'change agents'.
- In a learning organization, the idea of continuous improvement is taken seriously. One question asked often is: *'How can this be done better?'*
- Cross-functional learning through task forces, improvement teams, chimney-breaking and silo-busting are a way of life in the organization. The last two refer to the breaking down of vertical boundaries between different functional areas within organizations.

As we let go into the beautiful journey called life, and flow along with the river towards the ocean of love, we understand that life is one of the most beautiful 'custom-designed learning systems' there is. Everything that has happened to you or is happening to you has been designed by existence in its infinite compassion, to teach you the lessons that you need to learn. At times, these may appear harsh, at other times they may appear difficult. But they are appropriately aligned to your requirements of learning at this moment in your evolutionary journey.

The culmination of life's journey of learning is not a static dead end called 'perfection'. It is an endless truth, ever evolving and endlessly unfolding. It has no beginning and no end. It can be described as a timeless mystery unfolding in time, a divine play whose purpose itself is about celebrating the joy of knowing that God is all. If we forget this, we lose everything. If we remember this, we *are* everything.

Ideas for Playful Action

1. Look at anything in the room where you are sitting and write down what you can learn from it. (Be creative and playful.)

2. Identify your blocks to learning. Write them down.

3. Connecting silently with the peace of your self, seek its guidance on how to transcend these blocks. This may come in the form of an image which you may write down.

4. Seek further guidance to detail the image out into an action plan.

5. Scan through the list on enhancing individual learning. Pick up a few ideas for action for yourself.

6. How do you see learning in your organization today? List those things you can do to improve these right away. Put some 'alive lines' on these.

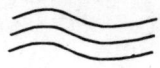

≈ 8 ≈

Teamwork

Working Together and Solving Problems Joyfully

See the world as yourself.
Have faith in the way things are.
Love the world as yourself;
Then you can care for all things.

Tao Te Ching

*E*xistence is one whole symphony of working together joyfully. From the thousands of plant and animal species in a rain forest, to the air and the clouds, everything in nature works smoothly as one interdependent whole. Rabindranath Tagore has expressed it this way, *'There is no such thing as absolute isolation in existence, and the only way of attaining truth is through the interpenetrating of our being into all objects'* (quoted in Zohar (1991)).

Our behaviour impacts the people we work with. When a person in an organization improves her time management, her colleagues, customers and subordinates, all begin to experience greater clarity of purpose. When she goes home on time, her family is delighted.

Work can never happen in isolation. Organizations are nothing but people working together. They learn and solve problems to achieve common objectives. This happens in teams of some kind.

In this chapter we will look at the 'inner view' of working together, and solving problems joyfully. Good thinking (Chapter 4), good communication (Chapter 5) and focused action (Chapter 6) are the building blocks of living and working joyfully. All that this chapter and the next one on leadership do is to put them together and show the connections.

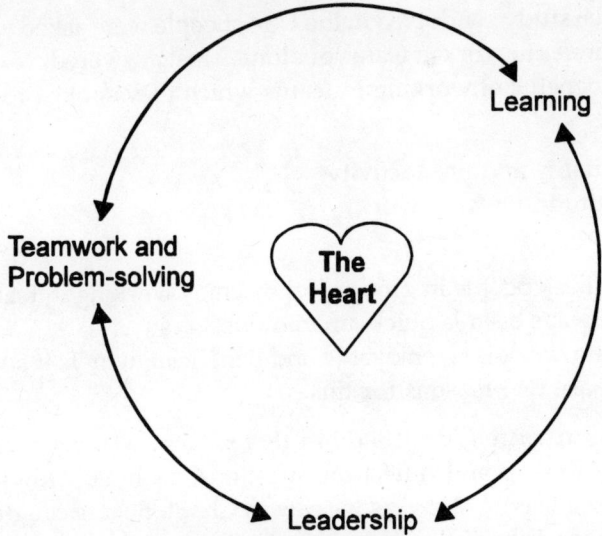

Learning happens when teams work well and solve problems. Leadership is about learning in individuals and teams. All this to unfold joy, and keep the frontiers of excellence expanding.

At the centre of all three is the Heart.

In the remaining part of this chapter we first look at:

- Two reasons why excellent teamworking does not happen
- Some principles and insights for action

We then look at:

- Problems, as blocks in the free flow of energy
- The inner look of how to solve them joyfully

When I look back on my life at moments of excellent teamwork, they seem magical. One thing common was a feeling of lightness and expansion, bringing with it a surprising increase in capacity. We could just go on working till late in the night, and get up reasonably fresh the next morning. Boundaries between the team members were non-existent. While we all did different things at different times, there was a clear feeling of oneness. A very peaceful and joyful emptiness premeated everything we did. It was this silent spirit which held us together. We were tuned into each others' needs and responded freely. These were moments when the garment of my limited self was consumed in the fire of joyful togetherness.

You would surely have experienced the magical exhilaration of working as part of a productive team. Stop for a moment and think of when you last experienced this magic.

In a research study conducted in the USA, people were asked whether they would prefer to work in teams or alone. Most answered, *'In teams'* Some of the benefits of working in teams which they spoke of were:

- Lower stress
- Higher quality and productivity
- Better attitude towards work
- Easier work

Whenever I ask people in groups if they enjoy working in teams, the answer has always been, a quick, unanimous, 'Yes'.

If good team work is so enjoyable and beneficial, why is it so rare? I believe there are two reasons for this:

1. *Conscious attention is not paid to this process.* Managers are usually too busy to stop and reflect on questions, such as, 'How are we functioning as a team?' Many, as we saw in Chapter 6, are caught up in routine activities. When we pay conscious attention to improving teamwork, it makes a positive difference.

I'm reminded of two recent experiences of team-building within the same organization.

A group of 30 managers met to discuss ways in which they could work better as a Regional Profit Centre. People from the commercial, manufacturing and sales functions needed to work better as an integrated team. From a state of frozen energy in which each person viewed the other with suspicion, and where problems and feedback were withheld from each other, in a period of two days, the team moved into a flowing, free and unified state with clear action plans. A shared understanding of how to function better as a team also emerged from the experience. The difference in the energy of the group was dramatic.

Snowflakes are one of nature's most fragile things, but just look what they can do when they stick together.
Vesta M. Kelly

Another example from the same organization was of members of a project team getting together to work better as a team. From an initial state of floundering, confusion and not knowing each other, they moved dramatically to a high-performing team over a few days. The joy meter showed a very different reading, and a lot of useful planning got done. In both cases, energy was released as thinking barriers melted and communication opened up.

2. The second reason why good teamwork is rare is because *all aspects of good teamworking are not paid attention together.* In other words, *this happens because teamworking is not wholesome.*

Let us first understand this useful concept a little better.

All of us are familiar with the concept of a balanced diet. We know that it is wholesome food that has all the ingredients required for nurturing and protecting our body and keeping it healthy.

Wholesomeness is simply being whole or complete. It is living life in a total, balanced and harmonious way. This happens when all aspects, all things, all types of people, all views and talents are held together in a beautiful oneness. It is like a garden full of different flowers, all adding to the beauty and fragrance of the whole.

Wholesomeness is about boundarylessness. It is holding apparent contradictions together and harmonising polarities. It is being comfortable with both night and day, with breathing in and breathing out, and peacefully integrating apparently opposite forces such as stability and progress. One of my favourite analogies to describe wholesome behaviour is of a painter with a palette of colours. While the brush and water are intrinsically colourless, any colour needed in a situation can be freely brought forth as required. Transition between colours is free and smooth. Since there is no like or dislike for any particular colour, a true painting can be made.

The diagram below illustrates the concept of wholesomeness symbolically:

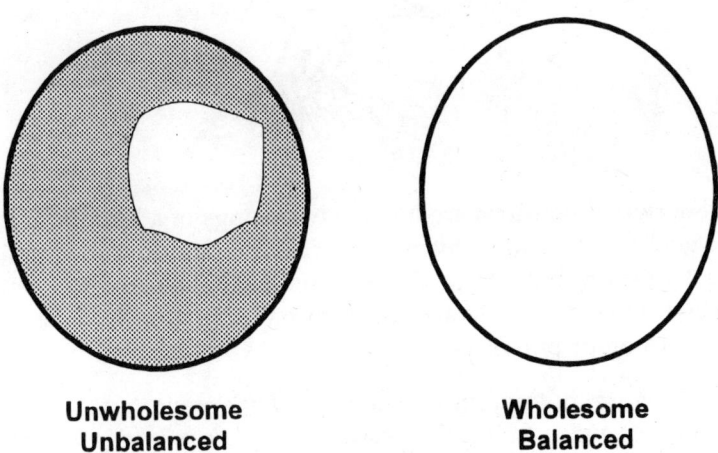

Unwholesome
Unbalanced

Wholesome
Balanced

Imagine that the whole range of possibilities is represented by the whole white disc. The disc on the left shows movement in a limited part of the possible range only. This is unwholesome or unbalanced operation. The disc on the right, however, represents a free movement all over the range of possibilities, that is, a free movement between opposites, not getting stuck anywhere, and therefore, dynamically balancing in each situation. Two aspects of teamworking which need balancing are:

- **Task dimension**, or *what* needs to be done. This is also known as the 'content' aspect of teamworking.
- **The process dimension**, or the *how* part of what we are doing? This is also known as the 'socio-emotional' or people aspect of working together in a team.

The task dimension would include doing things such as setting goals, giving directions, deciding using information, and concluding with action plans. The process dimension, on the other hand, would involve things such as involving all people in discussions, relieving tension with a joke, listening to peoples' feelings, and keeping communication lines open.

These two dimensions are like the two wings of a bird. Both have to work well together for a team to be effective and joyful. Good teams pay attention to both these dimensions and take steps to keep them balanced. However, they also need to pay attention to balancing between two other polarities:

- *Convergent thinking* and *Divergent thinking*
- *People giving feedback* and *People receiving feedback*

A good team is a wholesome team. It is diverse and flexible, and balances behaviour constantly between all the three polarities mentioned above.

We can use the disc shown earlier to illustrate the wholesome team as shown in the figure on the next page.

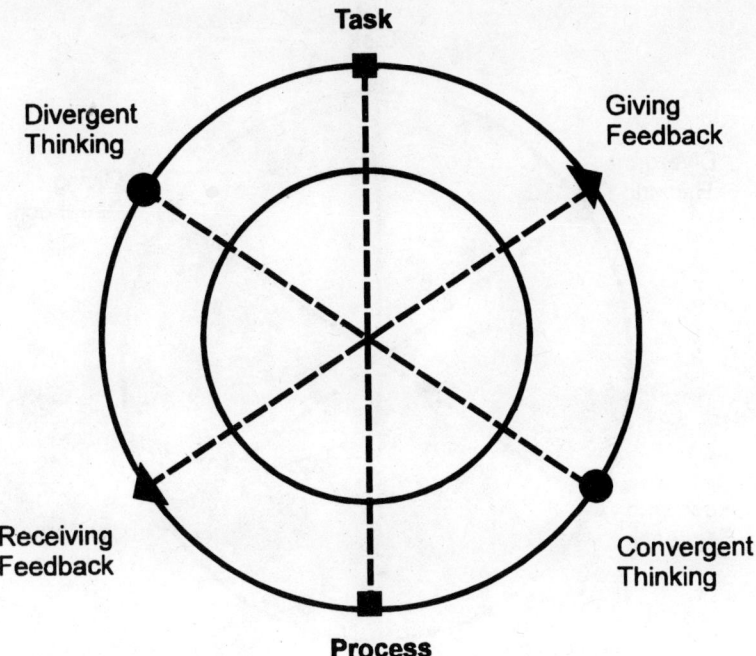

People in this team, freely and fully, pay attention to all the dimensions shown. They are free to move within the space encompassing all the three axes. The team is rich in diverse behaviour. Therefore, a whole range of possibilities, are available to the members of the team. Such a team, rich in possibilities, will be able to respond to situations in more appropriate ways. It will be more flexible compared to a team that is stuck in its behaviour to only a part of the whole range.

My own experience with groups in many organizations is that they tend to be predisposed towards the task, convergent thinking, and giving feedback parts of the whole. This unbalanced operation is shown in the figure on the following page.

When the teams are 'un-wholesome', as in the example above, its members are uneasy and stressed. The atmosphere is not joyful. On the other hand, when a team is wholesome, not only is it effective but also joyful. Work flows as easily as laughter.

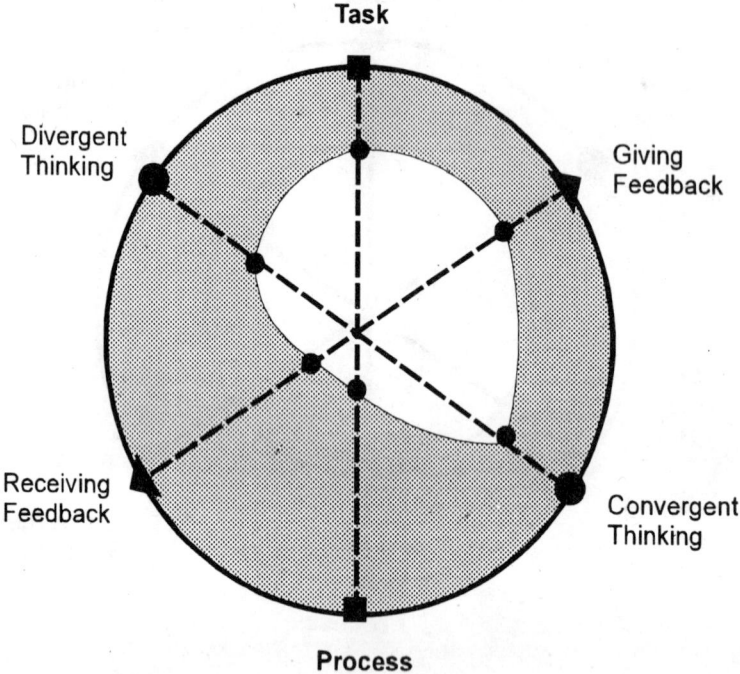

Task

Divergent Thinking

Giving Feedback

Receiving Feedback

Convergent Thinking

Process

Some Principles and Insights for Action

Besides wholesomeness, here are a few more characteristics of good teams. These may trigger some ideas for action in your own team:

1. The team is clear about what it wants to achieve. There is a clear vision. The values associated with the vision are clearly shaped by the members of the team. Aspirations are uniformly high amongst all members. The purpose is unified and noble. The strength of a common purpose and enabling vision creates a focused energy. The team members share a common struggle and journey and this gives them a sense of meaning and purpose.

2. There is strong partnership in the team and members show support for each other. There is a high level of openness and trust. The mutual understanding, love and respect that is shared in a good team creates an emotional support group, which helps the team to persevere in the face of challenges. Within the community of a high-performing team, individuals feel safe to explore new ideas and try out new ways of expressing themselves. They are, thus, encouraged to reach into their deeper reserves of talent, strength and confidence.

3. *Roles are clearly defined* and all members know how their work fits in with the big picture. Every member does real work. The experience, talents, knowledge, skills, contacts, spiritual and emotional strengths of all members combine and synergize into something far beyond the individual parts.

4. *Both collaboration and harmonizing differences* are used to get the best results. Differences are seen as opportunities for creative thinking and growth. Issues are always confronted and dealt with openly.

5. *There are sound and understood procedures* in the team as also a set of *agreed norms* that people have mutually worked out and follow. *A common working approach* is defined. Problem-solving and decision-making procedures are clear.

6. *Relationships with other groups and teams are sound.* The team is well integrated with its environment.

7. *The prevailing spirit in the team is strongly 'can do' and the commitment to team goals is high.* It has a powerful bias for inspired action. It focuses on its strengths and collectively looks at how it can create something of high value, which could contribute to the satisfaction of customers. Such teams set high standards and motivate themselves to 'walk their talk'. Since their actions come from the collective strength of the members, the total active contribution by the team is high.

8. *Individual and team development needs are regularly looked at and planned for.* Moreover, the group's positive influence and the example of one or more people in the team creates conditions for others to do their best. Each person is thus stretched to excel and supersede herself.

9. *The team has a high standard of leadership* and it is in the most appropriate hands.

10. *The team regularly reviews its progress* on the tasks against agreed performance standards and how it is functioning as a team. Regular reflection on experiences and conscious learning is a way of life.

11. In high-performing teams, *people hold themselves mutually accountable for results.* There is an atmosphere of joy and fun along with focus on the work at hand.

12. Finally, *a good team is held together by spirit.* It is the central dominion of the Heart, in the individual and collective life of the team which gives it the magical quality of a high performing team.

The closer the members of a team are to their own real self, the closer they come to each other. A wholesome team, because of its common spirit, is more like an organism rather than a hierarchical structure. Every one's thoughts, words and actions resonate with the same core. Boundaries melt away, and one's identity merges with that of the team. Each one's problem becomes everyone's problem. Everyone's strengths and resources are shared by all.

Such teams are *playful* because of this spirit of sharing and 'boundarylessness'. Learning is extremely high, since information and ideas are freely shared.

As we saw earlier, in wholesome teams there is free flow of information, energy and ideas. Because of this openness of thinking and communication, there is abundant insight into how things are. There is also integration and inspired action.

However, life is not always what we would like it to be. The things discussed in this book are still not so commonly seen. We encounter blocks in the free flow of energy in individuals and organizations. Society is beset with problems, many of which were yesterday's solutions.

What are Problems?

Problems arise because reality is not always what we would like it to be. We would like all our shops in India to sell pure food stuffs. They don't. We would like all the members of our team to be high performers. They are not always so. Take that train which I ride to work each day. It is not always on time. These are all problems that we face everyday.

A problem, therefore, is a gap between a desired situation and the present one.

Here are some examples of problems (as gaps):

Desired situation →	I experience ease/peace in my body	Machine X has zero breakdowns in a year	I want to have harmonious relations with Mr Y
	vs	vs	vs
Present situation →	I have a headache	Machine X has four breakdowns in a year	I have discord and friction with Mr Y

This is one way of looking at problems.

Another way of seeing problems is that they are pointers to something that needs our conscious attention. Through the resistance and difficulty they bring, they force us to grow. As Joseph Campbell (1968) has put it: *'Where you stumble, there your treasure lies.'*

Many times stumbling blocks create 'pain' or 'dis-ease'. Problem areas are, therefore, often referred to as 'pain areas' . Problems as we saw, are a reflection of a deviation from a desired state. If there was no preferred or desired situation, there would be no problems!

Problems can then be seen as our guides using pain to direct our attention. Any 'pain', 'dis-ease' or 'dis-comfort' in life can be seen as a signal from nature showing a deviation from how things ought to be. It is as if mother nature is gently signalling us to 'dissolve the gaps', make the necessary corrections in errors, and solve the required problems. This will restore us to our most natural condition of peace and ease.

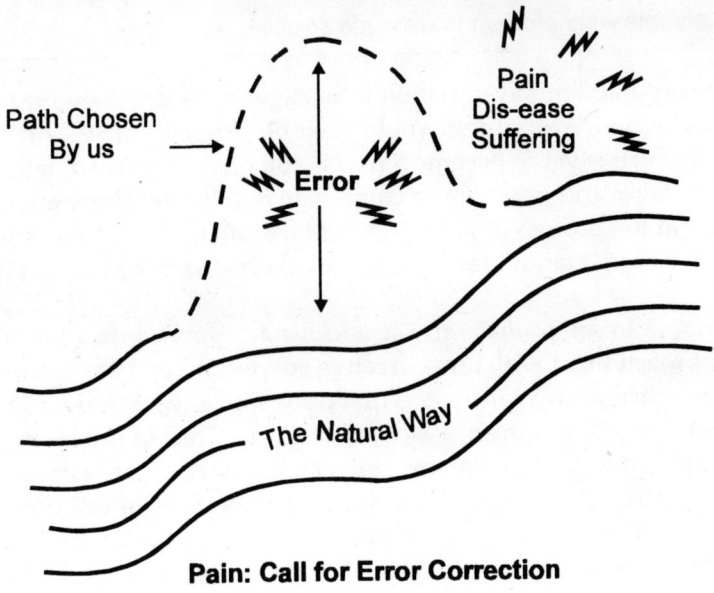

Pain: Call for Error Correction

'Pain' and 'dis-ease' are our teachers. They prompt us to restore the balance in our thoughts, words and actions.

Dissolving Problems

We can restore the balance and dissolve problems in two ways:

1. By changing our perception of the problem, or
2. By following a systematic step by step process to solve the problem.

P redictors—They help mould our future.

R eminders—We are not self-sufficient.
We need God and others to help.

O pportunities—They pull us out of our rut
and prod us to think creatively.

B lessings—They open up doors we usually don't go through.

L essons—Each new challenge will be our teacher.

E verywhere—No place or person is excluded from them.

M essages—They warn us about potential disaster.

S olvable—No problem is without a solution.

If we could accept any situation as a stage in the never-ending process of evolution, everything would then be perfectly okay as it is. A rose-bud which is yet to become a rose is still okay. A subordinate who makes mistakes and persistently comes late is still fine. These are natural stages in the process of growth. While we still may have work to do to improve the situation, taking this view keeps us peaceful and creative.

If I choose to see *problematic situations as opportunities for learning,* I approach them with more creative energy. When I see a problem from the peace at my centre, I radiate my soul's light outwards and allow nothing to affect my sense of peace. When I rest in my Heart, and remain open and loving no matter what another person does or no matter how severe the problem, I am drawing upon the highest power in the universe to solve the external problem.

The first step therefore for dissolving problems is to relax into my own ocean of inner peace.

Solving Problems Systematically

Having centred oneself in peace, how does one solve a problem systematically? Solving a problem involves two major steps:

1. The diagnostic step
2. The remedial step

The *diagnostic step* involves moving from the symptom to the root cause. It is about understanding the 'stated' problem manifested as a symptom, and getting to the root or the 'real' problem. The end of the diagnostic step is a clear understanding of the genesis of the problem.

The next stage is the *remedial step*, which seeks to move from the root cause to a remedy or solution. This is followed by a specific action plan that can bring about a cure. These two steps are shown in the diagram below:

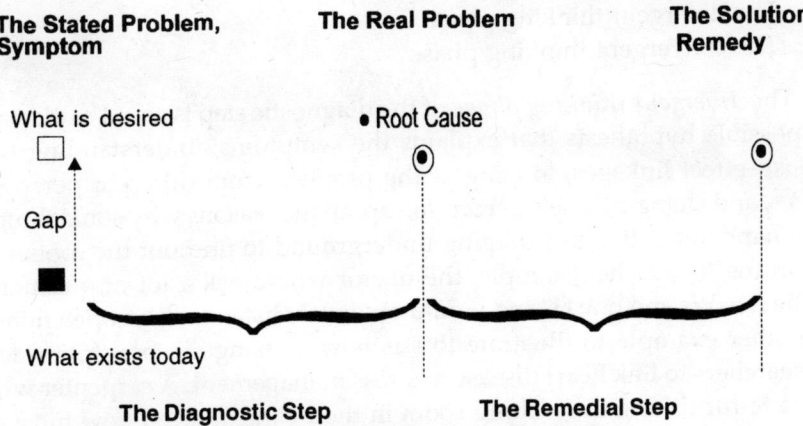

Let us take an example to illustrate these two steps. Imagine I go to a doctor saying I have a problem, say a headache (the symptom). The doctor would first take the *diagnostic step* to find out what the real problem is. He would try to find out the root cause of my headache. There could be many. Like a sleepless night, too much alcohol, a nose block, high blood pressure or poor eyesight. The purpose of finding the root cause is to solve the problem at its root. Doing this will dissolve the symptoms. If we attack only the symptoms without tackling the real cause, the symptoms can recur.

After it is discovered that my poor eyesight is the root cause of my persistent headaches, the doctor would now take the *remedial step* in the journey of treatment. This would involve generating solutions, such as:

- Using eye exercises to improve my eyesight
- Regularly using spectacles of a prescribed number
- Using contact lenses
- Going in for laser eye surgery to rectify the defects in my eye

- Improving intake of Vitamin A and other nutrients in my diet
- Doing yogic exercises for eyesight improvement
- A combination of the above

Having generated the above possibilities, the doctor would then use analytical thinking to converge onto a final solution. He would use objective criteria to select the best alternative. I would then be given a final prescription of remedial action and a schedule of follow-up. If I follow this treatment, my headache should be over.

Each phase of the two-step journey of problem-solving, in turn, has two separate components:

- The divergent thinking phase
- The convergent thinking phase

The *divergent thinking phase* of the diagnostic step is about exploring a possible hypothesis that explains the symptoms, understanding the cause–effect linkages, looking at the problem from different perspectives, and changing one's perception about the reasons why some things are happening. It is like digging underground to find out the roots.

In the 'headache' example, the doctor would ask a lot of questions (The five Ws and one H) and would obviously listen with an open mind. Another example to illustrate this is how a change in perception led researchers to link heart disease to stress management. A carpenter who was re-furnishing the waiting room in their clinic noticed how most of the chairs were worn out on the front edge of the seat rather than in the middle. He shared his rather unusual observation with the doctors. This led the doctors to hypothesize that most patients had been sitting on the edge of the chairs, which showed that they were extraordinarily tense compared to the rest of the population.

Besides questions and active listening, some of the other tools that are used in this phase are the cause–effect diagram, Ishikawa fish-bone diagram and brainstorming. (Description of these tools are widely available in the literature on total quality management (TQM).)

Having got a feel of the possible reasons for a symptom, the next task is to single out the most important cause.

The *convergent thinking phase*, as the name implies, uses logical and analytical thinking and data analysis. Our doctor friend may read my blood pressure, conduct an eye test, and thereby identify the root cause for the headache. Some common tools used in this phase are Pareto analysis, check-sheets and histograms, the details of which are available in TQM literature.

Both divergent and convergent thinking are required in the diagnostic step as well as the remedial step in problem-solving.

Once the best solution has been identified, the next step is to develop an action plan clearly specifying the list of actionable steps to be taken, people responsible, start and end dates, estimated hours and costs, and so on. The final step would be to implement the solution as reflected in the action plan, and review whether the original symptoms have actually diminished or not. This means a regular review of the original situation and a tracking of progress. If the symptom remains, the problem has not been solved. The whole sequence of systematic problem solving is shown in the diagram below:

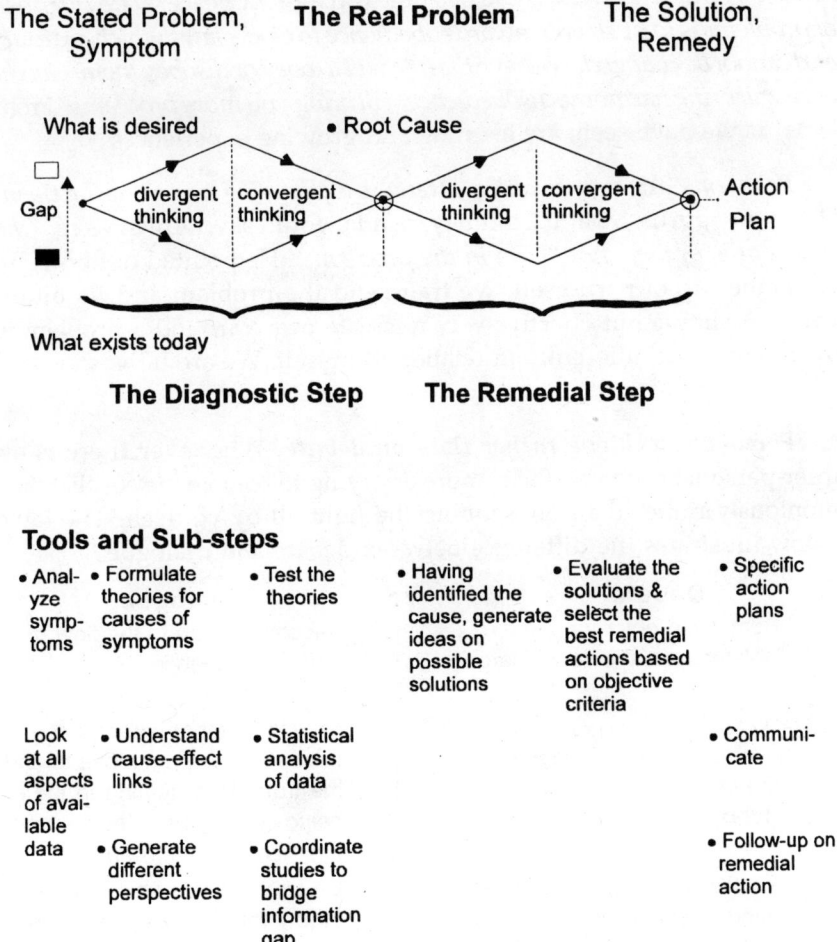

The Stated Problem, Symptom　　**The Real Problem**　　**The Solution, Remedy**

What is desired　　• Root Cause

Gap　　divergent thinking | convergent thinking　　divergent thinking | convergent thinking　　Action Plan

What exists today

The Diagnostic Step　　**The Remedial Step**

Tools and Sub-steps

• Analyze symptoms	• Formulate theories for causes of symptoms	• Test the theories	• Having identified the cause, generate ideas on possible solutions	• Evaluate the solutions & select the best remedial actions based on objective criteria	• Specific action plans
Look at all aspects of available data	• Understand cause-effect links	• Statistical analysis of data			• Communicate
	• Generate different perspectives	• Coordinate studies to bridge information gap			• Follow-up on remedial action

Systematic Problem-solving—Some Insights for Action

I'm sharing below a few points from my experience in problem-solving:

1. *Have a clear measure of the symptom you are trying to change.* '*What gets measured, gets done.*' The discipline of evolving a clear metric of what we are trying to change is very useful for tracking progress, and even for displaying it visually so that the entire team can see the improvements for themselves.

2. *Most problems have a built-in force for positive change.* To quote, Peace Pilgrim who walked 250,000 miles on foot for peace: '*The purpose of problems is to push you towards obedience to God's laws which are exact and cannot be changed. We have the free will to obey or disobey them. Obedience will bring harmony, disobedience will bring you more problems.*' Problems, as we have seen, are learning and growing experiences.

3. *Problems are significantly altered by changing our view of them.* One of my gurus, Swami Chinmayananda would say, '*Always say, "the problem is in me," not "I am in the problem."*' He pointed out how, by remembering our true self, we transcend the problem and its biting value. A simple but effective way to create peace around a problem is by looking at it differently in relation to myself. We are far vaster than what bothers us.

4. *Focus on dialogue rather than on debate.* Whenever there is an inter-personal problem, focus more on trying to resolve the conflict harmoniously rather than on winning the fight all by yourself. The table below illustrates the difference between debate and dialogue.

Debate	vs	Dialogue
☹ Remaining entrapped and isolated from the flow of larger intelligence.		☺ Becoming open to the flow of larger intelligence.
☹ Wanting my own view to prevail over the others. Antagonizing the other. The key issue is: '*Who is Right?*'		☺ Moving together in reverence, trust, friendship and love to find the truth. Participating in the being of the other. The search is for: '*What is the Truth?*'
☹ Forcing with a fixed, prepared mind—getting ready to contradict. Getting caught up in limited thinking. Prejudice: Theory ready.		☺ Understanding with an open, empty mind—active listening. Become an observer of thinking, including my own. Innocent mind:

Getting stuck with my assumptions through unawareness.	No theory. Suspending assumptions through awareness.
☹ Both remain limited/partial or are diminished. The perspective is partial. Sense of separation and fear.	☺ Both are enriched by the truth which surrounds them. The totality transcends both. The whole give meaning to the parts. Sense of oneness and love.

☹ Turns on the heat.	☺ Turns on the light.

5. The diagram below shows two different routes that a problem with another person can take. We can either attack problems or attack people. *Always focus on the problem, the behaviour, the situation that needs to be altered rather than putting down and attacking people*. The latter blocks the flow of creative intelligence required to resolve problems. Remember that you and the other person are one (at the level of the real self). From this loving space, see the problem as a common task to be worked through. I have found this a very smooth and easy way to dissolve conflicts.

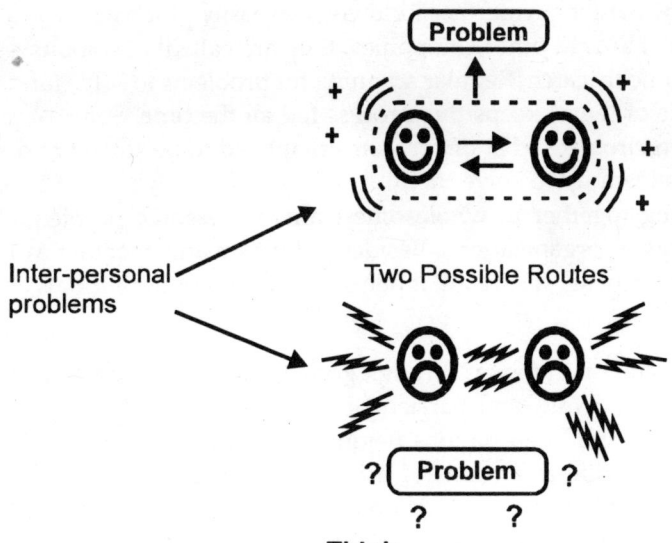

Inter-personal problems

Two Possible Routes

Think
- How can we work it out?
- There are always options
- I can control only what I do

6. *Always remember the incredible power of creative thinking*. There are always possibilities. Many problems evaporate with a shift in paradigm. Despair gives way to relief in a matter of seconds with a shift in thinking.

7. *Listen and seek first to understand* before you express your own viewpoint. It is no coincidence that Lord Ganesha, who is also known as Vigneshwara or the arch problem-solver, has very large ears. These are symbolic of excellent listening.

8. *Remember that time, sometimes, is the greatest problem-solver*. Maintaining an inner distance from a problem and silently saying to oneself, 'This too shall pass,' washes one heart in a wave of peace and equanimity. In the face of even grim challenges, one does not lose patience.

9. *Problem-solving needs to focus on the areas of highest payoffs for the organization*. Such areas can be identified through brainstorming and then evaluated for selection using criteria such as:
- How much benefit would the organization get from solving this problem?
- How quickly can the results be realized and with what ease?
- How visible are the results?

In General Electric (GE), problems that can be solved quickly are called 'low hanging fruit'. The kind you can easily pluck when you walk into an orchard. In other companies, they are called 'fat rabbits'—ones you can quickly catch. Regular scanning for problems to solve (and making a note of them) keeps this process fed all the time. Some organizations even circulate a list of problems that need to be solved and invite people to team up to solve them.

Working together in wholesome teams to dissolve problems liberates energy in organizations. Besides, it binds teams together around a common purpose. Above all, it helps the growth of individuals and the organization.

As integration increases through good teamworking, problems begin to melt away. Walls and barriers separating people, departments, organizations, and even nations begin to dissolve. A deep sensing and experience of life as a series of interdependent processes is unfolded. Energy is unblocked and spirit unfolds.

As one reflects on this beautiful interdependence, and how much we owe to 'others' for every single achievement, the Heart melts in gratitude. One is inspired to share more actively and work joyfully with others towards unfolding wholesomeness in life.

Ideas for Playful Action

1. Look at some team you are working in at present. What is working well in it and what is not? How is it working in respect of the *task* and *process* aspects? Use the points mentioned in this chapter to assess where you are on these dimensions.

2. If you had to think of your organization as a sport, what sport comes to your mind? (Boxing, football, chess, sword fencing, or kho-kho?) Why did you choose this sport? What does this image tell you about working in your organization?

3. Would you describe you team as wholesome? Plot where you think the team is and see for yourself:

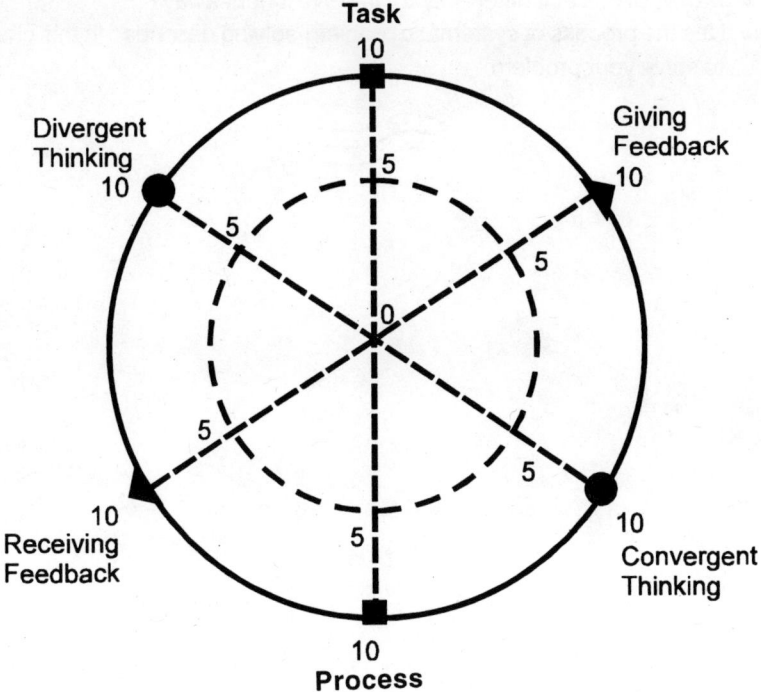

Put a dot on each of the six scales and join these points. A zero represents a low on that dimension, and a 10 a high. A wholesome and well-developed team would look like a balanced circle, close to the outer rim. What does your team look like?

4. Think of your own role in your team. Reflect on:
   - What am *I* bringing to the team?
   - What am *I* holding back from the team?
   - What can *I* do to help my team become more joyful and productive?

5. Brainstorm with your team to generate ideas for improvement projects:
   - List them up on a flip chart or a white board.
   - Prioritize these areas based on the marks received from the team.
   - Invite volunteers to work on these areas in teams using systematic problem-solving.

6. As a team think of the "low-hanging fruits" and "fat rabbits" in your department or organization. Agree on teams and action plans to start working on them.

7. What is the single-most pressing problem you are facing right now?
   - Can you look at it differently to dissolve it right away?
   - Use the process of systematic problem-solving described in this chapter to solve your problem.

≈ 9 ≈

Leadership

The Art of Wholesomeness

'I have three precious things which I hold fast and prize,' he said.
'The first is gentleness, the second is frugality, the third is humility.'
Be gentle and you can be bold.
Be frugal and you can be liberal.
Avoid putting yourself before others
And you can become a leader among them.

Lao-Tze

*D*elivering the Rabindranath Tagore Memorial Oration on 'The Servant Leader', this is what Danah Zohar (1997) said of servant leaders:

Rooted in the source of values and hence driven by love, his being and his doing leaves a space' where even the most impossible possibilities can be realized. When such leaders lead our great industries, the business of business no longer restricts itself to manipulating things and nature and people for profit. Rather, business becomes a spiritual vocation in the largest sense of the word, and its leaders serve the wonderful what can be of Reality.

Danah Zohar's vision of leadership as presented here resonates beautifully with wholesomeness. It is leadership by the whole, for the whole. With a deep connection to the Heart, the very source of life, the wholesome leader is grateful to be of service. His humility is not a 'stance' but a genuine expression of the mystery of being.

The world today needs wholesome leaders in almost all areas. We need people who, not only live full and inspired lives themselves, but know the paradoxical art of unfolding wholesomeness in others.

What is Leadership?

Leadership is the process of unfolding and channelizing human energies for worthwhile and life-affirming ends. It is the capacity to make things happen where people act in inspired ways to achieve common goals. It involves the processes of creatively combining three related aspects of work:

1. *Achieving the tasks towards a broad visionary purpose* for which a group has got together.
2. *Building and maintaining a wholesome team,* and making sure that all aspects of teamwork are given adequate attention.
3. *Developing and motivating people,* so that they are empowered and enriched.

Leaders are creators of a new reality. By shaping the collective mind of an organization, they influence the behaviour of people. This manifests as an organizational environment, which further shapes the behaviour of people.

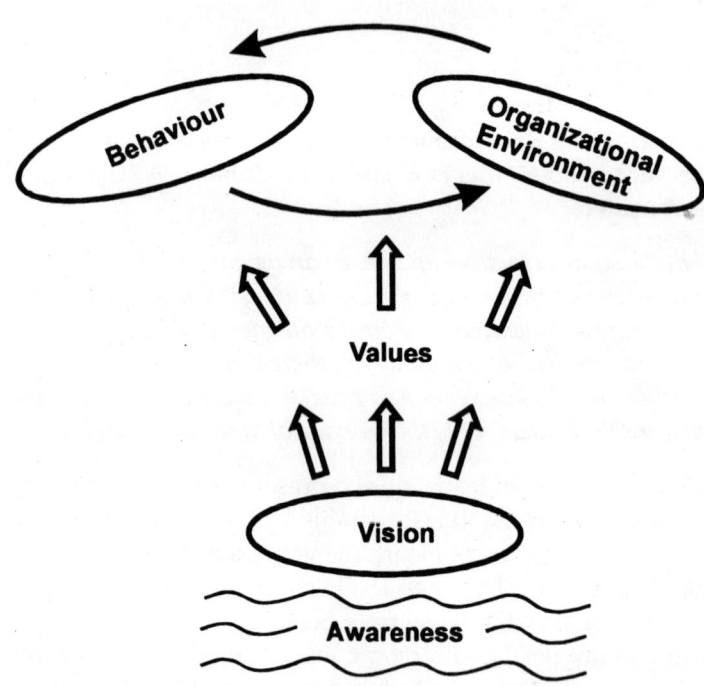

Leaders use the process of communication to shape the destiny of their organizations. Leaders stage revolutions. They are constantly challenging the status quo. They look around to see if people are doing the right things or if those things can be improved upon. They work at the roots of the organization, that is, the Hearts of people.

Today's business and social reality requires inspired change in ample measure. We need great leaders in almost every area of life. Leaders who can:

- See reality as it is in the here and now
- Mobilize the appropriate resources and responses to evolve things further
- Bring out the greatness in people

Luckily, there are people all over the world who are like this. Four examples of wholesome leadership in India come to mind. The 'Swadhay' movement of Pandurang Shastri Athavale is an example of how a single man with a vision of self-learning and value-based development has positively impacted the lives of hundreds of villages of fishermen and tribals in Western India. Similarly, the examples of outstanding leadership of J.R.D. Tata and Verghese Kurien, former Chairman of the National Dairy Development Board, show how single-minded dedication can create great industrial organizations benefiting millions of people.

Mother Teresa's 'Missionaries of Charity' has grown from a one-woman organization in 1952 to a worldwide dynamic organization of 169 educational establishments, 1369 clinics and about 755 homes (in 1997). It involves thousands of people in 120 countries. All this through the power of one frail woman with a message of love and service for the poorest of the poor.

Let us now begin to look at how leadership works and how we can unfold its power in ourselves and others.

Elements of Leadership

Leadership in all its forms has four common features:

1. *There has to be a vision or a goal* for leadership to make sense. Change, transformation and influencing always imply a preferred state or a valued destination. I cannot influence someone unless I know what I am influencing him towards, or for. Connected with this vision are a set of values.

2. *Leadership implies a team or a group* or at least one person who is influenced by the leader. It is a relationship between a person and others.

3. *Followership of the leader has to be voluntary.* A person herding a group of people towards robbing a bank under the threat of a loaded AK47 gun is not a true leader. This is coercion because there is no willing commitment or willing followership.

4. *Leaders inspire willing followership* because they:

- add value to the followers
- satisfy their needs
- give them benefits of some kind

> Most of us would like to change the world. The trouble is, too many of us want to do it 'our' way. Some people have the right diagnosis, but they bring the wrong cure. They reckon without God and without a change in the human nature—and change in the confusion, bitterness and war. Other people are quite sure they have the answer in theory; but always want somebody else or some other nation to begin—the result is frustration and despair.
>
> When the right diagnosis and the right cure come together the result is a miracle—human nature changes and human society changes!
>
> FRANK BUCHMAN

This is why people willingly follow the leader.

The last point is perhaps the most important. *Selfless service, based on an ideal or vision, is probably the hallmark of all good leaders.* The good leader is basically a person steeped in loving compassionate service. The leader gets people to enjoy contributing towards a big goal because doing so benefits them. People are fulfilling their own potential and destiny, satisfying their own needs, and working together to do what is required to be done.

This chemistry is catalyzed by good leaders. In that sense a good leader is like a connector. *He connects the potential of people with the needs of the organization after getting people to see their own power and potential.*

Power and Leadership

For leadership to be wholesome, the goals that the leader pursues must be aligned with the well-being of all. Leadership also involves influencing people. It involves having the capacity to make things happen. This capacity is also known as power. The word 'power' often evokes negative feelings in our

> Leadership is the capacity and will to rally people to a common purpose.
>
> J.M. MONTGOMERY

minds. It conjures up images of exploitation, manipulation and belittling people. However, power when seen as 'the capacity to do good' takes on a different meaning. Just as nuclear power by itself is neither good nor bad, power is also simply a capacity. It is potential which can be used positively or negatively. Positive power has been used extensively all over the world to make good things happen.

A person's power in organizations is derived from two basic sources:

- Positional power or authority
- Personal power or one's capacity to influence others

The total power that a person has can broadly be expressed as

$$P_T = P_A + P_P$$

where P_T is total power, P_A is positional power or authority, and P_P is personal power.

Positional power when exercised brings about compliance. The personal power component is about commitment. While positional power can give a person status in an organization, personal power gives him 'stature'. In many organizations I have seen cases of two

> Whatever you honour above all things, that which you so honour will have dominion over you. But if you give yourself to the domination of God, you will thus have dominion over all things.
>
> SEXTUS THE PYTHAGOREAN

people having the same designation and role and also reporting to the same boss, and yet having vastly different levels of total power. While one gets things done and has excellent relations with other people, the other is perpetually complaining of 'not having the requisite authority commensurate with my responsibility'. While one is a continuous learner and is always looking for ways to add value and give benefit to other people, the other is operating in the BMW (blaming, moaning and wailing) mode of managing. If there is one thing that people can do with proper understanding, it is to enhance their personal power. This book is also all about enhancing personal power.

Personal power, when used positively, can have a healing and inspiring influence. Power that stems from the peace within is expressed through humility. Truly powerful people are gentle, possess a sense of humour and are sources of loving compassion. They do not try to impress others or be influential. They are simply present. People are spontaneously attracted towards them. You would often find them very silent and conscious of their real self. They are aware that the outer world is simply a manifestation of their inner world. In fact, they see no split between the inner and the outer. They are playfully incharge of their destinies and do not try to convince or persuade anyone. They only invite and share. Manipulation and aggressiveness are alien to their nature. They listen deeply to others and help others to connect to their own source of power.

This is a new view of power. Such refined power recharges and regenerates people who come in contact with it. It leaves people feeling increased and expanded. If you have gained access to your deepest level of being, then you have experienced true power.

Managing vs Leading

I am often asked the difference between managers who are leaders and those who are not. Very simply, managers who are not leaders only rely on positional power to make things happen. They try to get things done only through the power of their post or position. Positional power, however, is rarely enough to bring about changes and sustain them in the long run.

Managers and leaders exhibit different mindsets. The table below gives you some of these differences.

Managing	Leading
• Producing orderly results	• Creating useful change
• Structuring work	• Inspiring vision
• Enforcing the work	• Encouraging innovation
• Following the business script	• Creating new business stories
• Tightly controlling the decision process	• Involving and empowering others to take decisions
• Monitoring what is going wrong	• Encouraging and stimulating the right things
• Getting compliance	• Creating commitment
• Following a clear path	• Forging a new path

From this table it is clear that we need both dimensions. While we need to envision change and inspire a shared vision of a desired future, we also need to run that future in an organized and orderly way to produce results. This involves structuring work, controlling processes and rewarding people to move forward towards the desired vision. It is said that managing uses more of the left hemisphere or convergent thinking (see Chapter 4) while leadership uses more of the right or divergent thinking mode.

My vision of a wholesome leader is one who is comfortable with both and free to respond to situations in whatever way is appropriate. A wholesome leader trusts the intrinsic order in life and aligns with its

**Leadership
Ensures
Balance and Focus**

**Peace
Joy
Ease**

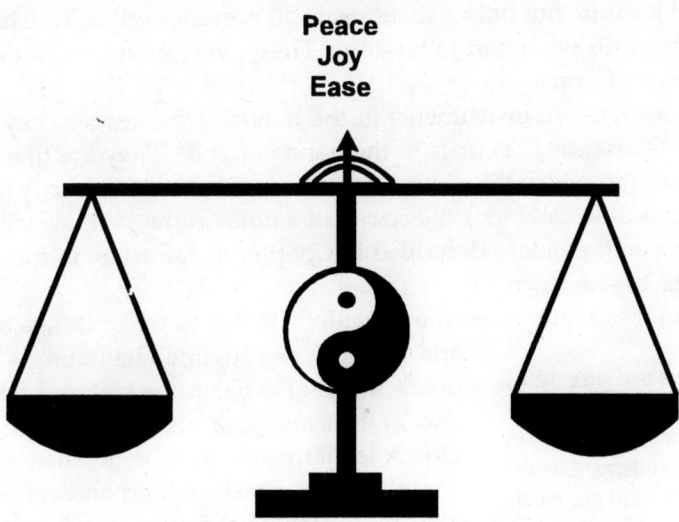

natural movement. There is a natural and inherent orderliness in life. It is born out of dynamic interrelatedness and constant churning.
A good leader understands this and trusts the
emergence of a spontaneous order in situations. This is not always as easy as it sounds. It
requires great courage to go through chaos
even though you know that a greater intelligence is guiding it all.

> **The world is not to be put in
> order; the world is order
> incarnate. It is for us to
> harmonize with this order.**
> HENRY MILLER

Good leadership is a lifelong challenge. Most practices of good leaders which we have discussed are easy to state but not so easy to follow
without the inner connection.

A good leader connects people to their own
source of power. He connects them to each
other and he also connects people to their surroundings and the environment. In that sense,
he is a healer or one who makes whole. And
yet, he really does nothing. A true leader is
more like a silent witness who allows life to
do what has to be done. He moves from doing things himself, to enabling others, and fi-

> **A dervish met a king. The king
> said: 'Ask a boon of me.' The
> dervish replied: 'I will not ask
> a boon from one of my slaves.
> I have two slaves who are thy
> masters; covetousness and
> expectation.'**
> HUJWIRI

nally to being. As mentioned earlier, this paradox of inaction and action coming together in a mysterious oneness is how it feels.

Some of my best moments have been when I truly felt I was doing nothing. My sense of 'I-ness' was a diffused unbounded awareness with no fixed location but only a silent peaceful presence which watched this body–mind do what had to be done. These were moments of deep inspiration and grace.

True leaders are instruments in the hands of Existence. They are as Mother Teresa said, 'Pencils in the hands of god'. They are like empty flutes through which the divine plays its music. A tiny impurity or drop of spit in a flute can block the clarity of a note. In the same way impurities (such as the blocks described in Chapter 4) can come in the way of the work of existence.

A leader is really a bit of a paradox. He has to make things happen and yet stay aloof while facilitating a group doing things. He has to be soft and feminine and, at the same time, also hard and business-like. A leader needs to be concerned with accomplishing the task at hand and yet he must also take care of the process. Leaders are empty inside with an almost creative nothingness and yet grapple with the tasks of leading a team and organization. These polar-opposites need to be integrated. While the mind wants to divide into 'either this or that', it is better to work with the magic of 'and'. The flexibility and ability to move freely between apparently contradictory polarities requires an open mind. This is the art of wholesomeness.

> The brave and wise man, who intends to overcome his foes, must first strive to subdue the internal enemies of his own heart and mind, and the members of his own body ... The kings of the earth in their earthly capitals are not as happy as are the Lords of the cities of their own bodies, and the masters of their own minds.
>
> SAGE VASHISHTA
> TO LORD RAMA

Being wholesome as a leader is vital because leaders need to use a whole range of behaviour depending on the situation. Young, inexperienced trainees may have to be handled with more firmness and direction than, say, people with 15 years' experience. Similarly, the same person may have to be treated differently at different points in time. Leaders, therefore, have to be capable of using different forms of behaviour in tune with different situations. *This comes easily if leaders are not stuck with or attached to any single idea of what a good leader should be*. They may have to be as soft and yielding as a ball of dough and yet be as tough and hard as a diamond. Above all, *all leaders must have the flexibility*

> God weeps ... over a leader who domineers over the community.
>
> TALMUD HAGIGA

to switch easily between the requirements of different situations. They must also have a vision that is aligned with nature's own unfolding design, and yet have no intrinsic deficiency or desire. You may find this contradictory. However, that is precisely what the paradoxical nature of leadership is.

Balancing comes naturally when one is not stuck in any fixed position. One is free to move from one end of the spectrum to another as easily as a piece of melting butter on a non-stick pan. The masculine and feminine energies are balanced. One can be as compassionate as a mother and as tough as a demanding father. One can be as playfully yielding as a blade of grass in the wind, and also embedded in the ground like a heavy boulder.

The inner signal of balance is a deep sense of ease and peace. It tells the leader moment to moment if the balance is right or not. It becomes an inner compass and touchstone of inner discernment. It is the silent barometer of existence which shines like an inner guide.

Good Leaders

- In the world, but not of it

- Centred and aware

- Have spirit of service

- Are connected to the Heart

Drawing upon 25 years of experience as consultants and teachers, Noel M. Tichy and Eli Cohen (1997) in their book *The Leadership Engine* assert that successful organizations win because they are run by people who cultivate leaders. Markets, products, and technologies come and go, but a company that continually produces leaders at all levels is here to stay because it has people who anticipate and know how to deal with change. According to the authors, *distinguished leaders are those who are willing to assume direct responsibility for developing other leaders.* They are facilitators of learning, who spend a lot of time and energy in imparting ideas, values and emotional energy by telling stories about their experiences to others. As Tichy and Cohen (1997) put it, *'A leader who aspires to be a winning leader organizes every meeting, makes every decision, and designs every organizational structure with developing others in mind.'*

Leadership and the facilitation of learning are almost identical processes. Both are about moving from where we are now to a new and desired future. Both are about people changing their behaviour. The leader is also a developer of people, and a good teacher is one who inspires and shows the way. Both have to be good facilitators who draw out what is already known by the student.

As Richard Bach (1977) says in the book *Illusions*, *'Learning is finding out what you already know. Doing is demonstrating that you know it. Teaching is reminding others that they know just as well as you. You are all learners, doers, teachers.'* Similarly, leadership is about enabling others to know their real potential. It is about developing other leaders.

I like to think of good leaders as being like the philosopher's stone, called Paras in Indian mythology, which turns things to gold. Paras is symbolic of the Heart. This is the true foundation of good leadership.

There is a beautiful ancient story, which I heard recently. *'A master once showed an iron box containing the fabulous Paras to his disciples. The stone turns everything it touches into gold. The disciples did not believe their master. They said that if what he claimed were really true, the iron box should have turned to gold. The master quietly opened the box and showed them the stone. He then picked it out, and sliding his finger on the floor of the box, cleaned out a patch of dust. He then put the stone back inside. The box instantly turned to gold.'*

The meaning of this story, as I interpret it, is that it's our identification with our ego (assumptions, prejudices, false notions and limiting beliefs which are like impurities) that breaks our connection with the fullness of life. The essence of these impurities is our mind. When we can transcend the mind, and thereby remove the dust, and enter into the holy space of our own inner purity, our life is transformed. Transcending the forms that limit us is purification. This is also liberation. This is the true work of a leader.

'Man is God veiled, and God is man revealed,' so said the Sufi masters of yore. While people are covered up in layers of conditioning and fear, the leader sees his work as 'dis-covering' and developing the full potential of people. *Leaders therefore must see this potential in people and have full faith in it*. One cannot see this potential in others unless one has seen it in oneself. Seen this way, the leader's work is to unfold the leader in others. This requires a capacity to delight in the unfolding of excellence and potentiality in others. Good leaders celebrate the unfolding of the divine wherever and whenever they see it. They seek the divine spark and revel in its expansion. Even a tiny indicator of positivity is noticed and given attention to. In people, they focus on the strengths

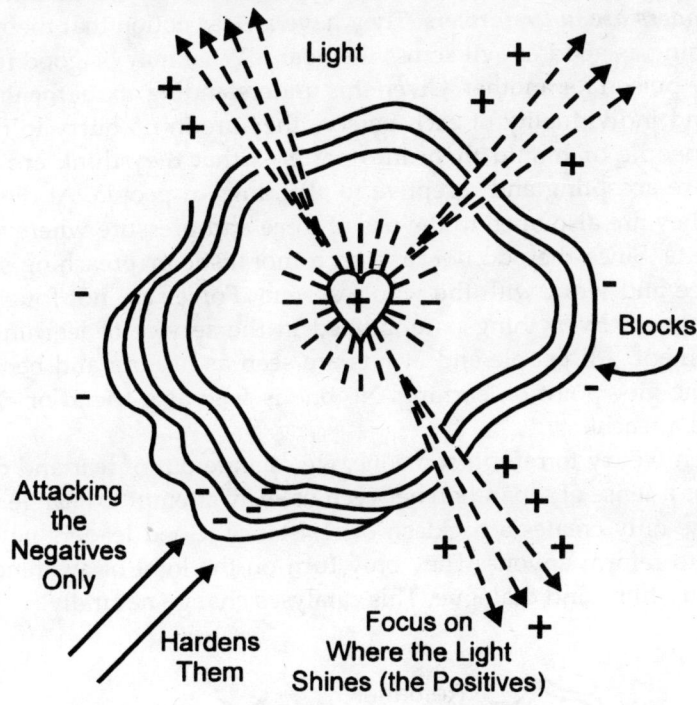

Good Leadership Focuses on Positives

and positives. This is like removing the crust covering a bright light starting from a point where the light is coming out.

They naturally gravitate towards the zones in a person's life from where the 'light' is radiating. They look for zones of energy, bliss, spirit. This is how they see where the openings are. They recognize that more can be achieved by appreciation than by hammering away at the negatives. They realize that the crust is weakest at the point from where light is already emerging, and so enter the openings at such points. This is the easiest approach to develop a person.

There is a story of prince Hui's cook, who being devoted to the Tao, would follow the natural openings or cavities while carving goats. He did not have to change his chopper for nineteen years because he was in perfect harmony with the situation. Skilful leaders also use natural openings and gaps to enlarge them. This, in turn, releases more energy and makes subsequent change easier. It unfolds spirit which is already there.

The leader's approach to developing people is very relaxed and natural. *Leaders are not reformers.* They have a clear notion that there is no such thing as good or evil across the board. What may be good for one may be poison for another. Given this understanding about the uniqueness and individuality of each person, they are in no hurry to reform other people or mould them into patterns that they think are good. They are accepting and receptive to all things in people. At the same time, they are also open to the use of force and pressure wherever appropriate. Since they do not take on a moralistic or preaching stance, they see and work with the whole system. Forces are not fought but channelized. Everything is mobilized in the service of learning and unfoldment. All people and events are seen as healing and beneficial from the viewpoint of learning. No one is seen as a friend or enemy, only as a teacher.

When we try to reform someone, we operate out of fear and desire. There is a sense of separation between us. Any attempt to change someone else only creates a backlash of resistance. Good leaders never attempt to reform anyone. They only turn on the light of awareness by their questions and dialogue. This catalyses change naturally.

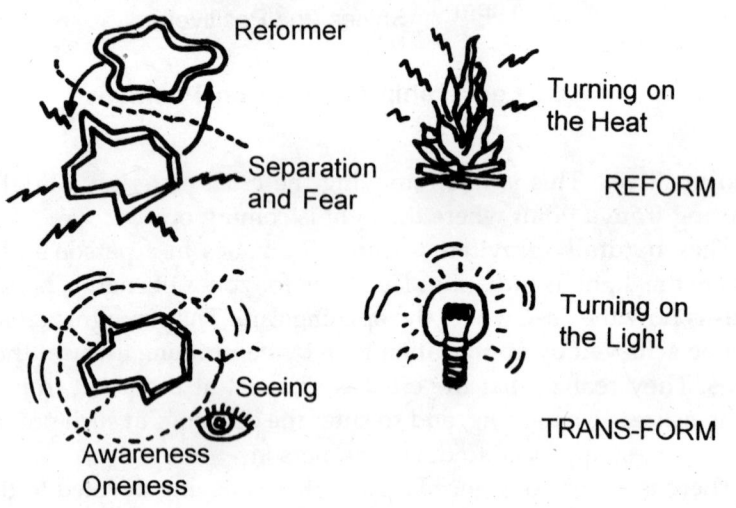

Reform vs. Trans-form

It is easy to think of 'trans-forming' as 'transc-ending' form. When the leader is free of all notions of limited identity, roles, images and ideas about right and wrong, he can operate with a natural ease which inspires and spontaneously creates change.

Leaders are focused on service. They revel in growing through sharing their talents and gifts in the service of others. They recognize that service aligned with a big cause unleashes energy and spirit, which in turn generates enormous capacity.

In 1995, Sathya Sai Baba and some 200 engineers and around 5000 unskilled labourers working along with 100 subcontracting agencies completed a drinking watersupply project for 3.8 million people of Anantapur district in Andhra Pradesh in a

> Religions which condemn the pleasures of sense, drive men to seek the pleasures of power. Throughout history, power has been the vice of the ascetic.
>
> BERTRAND RUSSELL

record eight months. It was a miracle and triumph of human endeavour! With Sathya Sai Baba being a constant source of confidence and inspiration, he exhorted people to give of themselves in a spirit of service. His model of a good leader is given below. The twin wings of knowledge and character hinge on the foundation of the divine Heart. It is this that lends energy to the selfless vision and to the means of accomplishing it. It is this spirit that opens the eyes of our understanding and helps us walk the journey of leadership.

In his book *Servant Leadership*, Robert Greenleaf (1983) says that the ultimate aim of the servant leader's quest is to find the resources of character to meet his or her destiny—to find the wisdom and power to serve others. Sai Baba's model shows us where to find that resource of character—at the source!

Whether it is a watersupply project or the creation of cooperatives for villagers, a spirit of service connected to a large vision inspires effort. More often than not, it creates miracles.

Traits of a Good Leader

We have already discussed some of the practices followed by good leaders. These are summarized below and some more added:

1. *Leaders inspire a shared vision and work for a large worthwhile cause.* This is one important factor that all good leaders have in common. While many people have ideals and goals, it is in the process of sharing these with others that leadership begins.

2. *They share responsibility and enable others to give out their best.* Leaders identify the natural gifts and strengths of people and entrust appropriate roles to them, matching their strengths. This is a process of creating conditions for people to give their very best and connect the sharing of their talents to a large worthwhile goal. They delegate competently, giving clear instructions, and regularly review the work of team members.

3. *Leaders are restless for improvement.* They have a quality of creative discontent and are prone to question the status quo. They challenge assumptions and processes, bringing to light the underlying assumptions and paradigms that hold organizations and society in place. They create a new order and are always sensitive to the needs of the times. Not only do they change in tune with present trends, but they are also in tune with their own vision of the future. They promote high standards of excellence setting clear criteria for success. They expect and demand the very best from themselves and from their teams. This helps them to call forth the very best in themselves and others.

4. *The raising of spirit and energy in a group is quite an important part of the leadership process.* Leaders celebrate success and encourage positive emotions. Through their caring words and human touch, they earn the respect and loyalty of their team and enable the growth of people alongwith the growth of the organization. Leaders are spirited

and enthusiastic (spirited = spiritual). Their spirituality is free from religion or sectarianism. It is universal and human. A leader's own vibrancy, and often unwarranted optimism, is infectious.

5. *Leaders inspire by their 'walking their talk'.* Inspiration comes from setting an example and modelling the way for others to emulate. Leaders are absolutely honest with their own self and others. Their authenticity is compelling. Good leaders transform others through their own example.

6. *They show tremendous care and respect for people.* A leader has a strong people-orientation and is excellent in interpersonal skills. He understands himself and his people, develops positive relationships with others and maintains contact.

7. *Leaders have a high demonstrable quality of integrity and character.* This is linked to the above quality of caring for people. Both these inspire trust in the leader. Because people know that a leader is fair and just and cares for them, they build a high degree of credibility in their relationship with him. This is vital for influencing people.

> He who knows much about others may be learned, but he who understands himself is more intelligent. He who controls others may be powerful, but he who has mastered himself is mightier still.
>
> LAO-TSU

8. *A leader needs to have great faith and self-confidence.* This can happen quite easily and naturally if the leader recognizes and lives from his own 'sacred self'. Doing this creates a space of deep trust within and an unchanging security in the face of even the most turbulent external trials. When others look to the leader for strength and solace in times of difficulty, he, in turn, looks at his own divine origin.

9. *A good leader ultimately creates other good leaders.* She helps connect other people to their own divine core and grow as leaders in their own right. She is like a candle lighting another candle. As against this, not so effective leaders are like huge searchlights that light up a place when they are around, but plunge the area into darkness when they are away.

10. *Leadership is action and not position.* It is courageous action and taking risks that finally makes things happen. Good leaders have a strong bias for informed action. They open their eyes of understanding and express their love in courageous acts.

11. *Good leaders keep themselves in good physical, emotional, intellectual and spiritual health.* They read Chapter 2 of this book regularly!

12. *They are excellent communicators with sound commonsense and an abundant sense of humour.* I have found humour to be a great lubricator of human relations and interaction. It serves a great need in these serious times. Cheerfulness and humour have been exemplified in the life of Mother Teresa and J.R.D. Tata. Humour implies a free spirit and a creative mind. It shows a vibrancy of soul and the absence of an ego. Being 'ego-less' paradoxically makes a greater leader. They are willing to let go, and let Existence do its work through them.

13. *The larger the vision to which the leader hitches his wagon, the smaller must his ego be to support that dream.* The larger the dream, the more the energy available to him.

14. *Above all, a leader has great love for people.* Her own core is loving compassion and she becomes a channel of nature's will. The ambit of her ambition dissolves to become one with the ambition of life itself. Just as, when a gardener has done his job we do not praise the trowel in his hand, similarly when a good leader does his work in tune with the flow of life, we do not praise him but the totality that worked through him.

Before you get the notion that good leaders are saints and superheros, let me state categorically that they are as human as you and me. They do not have any fixed notions of perfection or utopia. Nor are they immune from the difficulties of life. In fact, sometimes they have to face more than their normal share of such difficulties. The lives of leaders such as Gandhi, Socrates, Napolean and Akbar show that they had to go through a lot of travail. ***Leaders however use difficulties and challenges for growth.*** They recognize that kites rise against the wind and not with it. They also understand that suffering can be a great teacher and purifier and that life is truly a stream of learning opportunities.

Some women once asked a goldsmith how long he kept the gold in the fire. He replied, *'Until I see the reflection of my face in it.'* The same is true of human kind. Leaders recognize this and take difficulties with an attitude of gratitude. They hold fast to the affirmation that *'everything in life will purify me and will dissolve my ego'.* They see perfection in what is here and now. They see life as unfolding perfection itself.

Leaders do not seek followers just as flowers do not advertise for bees. The bees come naturally because they are attracted by the fragrance and colour of the flowers. In the same way, leaders spontaneously attract followers by their own thoughts, words and actions.

After reading this chapter, you would understand, perhaps, why their is a crisis in leadership in India and the rest of the world. As we saw in

Chapter 7, a crisis is also a hidden opportunity. *The opportunity points towards you.* Remember, that the first letter in the word India is 'I'. So, is the first letter in the words Initiative, Inspiration, Innovation and Integration. Drawing power from the most powerful source in the world, the LOVE which is your Heart, your real self, can we become channels for powerful transformational energies? Listen silently to the depths of your being for an answer. As wholesome leaders being whole ourselves is the first and last mantra.

Ideas for Playful Action

1. Read this beautiful Zen story (which I saw on page 23, of *The Corporate Mystic* by Gay Hendricks and Kate Ludeman):

    'Master,' said the student, 'where do you get
        your spiritual power?'
    'From being connected to the source,' said the Master.
    'You are connected to the source of Zen?'
    'Beyond that,' said the Master, 'I am Zen.
        The connection is complete.'
    'But isn't it arrogant to claim connection with
        the source?' asked the student.
    'Far from it,' said the Master, 'It's arrogant
        not to claim connection with the source.
    Everything is connected. If you think you are
    Not connected to the source you are thumbing
    Your nose at the universe itself.'

    Now write non-stop for five minutes whatever comes in response to the starting sentence: 'My connection to the source . . .' Do not censor. Whatever comes is okay. Let go and enjoy yourself. What insights does your sharing throw up?

2. To find out how wholesome your own style of leadership is, draw a disc of the kind you saw in Chapter 8. Put in your own axes of different polarities at equal angular intervals (as we had done for wholesome teams). Here are some ideas for you:

    - *Between* Being firm and tough *and* Being flexible and yielding
    - *Between* Time spent at work *and* Time spent on the family
      and professional goals   and personal goals
    - *Between* Being creative and *and* Being stable and secure
      innovative
    - *Between* Being people-oriented *and* Being task-oriented

- *Between*   Routine work   *and*   Developmental work
- *Between*   Inner growth (spiritual)   *and*   Outer growth (material)
- *Between*   Masculine energy   *and*   Feminine energy within us
- *Between*   Thinking   *and*   Feeling

Now plot how your style looks. Does it look like the full moon or a starved amoeba? What areas do you need to pay more attention to?

3. Slowly read the quotation below:

> *Until one is committed there is hesitancy,*
> *The chance to draw back, always ineffectiveness.*
> *Concerning all acts of initiative (and creation)*
> *There is one elementary truth, the ignorance of which*
> *Kills countless ideas and splendid plans:*
> *The moment one definitely commits oneself,*
> *Then providence moves too.*
> *All sorts of things occur to help one that would otherwise*
> *Never have occurred. A whole stream of events issues from the decision,*
> *Raising in one's favor all manner of unforeseen incidents and*
> *Meetings and material assistance,*
> *Which no man could have dreamed would have come his way.*
>
> W.N. Murray, *The Scottish Himalayan Expedition*

As a person, what are the few important things in your life that you need to commit yourself to? List them down. Now decide a few action steps you will take in the direction of your vision.

4. Challenge and stretch people out of their 'rest-houses' and request them to challenge yours. This implies being open to giving and receiving feedback. Challenge the assumptions and processes and always ask people, *'What are we doing today which will show us that our tomorrow's will be better than our todays?.'* Set up a meeting to do this with your team.

5. Good leaders systematically and regularly develop their people. This does not only mean sending them to training programmes. It also implies coaching them personally and using routine encounters at work as fuel for learning with your facilitation. Who are the people you need to sit with? What do you think they need to learn? Listen to what they think they need to learn.

6. On matters of values and basic principles, be honest and tough. Remember a good leader has to balance the qualities of nurturance and challenge. Are there any areas you need to 'get honest' on? List them down and take the risk to do it.

7. When was the last time you celebrated with your team? Plan one in the next two months.

≈ 10 ≈

Staying in Touch
Networking and Integration

*You are the center of your own
universe . . . where your universe intersects
or overlaps someone else's, your lines
cross that person's universe . . . if you
could draw a map of all universes, you'd
have a mesh or a web,
A huge fishnet . . . A NETWORK.
Everyone is set smackdab in the
middle of a vast network, if only
she realized it.*

MARY SCOTT WELCH

*A*ll of life is an interdependent whole. Your thoughts, words
and actions move outwards like the ripples on a lake and create their own vibrations and impacts. In our journey towards
a deep sense of oneness, we need to keep reminding ourselves of what
our life is all about and where we are going. We also need to stay in
touch not only with ourselves but also with other fellow travellers and
co-workers on our journey.

Staying in touch and focusing on action is not only important for our
evolution, but is also a vital need to meet the larger challenges facing us
today. When we join hands with other people and share our dreams,
aspirations and concerns, we find not only inner strengths in this kin-
ship but also practical help and ideas to carry our joint work forward.

To work from the Heart and create spirit in organizations, we need
to address two basic issues:

1. How do we stay in touch with people for collective learning and action?
2. How do we keep the process of action and growth alive in our own life?

Both these points are about ways to reinforce, build and expand our understanding. They are about networking with other people.

Staying in Touch with People—Networking for Learning

While it is useful to start inspired action on your own, there is also a power in working together with others for similar goals. This is what networking is all about. Networking is the new process of learning for the millennium. It is a beautiful way of staying in touch made much easier by the Internet and e-mail.

I am quoting below, some portions from *'A Collection of International Women's Tribune Centre (IWTC) Newsletter on Women's organizing and networking strategies'* (International Women's Tribune Centre, 777 United Nations Plaza, New York, NY 10017.) on Networking.

'Networking . . . .

- creates awareness,
- builds alliances, and
- pools resources.'

Networking can take on many forms. It can be formal with a definite organisational structure and a well-planned, well-financed, programme of action. Or, it can be informal—a coming together of people to share mutual interest and concerns, meeting when the need arises and lacking a structure or mode of operation. It can be unseen and invisible; conscious or unconscious.

Networking can be personal, to achieve personal growth and development objectives; political, to mobilize action around a specific issue; or professional, to link people with similar professional interest.

Networking can be international, joining people from different regions of the world; regional, bringing people together based on concerns unique to conditions in that country, such as legal or economic problems; national, bringing people together based on concerns unique to conditions in that country, such as legal or economic problems; or local, linking people within a community for action on a specific issue of local concern.

Networking can be individual, putting one person in touch with another person with similar interests. These people may have similar professional skills, or they may have different skills which are complementary and necessary for resolving a problem. Or, it may be institutional, among organizations which have agreed to join forces in resolving a common problem.

You are not alone!

Some Benefits of Networking

Networking . . .

- Puts you in touch with other people concerned about the same issues
- Gives you specific information which you won't find in the mass media
- Gives you a broad picture of the issue you are dealing with
- Informs you how other individuals or groups are resolving the problems
- Provides you with the names of people and/or organizations who can help you by providing technical or financial assistance
- Assures you that you are not acting in isolation, but are part of a larger group struggling with similar issues
- Informs you of the various options or directions you have before you
- Pools efforts and energies to create a collective front to problems
- Gives greater visibility to the issue through collective action
- Informs you of training opportunities, workshops, meetings, which may be of interest
- Gives you new ideas and perspectives on a problem
- Provides a channel of communication at local, national, regional, or worldwide levels.

Networking Exists. Use It!
My own 'feeling level' of experience with networking has been:

- *A feeling of joy* at discovering that other people are also struggling with some of the issues dear to my heart. Also, a sense of satisfaction at finding new solutions and new insights into problems where I was stuck.

- *A feeling of solidarity and oneness.* A feeling of belonging to something vast, beyond my own small role and organizational boundaries. My first experience of feeling like a global citizen came through networking. I experienced the same feeling of warmth and hope that happens when I see a picture of planet earth taken from outer space.

- *A sense of richness and abundance* because I see that I am not isolated or alone but am deeply connected to other people, other resources, other ideas and information bases.

- *A feeling of* A-HA! *and surprise,* when one wakes up to new possibilities through networking.

My favourite example of networking is how we discovered another person working in a field similar to ours via a database network located in New York. She happens to live in the next lane from our office!

In a recent International Conference on 'Sustainable Village Based Development', held at Fort Collins, USA, it came to light that the world has many living examples of excellent practical solutions to the problems of sustainable village development. All people in the same field were, however, not aware of them. Think of how much can be achieved if all people in the field had access to the collective wisdom of all successful examples.

In a training programme for a well-known engineering organization, we found that two people, whose workplaces were only a hundred metres away from each other (on different production lines), had both struggled with the same problem. One had solved it successfully four years ago while the other was still struggling with it! They were not aware about this. Think of the opportunity lost.

The principals and teachers of a few schools in Pune came together at a meeting organized under the 'HRD in the Classroom' project of the HRD Network. They were amazed at how much they could learn from each other's experiences. They decided to meet regularly, and stay in touch through a newsletter.

These examples are illustrative of the need to stay in touch with people and to learn from their experiences.

Wherever we have tried to network with people for positive ends, the results have been encouraging. People enjoy sharing their stories amongst a group of friends and fellow travellers. If I have been slack in my work, my friends' story inspires me to make more effort. Sharing about concepts refires the neural circuits in my brain connected with that concept. It brings my attention back to the ideas which I want to see materialized in my own life. *Whatever you pay attention to grows.* As Linda Goodman says quaintly in her book *Star Signs*, *'If you mind it, it matters.'*

To me, learning through networking is the new form of empowerment that we need so much in the world today. I am reminded of the words of the famous German poet Goethe who said: *'Connect, always connect'.*

Networking is nothing short of seeing life in new ways, seeing ourselves in new ways, and above all, being open to the vast resources of learning and experiences that are available provided we see them. It is like an opportunity that exists only if you see it.

It is a bringing together of needs and capabilities, of opportunities for expression and the strengths of people. To me, it is one of the finest forms of saying that we are one world with one common destiny.

Decide to network.
Use every letter you write
Every conversation you have
Every meeting you attend
To express your fundamental
beliefs and dreams.
Affirm to others the vision of the
world you want.
Network through thought
Network through action
Network through the spirit
Network through love.
You are the centre of the world
You are a free, immensely
powerful source
of life and goodness
Affirm it
Spread it
Radiate it
Think day and night about it
And you will see a miracle
happen;
the greatness of your own life,
In the world of big powers, media,
and monopolies
But of four and half billion
individuals
Networking is the new freedom
the new democracy
a new form of happiness.

ROBERT MULLER

When I Dream alone It Is
just a dream. But When We
Dream Together It Is The
Beginning of REALITY.

BRAZILIAN PROVERB

Making Networking Work—Some Ideas for Action

- TALK with people in your community or with whom you work. Ask for names and addresses of individual/groups involved in projects similar to yours.
- TALK or write to government ministries, university personnel, and

non-governmental organizations in your area. Try to learn if they are networking, and, if so, with whom.

- LOOK AT directories, resource books, information brochures, etc. to locate additional names and addresses of people you should know about.
- WRITE letters requesting information from groups/individuals you've identified. When possible, a personal visit is most effective. REMEMBER , whenever you talk or write to anyone, ask for additional names of individuals/groups that you should be in touch with as well as their suggestions for resource materials that will help you uncover more network members.
- SEND any publications, notices, or materials that you produce or that describe your organization, project, or interests to your network. Ask that you be put on their mailing list to receive their free publications regularly. If you have regular publications, ask them if they would be interested in establishing an exchange agreement with you.
- ASK for advice from groups you've learned about, and begin exchanging materials. This strengthens the process of building an information and contact base that is so important to good networking.
- INVITE people or groups you are in contact with to drop in on your organization or project when they are in your area.
- ATTEND conferences, seminars and workshops at which the people with whom you've begun to network will be present, particularly regional meetings.

Having got a feel of how networking can help us, and how to do it, let us now focus our attention on other ways to keep the process of learning and growth alive in our lives.

Keeping Action and Growth Alive in Our Life

The value of this book is directly proportional to how much of it you put into practice. *We are nourished not by what we stuff into our mouth, but by what we chew and digest.*

> Regular practice can sharpen even the mind of a dull man, Just as a small rope going back and forth on a stone leaves a mark.
>
> KABIR

This book has perhaps given you a new vision of possibilities. I have attempted to keep things simple and focused on specific actions. The challenge now is to joyfully implement some of these ideas so that they bear positive fruit in our lives. What we need are simple ways to stay in touch with these ideas regularly, try out new actions based on them, and expand the circle of awareness and blissfulness in our own and other peoples' lives.

As we saw in Chapter 7, learning a new habit requires continuous effort and practice. As Ray Crock, the CEO of McDonald, says *'Nothing is as important as perseverance.'* If we do not put some of these ideas into action, the memory of these will fade away like a spinning potter's wheel which slowly loses energy and comes to a halt.

The diagram below shows the effects of continuous reminders and action. What was initially just a vision of new possibilities finally gets established as a way of life. Continuous attention actually materializes a habit. Little drops of water dropping continuously on a rock can make a dent in it.

Vision of New Possibilities

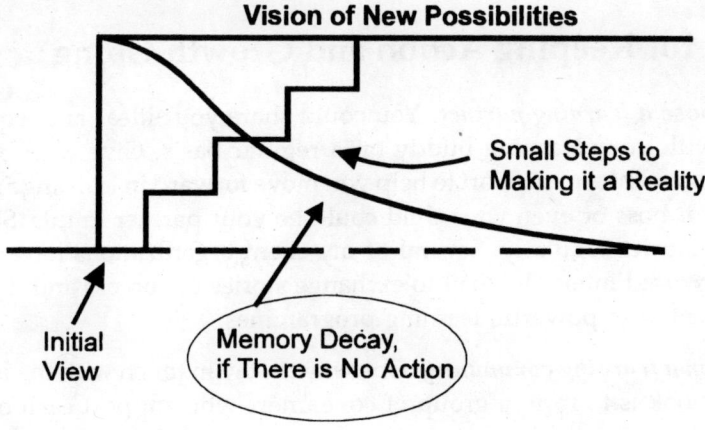

About 23 years ago, I was a very poor listener. Today, after years of practice and reminders, I am reasonably good at it. When I started trying to use a time management diary five years ago, it was a 'trying' experience. For many months and years I would make some progress and then slip back. There were days when I thought I would never be able to use a diary well, let alone getting a grip on what my life and values were all about. It seemed futile to try again.

I'am happy to share that after years of continuous and imperfect trying, my time management is now above average. I have begun to enjoy the pleasure of knowing what I have to achieve in the next one or two years and managing each day in a balanced way, celebrating the 'now' while also moving towards my goals. This joyful energy, in turn, propels me to reach out for still higher goals and achievements.

Successful implementation of new ideas releases energy. This is an important point to remember. It makes it easier to implement action further because one is more enthusiastic and joyful, having tasted success! This is fuel for further victories. Try to tap into this upward moving spiral of growth and creative action. It is like the engine of a car firing on its own after the starter motor has done its job. Persist until you tap into this magical movement. Remember that it is there waiting for you to discover it. Also remember that the very nature of life is to grow. Existence is waiting for you to take a few more steps out of your current 'rest-house'. You take one step and existence takes five. It waits with an adventure if we venture!

> It's not because things are difficult that we do not dare. It is because we do not dare that they are difficult.
>
> SENECA

Ideas for Keeping Action and Growth Going

1. *Choose a learning partner.* You could share your ideas and experiences with your learning buddy on a regular basis. Give each other encouragement and support to help you move forward in learning. Your spouse or boss or even your child could be your partner in this. Share success stories regularly. Several of my client organizations have successfully used internal e-mail to exchange stories of success and disappointment after powerful learning programmes.

2. *Form a learning community.* One way to stay in touch with the ideas in this book is to form a group of co-learners who support each other and share their experiences as a part of a collective process of learning. Such a group could meet regularly to keep sharing their experiences and to gently remind each other to keep moving forward. If, in a group of people who want to stay awake, someone falls asleep, another person can wake him up. Tomorrow, the one who awoke, in turn, can wake up someone else!

You could initiate action to form a learning community by starting a study group. In it, some of the ideas in this book can be discussed and joint thinking concretized on how we could do something together to get these ideas into action. Success stories and setbacks can be shared. The study group can slowly evolve into an action group. Remember the power of people with pure intention working together. It is important to work for the positive rather than against the negative.

3. *Hold a departmental or family meeting every month.* Discuss the progress on initiatives and examine the process of working together at such meetings. Use tips for better meetings framed up or shared to improve the quality of these meetings.

4. *Teach others something that you feel passionately about.* It is said that we have finally learnt something when we can teach it to others. You can teach your colleagues, subordinates, your boss and your family members. They learn something new and the learning is reinforced in your mind.

5. *Create your own reminder systems.* Continuous repetition is a powerful way to cultivate a habit. I remember my first lessons on the tabla. A *kaida* has to be practised over and over again until it becomes a natural part of you. We can 'remind' ourselves in several ways:

- Colour posters and charts stuck up on the wall or under the glass top on your table.
- Little reminder cards capturing the essence or key action points which need to be followed.
- A log-in-reminder on the computer which is part of your first screen or wall-paper.
- Tips on salary slips.
- Pre-recorded messages on the phone set to music.
- Inspiring quotations, shared values and ideas for action on planners, calendars and diaries.
- Self-recorded messages played on to a tape-recorder and replayed once in a while. Try to do this in a hypnotic voice so that it goes deep into your subconscious.

6. *Managing yourself and focusing on growthful action.* Maintain a learning journal. Record important events, meetings, feelings, insights, ideas and dreams as they come in the journal. This is a powerful way to stay in touch with your feelings and expand your awareness through conscious reflection. The content of the experiences is not important but the process is. Some of my most beautiful moments are when I unravel my own inner world between the loving folds of pure white sheets of paper on the one hand and silent peaceful awareness on the other. It is delightful to read your own journey and see your own progress towards integrity.

Monthly check-ups in the form of self-evaluation checklists can be a powerful reminder. An excellent system devised by Swami Shivananda (and also used by Benjamin Franklin) is to keep a daily track record of performance on critical issues for growth. A sample format is as follows:

Daily Matrix	Exercise	Listening	Meditation	Reading				
1	✓	✓	✓	✗				
2	✓	✗	✓	✗				
3	✓	✗	✗	✓				
4								
5								
6								
7								
8								
9								
10								
11								

This forms part of the PLS Time and Life Management Planner System. Every evening when I look at the points I had chosen to work on, I reflect on how I have performed on those and am also reminded of them once again.

Visualize yourself actually carrying out new actions and achieving them. Also visualize and write down the specific things you will need to do to make things happen differently. Reserve at least one to two hours per week to review your learning goals and set new ones. Some books serve as vibrant reminders to rouse the spirit and inspire positive action. For daily reminders, some of these books have a salient thought for each day. Read a page every day of the year, reflect on the import of the message, and commit yourself to action based on the insights. You can have a beautiful visual to brighten your day. A thought in one such book is, 'Complete faith and surrender are perfectly practical in the spiritual life.' Two such useful books are: *Books of Daily Thoughts and Prayers* by Swami Paramananda (1926) and *Reflections in the Light* by Shakti Gawain (1988).

7. *Invite feedback regularly.* Feedback is the breakfast of champions. You can do this in several ways:

- Ask your colleague, spouse, friend or subordinate for feedback (and then listen to them without pouncing on them!)
- 360° appraisal or the process of being given feedback by people above, below and around you is another powerful way to keep one 'awake' to the learning process in one's life. When my internal customers, subordinates, boss and colleagues all tell me in writing how my behaviour is affecting them, I have a clear multi-dimensional snapshot of myself. This is valuable for learning.
- A lovely way of receiving feedback which I have used successfully in several organizations is the 'light seat' exercise. (It throws a lot of light on your behaviour, your attitudes, and at the end of it, everyone feels lighter!) In this method, you sit with your back towards a circle of people who know you well. They converse among themselves about you as if you are not there. You are to be like a fly on the wall, that is, totally silent. Of course, if you want to remember what they are saying, for constructive action later on, you can make some notes. In my experience, the 'light seat' method evens out different perceptions and you end up getting a fair, balanced and honest picture of your behaviour as perceived by others. In our programmes, this has often been rated as the most valuable learning device. It is something like the 360° appraisal in real time.

8. *Stay in touch with your body and nature.* This important part of being whole has been described in Chapter 3. Daily exercise, yoga, walks, being in touch with trees, forests, parks, etc. would be part of this.

9. *Meditate.* For me, the singlemost vital daily reminder is regular meditation. When I meditate, I connect back to the ease and essence which is my own self. In that wholeness and silence, I remember the very purpose and source of life. The fragrance of this understanding stays with my body–mind the whole day and subtly guides all that I think, say and do.

A note of caution at this point. Take on only as much as you can handle. Stay focused on the most critical bottlenecks. Do those few things that will have the maximum pay-offs for you in your life. Take one step at a time.

As we discovered in Chapter 6, making things happen requires a definite plan. Having gone through this book and experimented with the 'Ideas for Playful Action' at the end of each chapter, it is time now to prepare a plan of action for yourself. Before you do this, you could expand your awareness through some questions and ideas. These will enable you to reflect on your present situations and plan specific actions for the future.

Ideas to Expand Your Awareness

1. ***Decide on the issues you want to focus on.*** What are the issues or problems you want to look at a little more closely? Try to be as specific as possible and be compassionate with yourself (go slowly).

Set **S** specific goals
M easurable
A ttainable
R elevant
T imebound

2. What are the strengths/positive aspects you can build upon? What are you already doing which you feel helps you with your issue/problem?

3. ***Set objectives.*** Decide on very clear, specific objectives (for example, to improve your fitness level by taking more exercise).

4. ***Make a plan.*** What action needs to be taken to achieve your objectives? (What specific changes in your lifestyle will you need to make?):
   I will do more of (something you are already doing):

IMAGINE
Visualize yourself actually carrying out the action and achieving it.

   _____

   _____

   _____

☊ **Start.**   I will begin to (something you can realistically add to your life):

   _____

   _____

   _____

☋ **Reduce.** I will do less (something you know is unhealthy and that you can do something about):

   _____

   _____

   _____

⊠ **STOP.** I will stop (something you feel capable of immediately eliminating from your life):

_____

_____

_____

5. **Implementation picture.** What has happened so far? What is happening?

> Reserve one hour for reflection and two hours for review and setting new goals every week

6. **Support.** What support do you need from others, and whose support do you need? (consider family members, co-workers, etc.)

> Discuss your goals and progress every week with one person

7. **Who can you talk this over with to support your efforts and results ?**

8. Make a type of poster for your home or workplace which has some words of inspiration to help you when you are experiencing difficulties in making changes. What key words would be helpful for you ?

> Use colour codes
> * Green—did it well
> * Red—Need to improve

9. How will you know if you have successfully **implemented** your plan? What will be some of the external signals of your success? What about internally?

10. What are the ways you will **celebrate** your success?

> Reward yourself every time you achieve a goal

Connecting with You

Having said so much about networking, integration, and planning for action, it would be great to be in touch with you. Your suggestions for improvement of this book, ideas, comments and stories are welcome.

Some of the stories of your own initiatives and application of these ideas may be published in the next edition of this book.

I would be delighted to hear from you. Feel free to get in touch. My address is:

Arun Wakhlu
Pragati Learning System (P) Ltd
11, Ganesh Krupa, ITI Road,
Sanewadi, Aundh, Pune 411 007, India
Tel.No: +91-212-387773, 381217
Fax No: + 91-212-382246
e-mail: <oshiana@bom3.vsnl.net.in>

I am convinced that many of these simple ideas have the power to transform your personal, family and work life.

As more and more of us begin to unfold peace and productivity in our lives, our nation can undergo a major change. India is destined to show the world the path of wholesome development and total living. You can be a creative contributor to this process.

You can revel in the divine core of your 'I', and stay in touch with others and with nature. As your life unfolds it will become an inspiration for others. I pray that this unfoldment happens through your own efforts and also by the grace of Existence.

All good wishes for life-long learning and joyful contribution.

≈ References ≈

Bach, Richard (1977), *Illusions: The Adventures of a Reluctant Messiah*, Dell, New York.

Bohm, David (1980), *Wholeness and the Implicate Order*, Routledge and Kegan Paul, London.

Brunton, Paul (1975), *The Spiritual Crisis of Man*, B.I. Publications, New Delhi.

Buzan, Tony (1993), *The Mind Map Book*, BBC Books, London.

Campbell, Joseph (1968), *The Hero with a Thousand Faces*, Princeton University Press, New Jersey.

Cameron, Julia (1994), *The Artist's Way*, Pan Books, London.

Canfield, Jack and Hansen, Mark Victor (1993), *Chicken Soup for the Soul*, Health Communication, Deerfield Beach.

Canfield, Jack and Miller, Jacqueline (1996), *Heart at Work*, McGraw-Hill, New York.

Capra, Fritjof (1989), *Uncommon Wisdom*, Fontana Paperbacks, London.

Chakraborty, S.K. (1987), *Managerial Effectiveness and Quality of Work-Life: Indian Insights*, Tata McGraw-Hill, New Delhi.

_____ (1989), *Foundations of Managerial Work: Contributions from Indian Thought*, Himalaya Publishing House, Bombay.

_____ (1991), *Management by Values: Towards Cultural Congruence*, Oxford University Press, New Delhi.

Chibber, M.L. (1987), *Sai Baba's Mahavakya on Leadership*, Sri Sathya Sai Books & Publications Trust, Puttaparthi.

Chopra, Deepak (1989), *Quantum Healing*, Bantam Books, New York.

_____ (1997), *Creating Affluence*, Excel Books, New Delhi.

Chung, Tsai Chih (1994), *Zen Speaks*, Harper Collins, London.

Collins, James C. and Porras, Jerry I. (1994), *Built to Last*, Harper Collins, New York.

Connelly, Dianne M. (1986), *All Sickness is Home Sickness*, Centre for Traditional Acupuncture, Columbia.

Cousins, Norman (1991), *Anatomy of an Illness*, Bantam, London.

Covey, Stephen R. (1989), *The Seven Habits of Highly Effective People*, Simon & Schuster, New York.

Csikszentmihalyi, Mihaly (1990), *Flow: The Psychology of Optimal Experience,* Harper and Row, New York.

Dayer, Wayne W. (1995), *Your Sacred Self,* Harper Collins, New York.

Eccles, R G. and Nohria, Nitin (1993), *Beyond the Hype,* Tata McGraw-Hill, New Delhi.

Garratt, Bob (1994), *The Learning Organization,* Harper Collins, London.

Gawain, Shakti (1982), *Creative Visualization,* Bantam Books, New York.

_____ (1988), *Reflections in the Light: Daily Thoughts and Affirmations,* New World Library, Novato.

Godman, David (Ed.) (1992), *Be As You Are: The Teaching of Sri Ramana Maharishi,* Penguin Books, New Delhi.

Goodman, Linda (1987), *Star Signs,* Pan Books, London.

Greenleaf, Robert K. (1983), *Servant Leadership: A Journey into the Nature of Legitimate Power and Greatness,* Paulist Press, Mahwah.

Handy, Charles (1995), *The Age of Paradox,* The Harvard Business School Press, Boston.

_____ (1997), *The Hungry Spirit,* Hutchinson, London.

Hart, William (1990), *The Art of Living—Vipassana Meditation As Taught By S.N. Goenka,* Vipassana Publications, Singapore.

Hassija, Jagdish Chander (1995a), *Twelve Wonder Values,* Brahmakumaris Ishwariya Vishwa-Vidyalaya, Mount Abu.

_____ (1995b), *Business and Industry Based on Human and Moral Values,* Brahmakumaris Ishwariya Vishwa-Vidyalaya, Mount Abu.

Hendricks, Gay and Ludeman, Kate (1996), *The Corporate Mystic,* Bantam Books, New York.

Hewitt, James (1978), *Teach Yourself Meditation,* Hodder & Stoughton, Seven Oaks.

Isherwood, Christopher (1972), *Vedanta for Modern Man,* New American Library, New York.

Jaworski, Joseph (1996), *Synchronicity,* Berrett-Koehler Publishers, San Francisco.

Khandwalla, Pradip N. (1984), *Fourth Eye: Excellence Through Creativity,* A.H. Wheeler & Co., Allahabad.

Knight, Sue (1995), *NLP At Work,* Nicholas Brearely, London.

Kouzes, James M. and Posner, Barry Z. (1995), *The Leadership Challenge,* Jossey-Bass Publishers, San Francisco.

Krishnamurti, J. (1980), *Meditation,* Krishnamurti Foundation India, Madras.

Lala, Russi M. (1986), *In Search of Leadership,* Vision Books, New Delhi.

_____ (1995), *The Joy of Achievement,* Penguin India, New Delhi.

Maharishi, Mahesh Yogi (1968), *Transcendental Meditation,* New American Library, New York.

_____ (1995), *Wholeness on the Move,* 2nd Edition, Maharishi Prakashan, New Delhi.

Mascaro, Juan (1965), *The Upanishads,* Penguin Books, New Delhi.

Millman, Dan (1983), *The Life You Were Born To Live—A Guide to Finding Your Life Purpose,* H.J. Kramer, Tiburon.

Mother Teresa (1975), *A Gift for God,* Harper Collins, London.

Naimy, Mikhail (1971), *The Book of Mirdad,* Penguin Arkana, London.

Noe, John R. (1984), *Peak Performance Principles For High Achievers,* Berkley Books, New York.

Ornish, Dean (1990), *Reversing Heart Disease,* Ballantine Books, New York.

Owen, Harrison (1992), *Open Space Technology: A User's Guide,* Abbot Publishing, Potomac.

_____ (1994), *The Millennium Organization,* Abbot Publishing, Potomac.

Paramananda, Swami (1926), *Book of Daily Thoughts,* Sri Ramakrishna Math, Madras.

Peace Pilgrim (1994), *Peace Pilgrim,* Ocean Tree Books, Santa Fe.

Radhakrishnan, S. (1987), *Towards a New World,* Orient Paperbacks, New Delhi.

Rajneesh, Bhagwan Shree (1977), *Meditation—The Art of Inner Ecstacy,* Rajneesh Foundation, Pune.

_____ (1983), *Hsin Hsin Ming: The Book of Nothing,* Rajneesh Foundation International, Rajneeshpuram.

Rajneesh, Osho (1989), *Meditation: The First and Last Freedom,* The Rebel Publishing House, Cologne.

Rastogi, P.N. (1988), *Productivity, Innovation, Management and Development,* Sage Publications, New Delhi.

Remen, Rachel Naomi (1988), *On Defining Spirit,* Noetic Sciences Review, Originally Autum 1988, Reprinted in No. 27, Autumn 1993, p. 41.

Renesch, John (Ed.) (1992), *New Traditions in Business,* Berret-Koehler Publishers, San Francisco.

Rose, Colin and Nicholl, Malcolm J. (1997), *Accelerated Learning for the 21st Century,* Dell Publishing, New York.

Secretan, Lance H.K. (1996), *Reclaiming Higher Ground,* Response Books/Sage Publications, New Delhi.

Shukla, Madhukar (1997), *Competing Through Knowledge,* Response Books/Sage Publications, New Delhi.

Smith, Hyrum W. (1994), *The 10 Natural Laws of Successful Time & Life Management,* Nicholas Brealey, London.

Sajandas, Gangaram (1986), *An Equation of Health,* Mira Publications, Pune.

Stevens, D.E. (1985), *Listen! The New Humanity,* Companion Books, Jersey Islands.

Talbot, Michael (1996), *The Holographic Universe,* Harper Collins, London.

Thakkar, Vimla (1985), *Meditation—A Way Of Life,* Vimal Prakashan Trust, Ahmedabad.

Tichy, Noel M. and Cohen, Eli (1997), *The Leadership Engine: How Winning Companies Build Leaders at Every Level,* Harper Collins, New York.

Tournier, Paul (1983), *The Adventure of Living,* Highland Publishers, London.

Verifone, (1990), *The Verifone Philosophy,* Redwood City.

Vivekananda, Swami (1959), *The Complete Works,* Advaita Ashram, Calcutta.

Wakhlu, Arun and Wakhlu, Omkar N. (1993), *A New Paradigm of Wholesome Development,* Proceedings of the International Conference on Sustainable Village-Based Development, Colorado State University, Fort Collins (Sept 27–Oct 1, 93), pp 1531–55.

Wakhlu, Anu and Wakhlu, Arun (1996), *Time And Life Management,* Pragati Learning System, Pune.

Wakhlu, Bharat (1994), *Total Quality: Excellence Through Organization—Wide Transformation,* Wheeler Publishing, New Delhi.

Wakhlu, O.N. (1984), *Society, Technology and Development,* B.R. Publishing Corporation, New Delhi.

Walker, Anne S. (Ed.) (1984), *Women Organizing: A Collection of IWTC Newsletters on Women's Organizing and Networking Strategies,* International Women's Tribune Centre, New York.

Wheatley, Margaret J. (1992), *Leadership and the New Science,* Berret-Koehler Publishers, San Francisco.

Woods, Bernard (1993), *Communication, Technology and the Development of People,* Routledge, London.

Zohar, Danah (1991), *The Quantum Self,* Harper Collins, London.

_____ (1997), *The Servant Leader,* Rabindranath Tagore Memorial Orientation, Management Centre for Human Values, IIM (Calcutta), Jan. 9, 1997 (paper seen).

≈ *Index* ≈

≈ About the Author ≈

Arun Wakhlu is the founder Managing Director of Pragati Learning System (P) Ltd, a management training and consulting firm based in Pune. An electrical engineering graduate from the Indian Institute of Technology (IIT), Delhi, he obtained a postgraduate diploma in management from the Indian Institute of Management (IIM), Ahmedabad. He has also attended many training programmes in management and is a certified facilitator of the Covey Leadership Center, USA.

Mr Wakhlu began his professional career with the National Radio and Electronics Co. Ltd (NELCO), Bombay. Later, as a member of the Tata Administrative Service, he worked with the Tata Engineering and Locomotive Company Ltd (TELCO), Jamshedpur, before setting up Pragati at Pune in 1986. For the past 13 years, as head of Pragati, he has led consulting and training assignments in leading Indian and international organizations. An acknowledged expert in the area of human resource development and organization development, he has designed and facilitated over 600 management development programmes and trained more than 12,000 executives. A much sought after speaker and presenter, he has given numerous invited talks and presentations.

Arun Wakhlu has been a visiting faculty at IIM Ahmedabad, XLRI Jamshedpur, the Symbiosis Institute of Business Management, Pune, and also at the Tata Management Training Centre, Pune. He has published more than 20 papers and articles and co-authored two books. A sincere student and proponent of spiritual development in organizations, Mr Wakhlu devotes a quarter of his time to socially relevant projects. Widely travelled, he is fluent in five languages.